I0810579

IMAGES
of America

Lighthouses and Life Saving at Oswego

On the Cover: A group of fishermen test their luck along Oswego Harbor's west inner harbor breakwater in the late 1800s just west of the second Oswego Harbor Lighthouse, completed in 1837. In the background at the mouth of the Oswego River on its east side is Fort Ontario, which has guarded Oswego Harbor for over 200 years. Below Fort Ontario is the US Life-Saving Service station at Oswego, which operated between 1876 and 1915. (Courtesy of the Library of Congress.)

IMAGES
of America

LIGHTHOUSES AND LIFE SAVING AT OSWEGO

Theodore J. Panayotoff
and Michael R. Pittavino

ARCADIA
PUBLISHING

ISBN 978-1-4671-2851-3

Published by Arcadia Publishing
Charleston, South Carolina

Printed in the United States of America

Library of Congress Control Number: 2017954554

For all general information, please contact Arcadia Publishing:
Telephone 843-853-2070
Fax 843-853-0044
E-mail sales@arcadiapublishing.com
For customer service and orders:
Toll-Free 1-888-313-2665

Visit us on the Internet at www.arcadiapublishing.com

This book is dedicated to the members of the US Lighthouse Service, Life-Saving Service, and Coast Guard who have given their lives while in service at Oswego, New York:

Surfman Robert Wright, US Life-Saving Service, December 2, 1886; Keeper George Greenfield, US Lighthouse Service, July 3, 1903; Lt. (jg) Altson Wilson, BM1 Karl Jackson, BM2 Eugene J. Sisson, MM2 Ralph J. Sprau, S1c. Leslie J. Holdsworth, and S2c. Irving Ginsburg, US Coast Guard, December 4, 1942; and SA James Kwiatkowski, US Coast Guard, July 13, 1973.

Contents

Acknowledgments

Unless otherwise noted, all images appear courtesy of the archives at the H. Lee White Maritime Museum at Oswego. The authors would further like to acknowledge City of Oswego historian Mark Slosek, BM1 Jason Gwiazdzinski of US Coast Guard Station Oswego, the Oswego County Historical Society, and all others who, big or small, contributed to the contents of this book.

INTRODUCTION

Nothing indicates the liberality, prosperity and intelligence of a nation more clearly than the facilities which it affords for the safe approach of the mariner to its shores.

—*Report of the Unites States Lighthouse Board, 1868*

Mariners have approached shores since ancient times, and facilities have existed to safely guide them there. The Pharos of Alexandria and the Colossus of Rhodes—two of the seven wonders of the ancient world—were lighthouses in the eastern Mediterranean that were destroyed by earthquakes and Roman invasion, respectively. Similar to those ancient mariners engaging in commerce and trade, mariners have sailed the Great Lakes for nearly four centuries. The first official lighthouse on the Great Lakes, though, was not built until 1821. Lakes they may be in name, but as any mariner who has sailed one of the Great Lakes during a storm can attest, they can be as unforgiving and treacherous as any of the world's oceans.

The Great Lakes have served as a vital maritime trade route into the interior of the North American continent since their discovery. With the founding of the United States, trade was further facilitated by the Erie Canal, stretching from the Hudson River to Buffalo, New York, on Lake Erie, and the Oswego Canal, which connects Lake Ontario to the Erie Canal at Syracuse, New York. The early-19th-century commercial boom brought lumber, grain, salt, and coal to and through Oswego, New York. As such, the grain elevator, shipbuilding, and fishing industries further contributed to Oswego's maritime commercial growth, echoing the need for enhanced facilities to guide the mariners' safe passage.

As commercial interest in the lakes grew, the mariners, ship owners, and merchants who engaged in maritime commerce on the Great Lakes soon petitioned for lighted aids to navigation to guide their safe approach to lake shores. The US Lighthouse Establishment, later known as the US Lighthouse Service, obliged, and plans were formulated for lighthouses that were later supported by congressional appropriations. At Oswego, the first lighthouse was completed in 1822 and was followed by three others, culminating in the present Oswego West Pierhead Lighthouse.

In spite of lighthouses, though, maritime accidents were inevitable, and the need to assist mariners in distress was evident. Created in 1790 and serving on the Great Lakes beginning in the early 19th century, the US Revenue Cutter Service had the principal mission of enforcing customs regulations but also assisted distressed mariners offshore. Later, in the 1870s, the US Life-Saving Service began constructing and staffing Life-Saving stations along the coastal waterways and Great Lakes of the United States. Commanded by a keeper and staffed by a team of surfmen during the shipping season (usually late March through early December), these stations provided the resources and manpower necessary to rescue distressed mariners within their area of operation. In January 1915, the US Revenue Cutter Service and the US Life-Saving Service merged, forming the US Coast Guard.

Like others on the Great Lakes, the Life-Saving station at Oswego was expanded to accommodate the new missions and larger staff of the Coast Guard. Prohibition in the early 1920s, for example, created increased law enforcement demands and necessitated new cutters and patrol boats, with some of the latter being based in Oswego. Special motorized rescue vessels replaced the early pulling surfboats and lifeboats and greatly improved stations' ability to respond to maritime disasters.

In 1939, the US Lighthouse Service was disbanded, and the US Coast Guard assumed responsibility for all federal aids to navigation, which included lighthouses, beacons, buoys, and day-marks along the coastal waterways and Great Lakes of the United States. Additionally, the Coast Guard inherited a fleet of lighthouse tenders to support and maintain the aids to navigation. At that time, all Lighthouse Service personnel became civilian employees of the Coast Guard and were given the option to remain civilians or enlist in the Coast Guard with a rank or rate commensurate with their former position in the Lighthouse Service. Indications suggest that roughly 50 percent of Lighthouse Service personnel enlisted in the Coast Guard at that time. That decision was not required immediately, though, as the keeper and two assistant keepers at Oswego waited over two years before enlisting. After World War II, the Coast Guard did not hire any civilian lighthouse keepers, and by the 1960s, most civilian lighthouse keepers had retired.

Beginning in the early 1930s, the Lighthouse Service began experimenting with the automation of lighthouse operations. Technology became available to automate the beacon, but the fog signal still required a human operator. After World War II, though, the technology for the fog signal had matured sufficiently, and by the 1960s, full automation of a lighthouse was possible. Faced with the difficulty of staffing lighthouses with military personnel, especially in remote areas, the US Coast Guard accelerated automation so that by the 1990s, there were no longer lighthouse keepers on duty at any lighthouse. With no Coast Guard keepers onsite and no staff or funding to maintain them, the nation's lighthouses tended to fall into disrepair. Some were demolished, as were many ancillary structures such as keepers' homes.

In the 1980s, the public began viewing lighthouses as enduring symbols of the nation's history and maritime heritage, and they soon became valued assets to be restored, preserved, and when possible made available to the public for historic interpretation. Nearly all of the nation's lighthouses are now listed in the National Register of Historic Places, and Congress has provided for their transfer to other entities for restoration, preservation, and historic interpretation. Where lighthouses are still active aids to navigation, the Coast Guard retains the responsibility for that function. Recently, the remaining US Life-Saving stations are also being recognized as similar assets worthy of preservation. It is the authors' goal to share with the reader, through these many historic photographs, the deeply rooted history and culture of the US Lighthouse Service, Revenue Cutter Service, Life-Saving Service, and Coast Guard at Oswego.

One

Oswego Harbor's First Lighthouse 1822–1837

The US Lighthouse Service was formed on August 7, 1789, when Pres. George Washington signed the ninth act passed by the first US Congress, which transferred all lighthouses from the states to the federal government. The first lighthouse on the Great Lakes was completed in 1821 on Lake Erie, and the first lighthouse at Oswego was constructed the following year.

On March 3, 1821, Congress appropriated $3,500 for "A Lighthouse at the mouth of the Oswego River, at a place as shall be designated by the Secretary of the Treasury, in the State of New York," and thus the US Lighthouse Service officially began its long association with Oswego. The legislation further stated that "no lighthouse shall be built on any site previous to the cession of jurisdiction over the same to the United States," requiring New York State to cede the land for the lighthouse to the federal government. The state did just that on March 27, 1821, providing the federal government with "so much land, lying at or near the mouth of the Oswego River, in the county of Oswego, as they shall deem necessary for the purpose of erecting a light-house thereon, not to exceed six acres in the whole." New York governor Dewitt Clinton signed the document, and it was recorded in the Book of Patents on July 13, 1821. The legal description of the ceded property stated, "Beginning at a stake and stones marked 'LH' standing south thirty five degrees west from the south west angle of the fort" and described the location of three additional markers.

The lighthouse tower, in the shape of an octagon, was of stone construction and 20 feet high, with a four-foot, 10-inch lantern on the top. The base of the tower was 16 feet in diameter and tapered to nine feet, three inches at the top. The keeper's dwelling was also built of stone and was a two-room, single-story structure 34 feet long by 20 feet wide with 20-inch-thick walls. The dwelling is still in use today and is thought to be the oldest surviving keeper's dwelling on the Great Lakes.

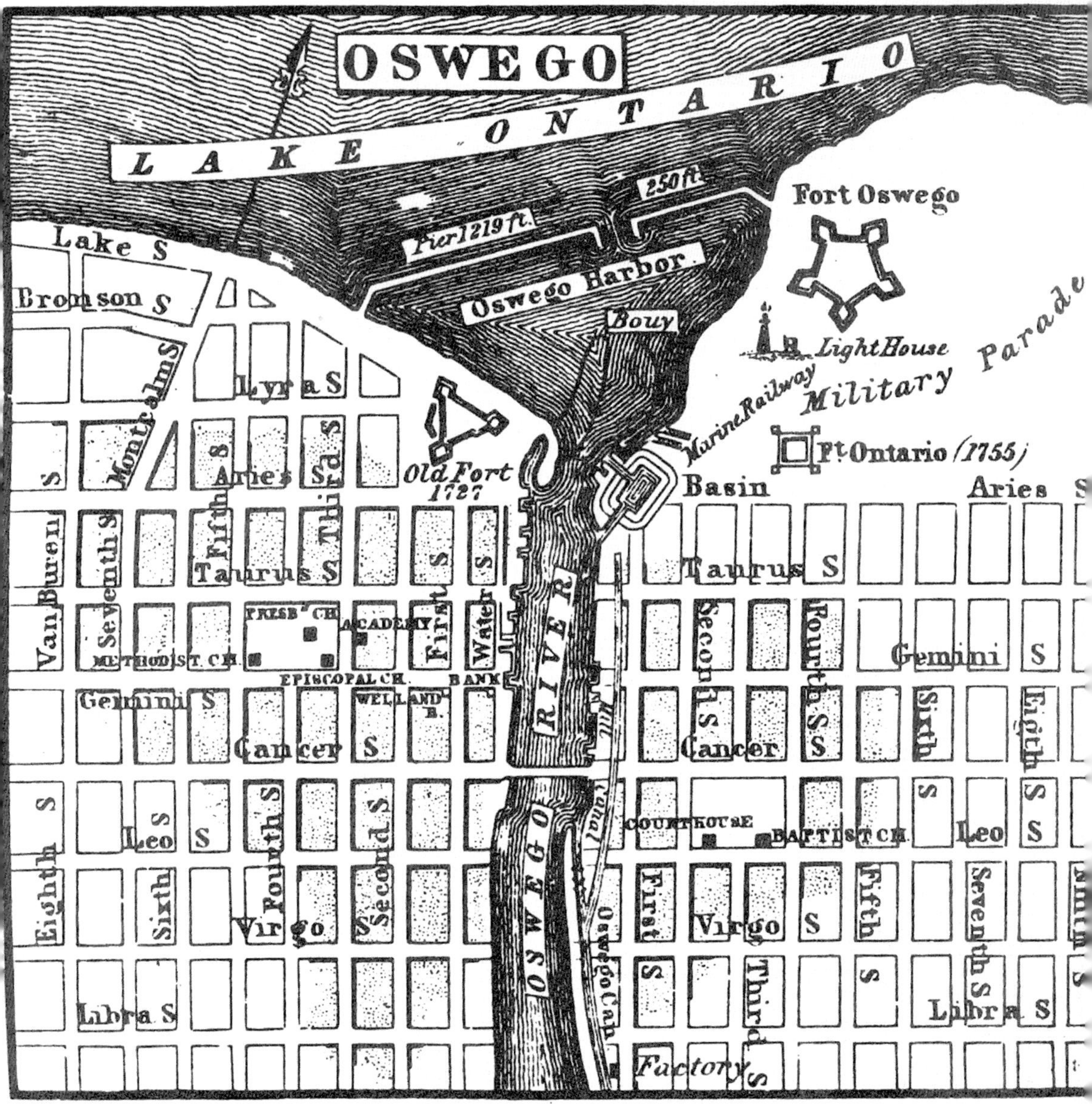

This 1836 map depicts Fort Ontario, Oswego Harbor, and the original city of Oswego. Although many of the east-west streets have been renamed, the basic layout of the city is recognizable. The 1822 Oswego Harbor Lighthouse tower and keeper's dwelling are shown in their correct relationship to Fort Ontario. The Oswego Canal is seen on the east side of the Oswego River, as is the Oswego Harbor breakwater.

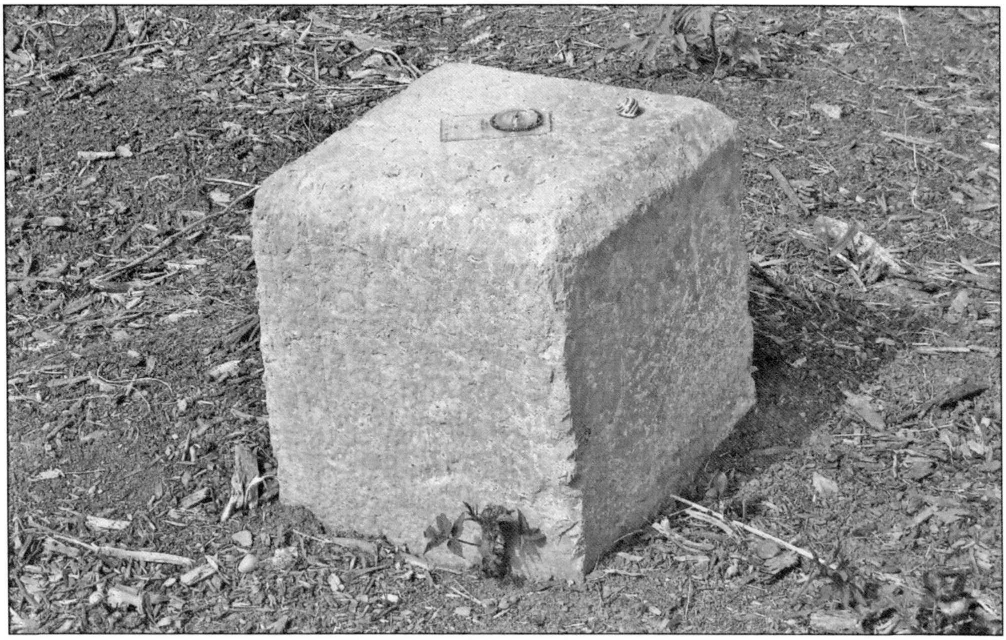

The first granite "LH" marker still exists on the grounds of Fort Ontario State Historic Site where it was originally placed; however, the other three have not survived. Once the cession act was passed by New York State, the collector and superintendent of lighthouses on Lake Ontario, John Canfield, was free to place ads in the *Oswego Palladium*. On May 25, 1821, the *Palladium* ad read "Proposals will be received at the office of the Collector of Customs at Sacket's Harbor for building a Light House and dwelling house on the east side of the mouth of the Oswego river in the state of New York." A lengthy verbal description of the required lighthouse and dwelling followed. As was custom at the time, there were no drawings provided to the building contractor.

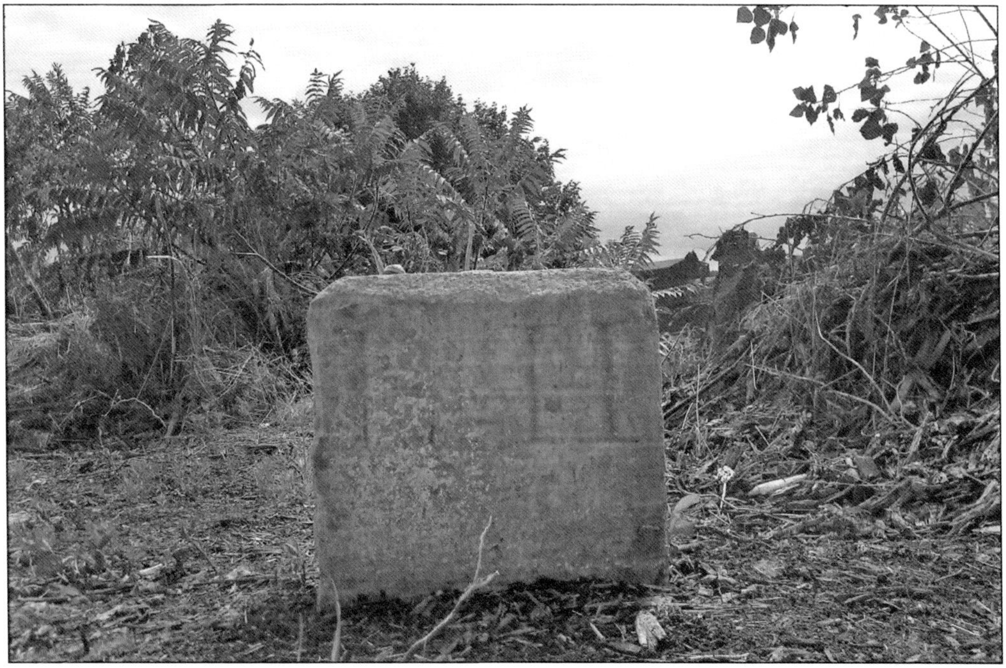

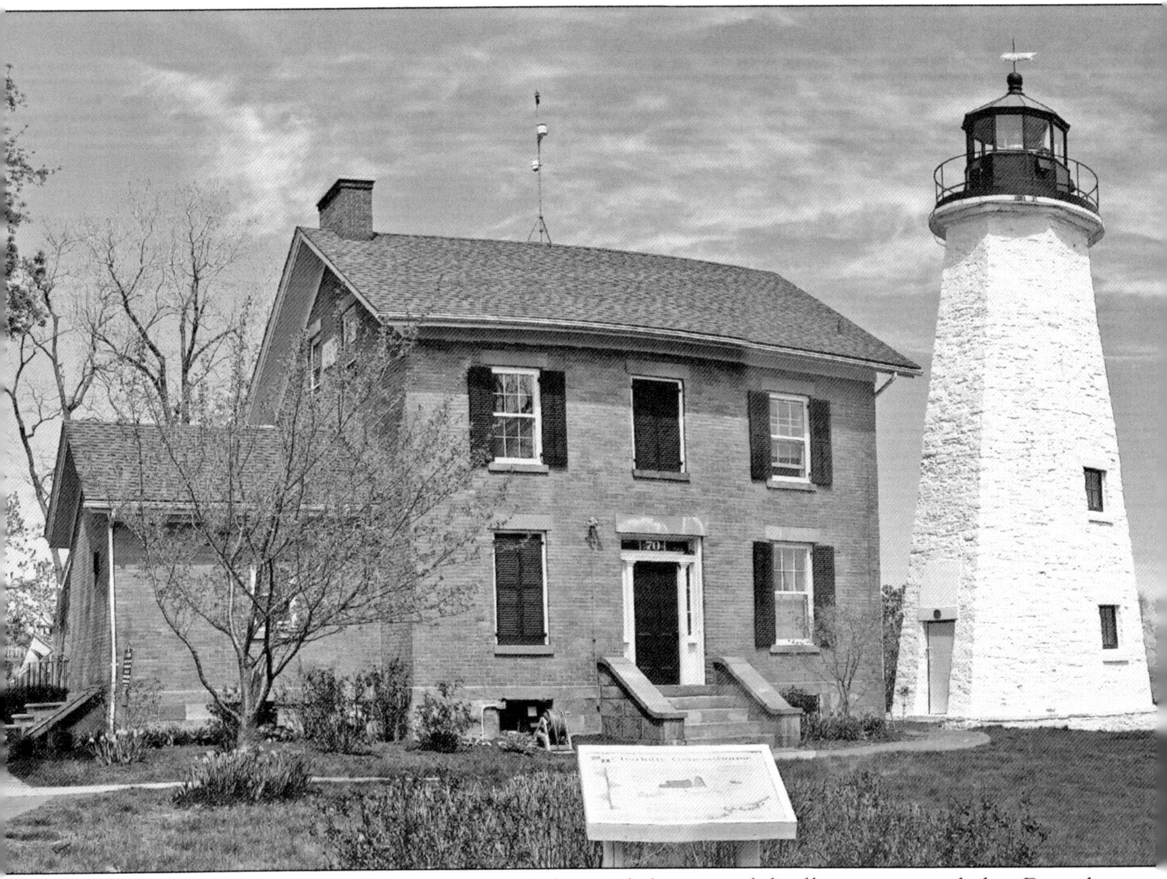

The contract to build the 1822 Oswego Harbor Lighthouse and dwelling was awarded to Daniel Warren and William Cobb of Rochester, New York, on August 6, 1821. It was to be completed by November 1, 1821, with an additional 30 days to outfit the lighting equipment. The lighthouse began operation in 1822, and the final contract payment was made to Warren and Cobb on April 10, 1822. The 1822 lighthouse was extinguished in 1837 upon the activation of the second Oswego Harbor Lighthouse, and the tower was sold and demolished in 1841. As a result, no photographs of the 1822 tower exist. Fortunately, the nearby, still-standing Charlotte-Genesee Lighthouse tower at Rochester was also built in 1822 and has almost identical dimensions as the 1822 Oswego tower. This photograph shows the Charlotte-Genesee Lighthouse tower today. The original keeper's dwelling, which was like the 1822 Oswego keeper's dwelling, was replaced in 1863 by the two-story brick house seen here. (Courtesy of the Charlotte-Genesee Lighthouse Historical Society.)

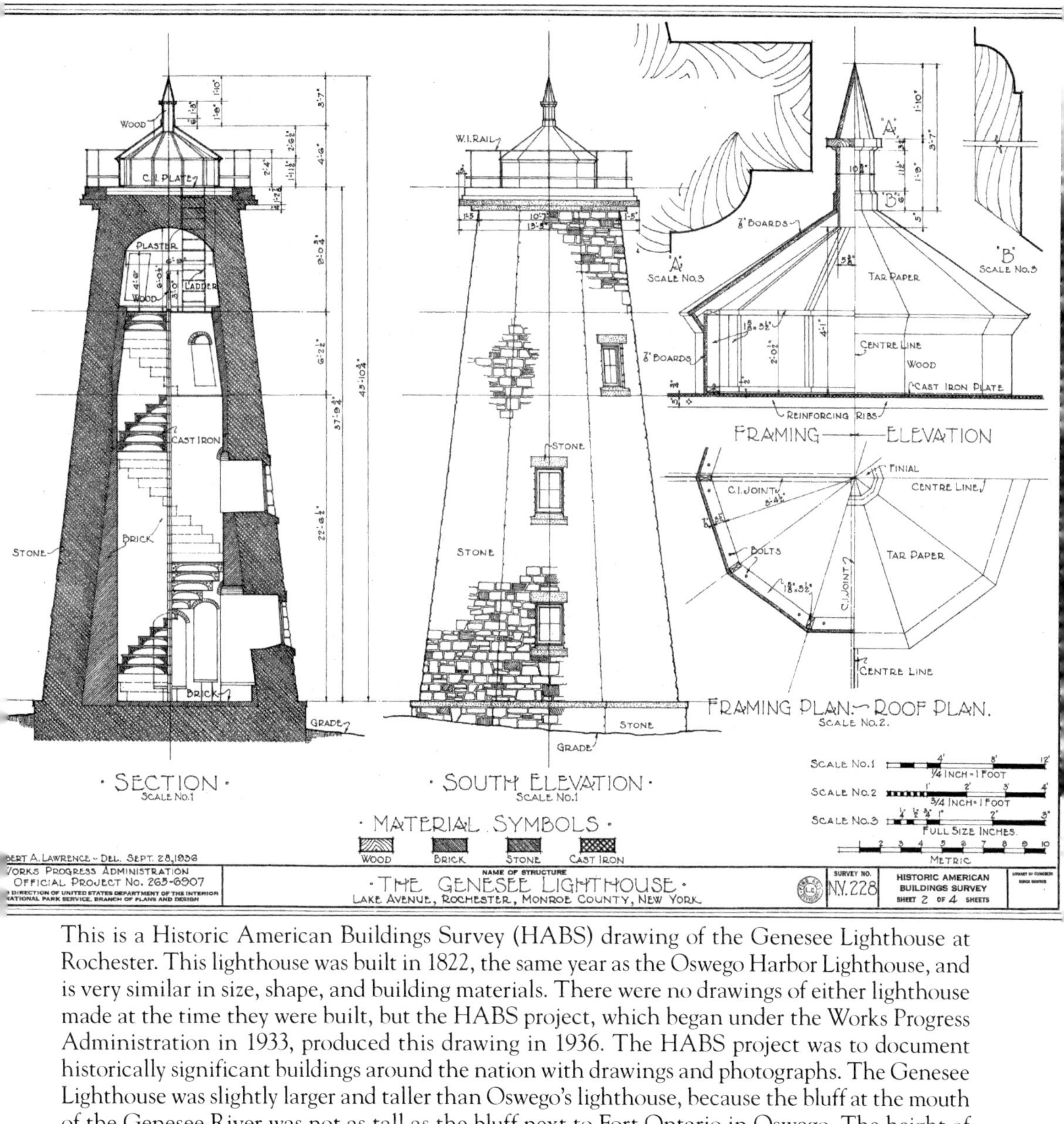

This is a Historic American Buildings Survey (HABS) drawing of the Genesee Lighthouse at Rochester. This lighthouse was built in 1822, the same year as the Oswego Harbor Lighthouse, and is very similar in size, shape, and building materials. There were no drawings of either lighthouse made at the time they were built, but the HABS project, which began under the Works Progress Administration in 1933, produced this drawing in 1936. The HABS project was to document historically significant buildings around the nation with drawings and photographs. The Genesee Lighthouse was slightly larger and taller than Oswego's lighthouse, because the bluff at the mouth of the Genesee River was not as tall as the bluff next to Fort Ontario in Oswego. The height of the focal plane of the lamp above the level of the lake determined the desired tower height. The original keeper's dwelling, replaced in 1863, was exactly like the one that still exists in Oswego. The lantern at the top of the tower was removed in 1884 and transferred to a new tower on the north end of the west breakwater at the mouth of the Genesee River. This drawing shows a roof that was added in place of the original lantern to protect the tower's interior. In 1984, a replica lantern with a fourth-order lens on loan from the Coast Guard returned the lighthouse to its original configuration. In 2014, that lens was returned to the Coast Guard and replaced by a replica fourth-order lens. (Courtesy of the Library of Congress, HABS Collection.)

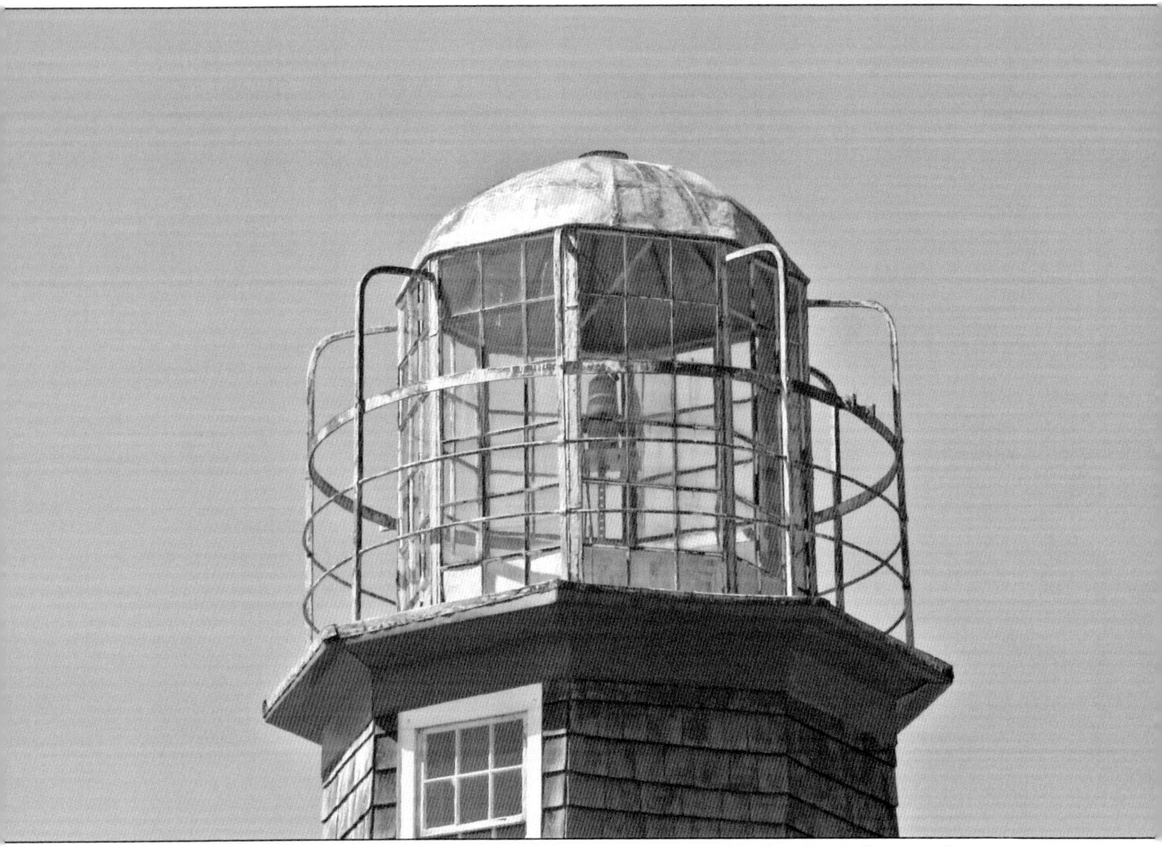

Nearly identical to the birdcage lantern of the 1822 Oswego Harbor Lighthouse, this equipment is from the Salmon River Lighthouse at Selkirk, New York, built in 1838. The birdcage name stems from the multitude of small windowpanes, a result of the glass-making technology of the time. By the late 1850s, glass-making technology had improved, allowing larger windowpanes to be made. The Salmon River Lighthouse was decommissioned in 1858 and was never upgraded to lager panes, making it one of the few remaining examples of a birdcage lantern.

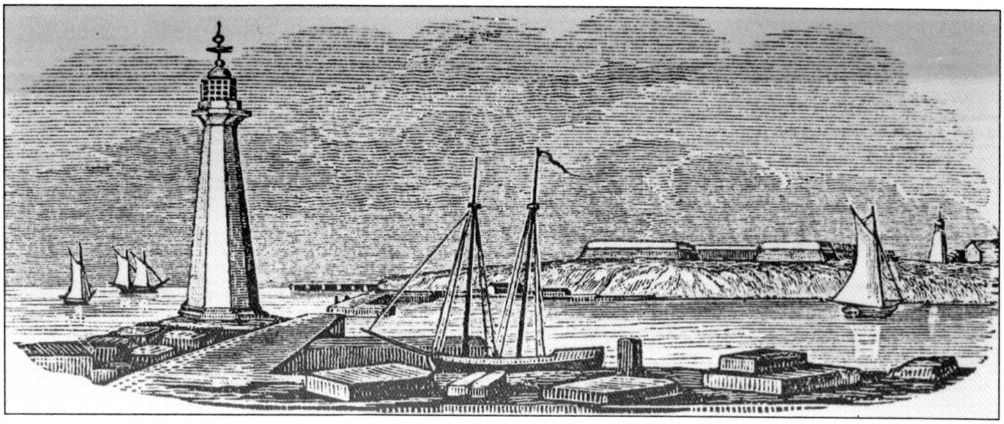

While no photographs of the 1822 Oswego Harbor Lighthouse exist, it is frequently depicted in the many paintings, illustrations, and drawings of the time. The etching above shows the mouth of the Oswego River looking east toward Fort Ontario from Oswego's west side sometime between 1837 and 1841. Both the 1822 (right) and 1837 (left) Oswego Harbor Lighthouses can be seen along with the keeper's dwelling, at far right. The painting below, by Capt. James Van Cleve (1808–1888), depicts the mouth of the Oswego River with the 1822 lighthouse on the east side of the river just south of Fort Ontario. The keeper's dwelling can be seen to the left of the tower, and to the right is a barn, a common addition to light stations. (Above, courtesy of Mark Slosek, City of Oswego historian.)

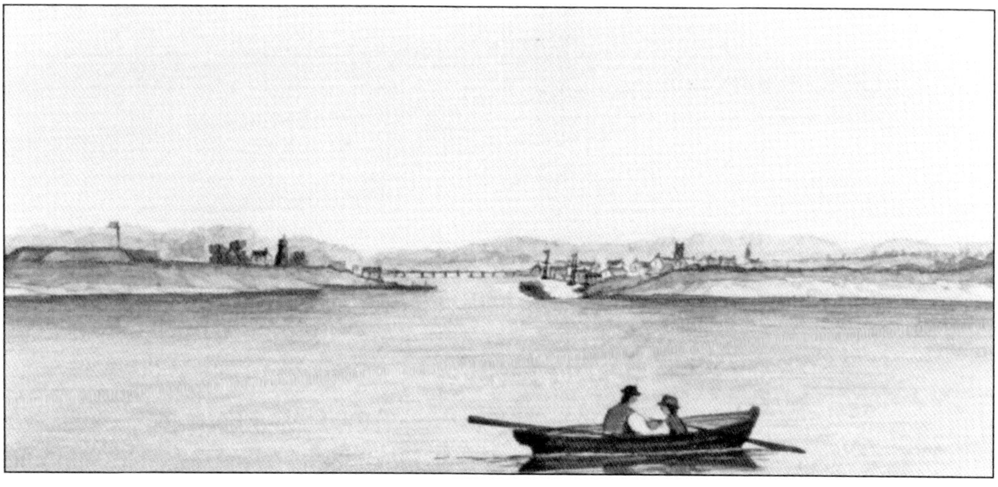

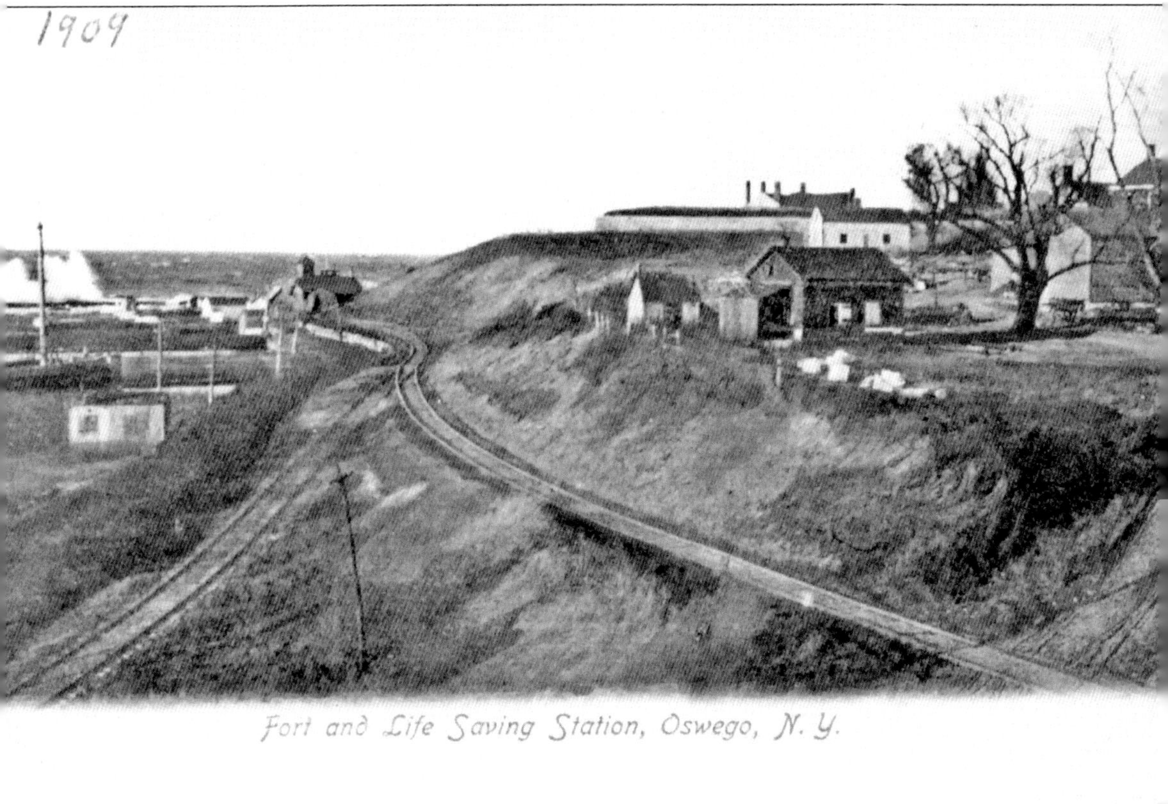

Looking north along the east side of the Oswego River, this c. 1909 postcard captures the 1822 keeper's dwelling (white) just south of Fort Ontario. The Lighthouse Service gave up the dwelling when the 1837 Oswego Harbor Lighthouse was commissioned on the west side of the Oswego River. The US Army, which had regarrisoned Fort Ontario in 1836, retained the dwelling.

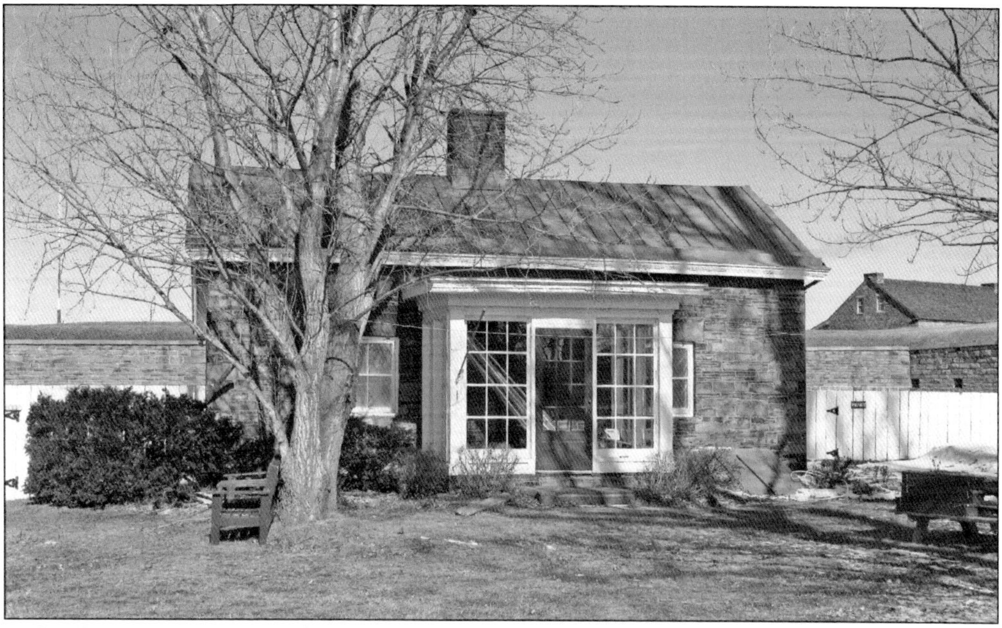

Today, Fort Ontario is a state historic site, and a member of the park staff occupies the old keeper's dwelling. Viewed in 2010, the small home has four rooms: two rooms occupy the first floor on each side of the large double central fireplace, and two bedrooms occupy the attic. A stone kitchen attached to the rear of the house was added later. This dwelling was of standard US Lighthouse Service design and was repeated at many light stations on the Great Lakes and in New England. Oswego's keeper's dwelling is believed to be the oldest such structure still in existence on the Great Lakes and almost the oldest in the entire nation.

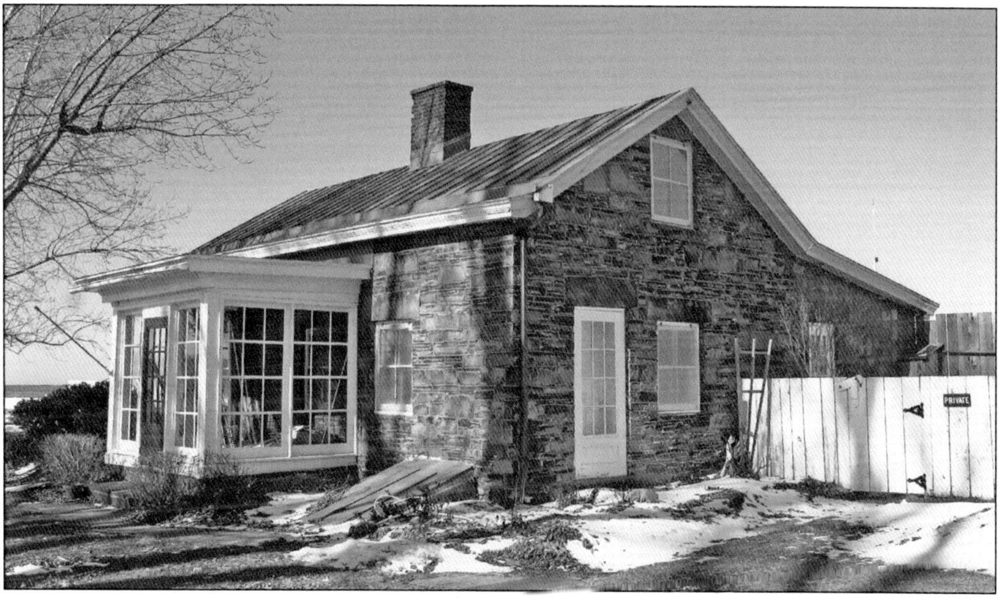

Also in 2010, the attached stone kitchen and new front porch can be seen. The porch is suspected to have been added when New York State acquired Fort Ontario in the late 1940s. The stone was quarry rubble, an inexpensive material of the day, but was effective, as it still stands nearly 200 years later.

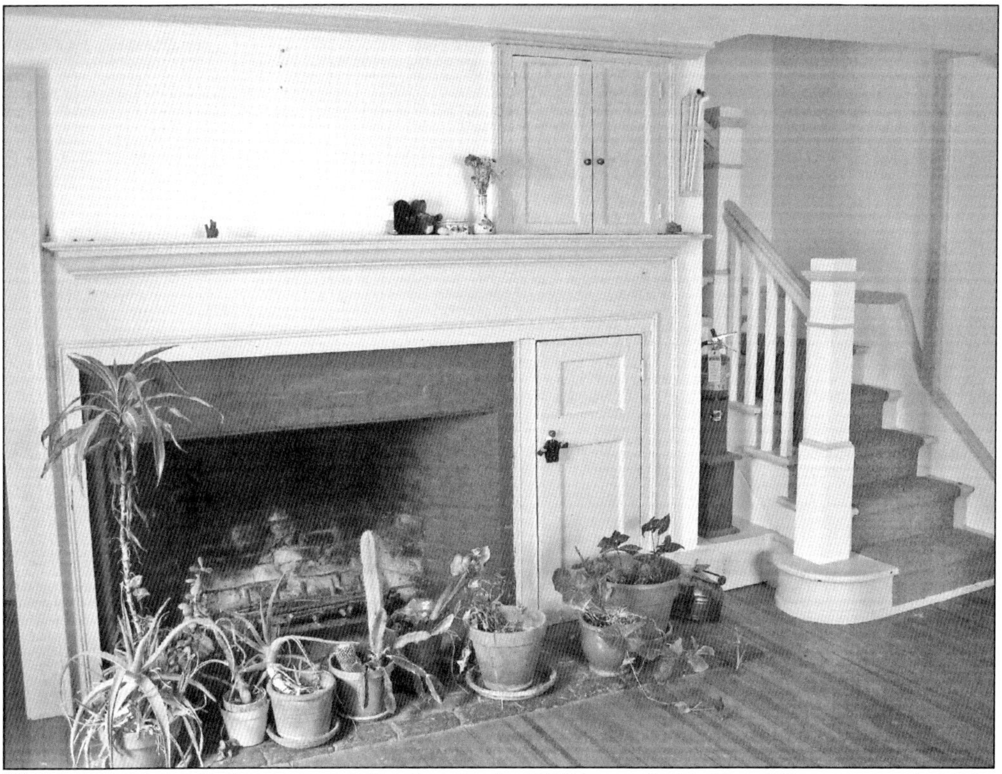

This is one side of the large central fireplace in the 1822 keeper's dwelling. The stairs to the right go up to the two small bedrooms in the attic. Prior to the addition of the kitchen, meals were prepared here or in the room on the other side of the double fireplace.

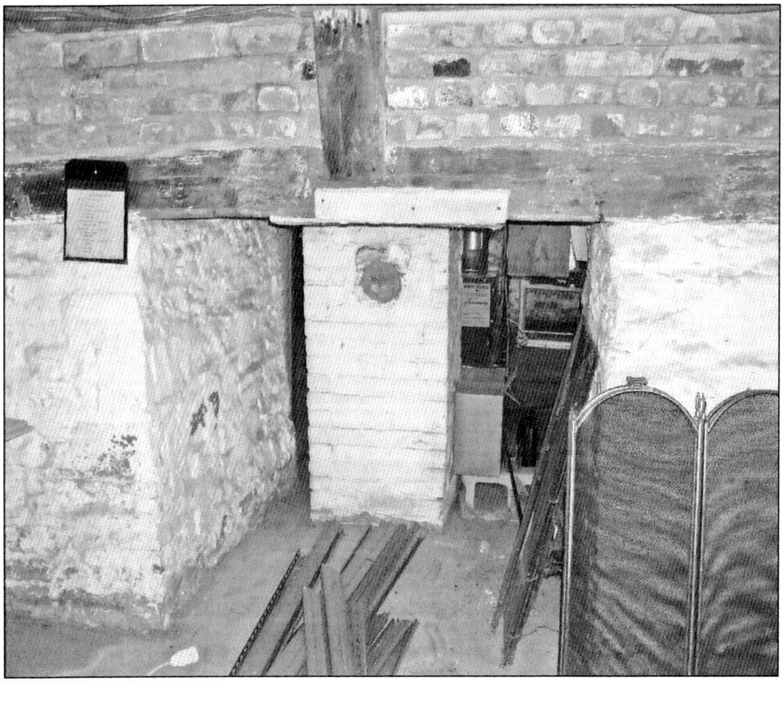

This image of the basement of the keeper's dwelling shows the massive support structure for the double central fireplace. The stone walls of the dwelling are 20 inches thick and extend two feet above the attic floor.

Two

Oswego Harbor's Second Lighthouse 1837–1917

The Oswego Canal (1828) is the economic engine that drove the development of the Port of Oswego and is thus inextricably linked to the development of Oswego's lighthouses and harbor facilities. The Oswego Canal provides a direct link to the Erie Canal at Syracuse and therefore provides access between Lake Ontario and New York City. Similarly, the Welland Canal (1829) connects Lake Erie and Lake Ontario by bypassing Niagara Falls, creating greater access to Great Lakes commerce and further generating commercial growth in Oswego as a major shipping hub.

With the Rivers and Harbors Act of 1826, the US Army Corps of Engineers began development of Oswego Harbor in anticipation of the Oswego Canal's opening. For a decade thereafter, the United States spent over $200,000 building stone-filled timber-crib breakwaters on each side of the mouth of the Oswego River, ultimately creating a usable and safe harbor. Such development rendered the 1822 Oswego Harbor Lighthouse ineffective.

On June 30, 1834, the Lighthouse Appropriations Act was signed; it included $3,666 "For a lighthouse or beacon light on one of the piers at the harbor of Oswego, on Lake Ontario." Thus the project to build Oswego's second lighthouse began, and the light was first lit on July 15, 1837. The *Oswego Palladium* indicated the new lighthouse had cost $15,000, so additional funds must have been appropriated in 1835 and 1836 to support the increased project cost. The result was a 45-foot-high cut-stone octagonal tower lit by seven Winslow Lewis patent reflector lamps. By 1849, the number of lamps had increased to 13, giving the light a 16-mile visibility offshore.

The commercial prominence of the Port of Oswego continued to increase, and the 1837 Oswego Harbor Lighthouse was upgraded accordingly. In 1855, the 13 reflector lamps were replaced by a fourth-order Fresnel lens housed in a new lantern. In 1869, the tower height was increased by 14 feet, and a larger third-order Fresnel lens was installed in a new, larger lantern. The 1837 Oswego Harbor Lighthouse was discontinued in 1917 and replaced by a red lens lantern on a pole called the Oswego Inner Light. Fear of the deteriorating tower's collapse prompted its removal in 1927. It was Oswego's longest serving lighthouse.

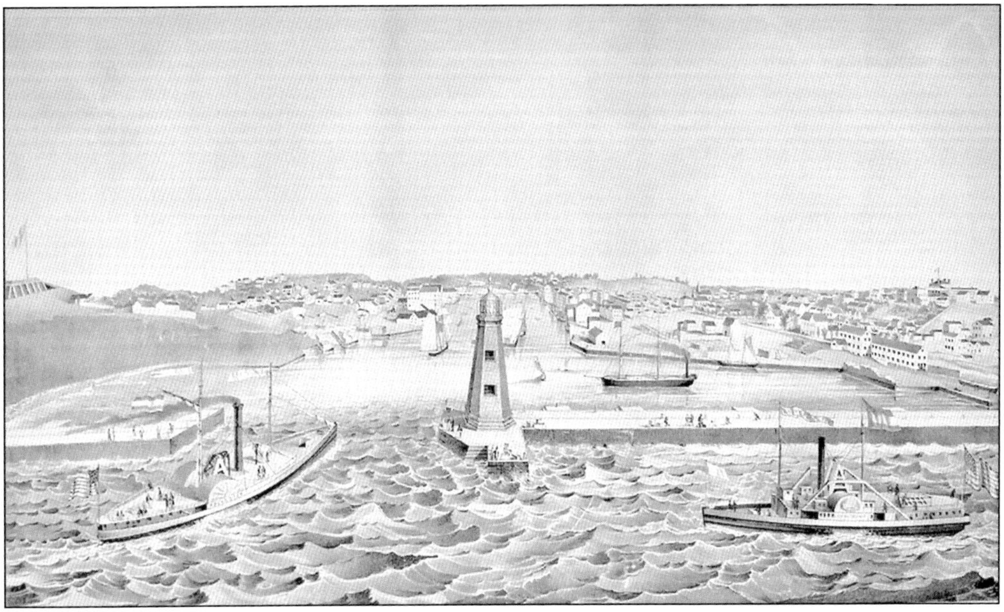

Like the 1822 Oswego Harbor Lighthouse, all that is left are illustrations and drawings to gather visual information about the early period of the 1837 Oswego Harbor Lighthouse. According to the 1839 Light List, and similar to the 1822 lighthouse, the 1837 lighthouse was equipped with seven reflector lamps. The 1849 Light List indicates it was upgraded to a 13-reflector lamp array in a birdcage lantern, as portrayed in this 1843 George Endicott lithograph. This extended the visibility of the beacon to 16 miles, indicating the growing commercial importance of Oswego Harbor.

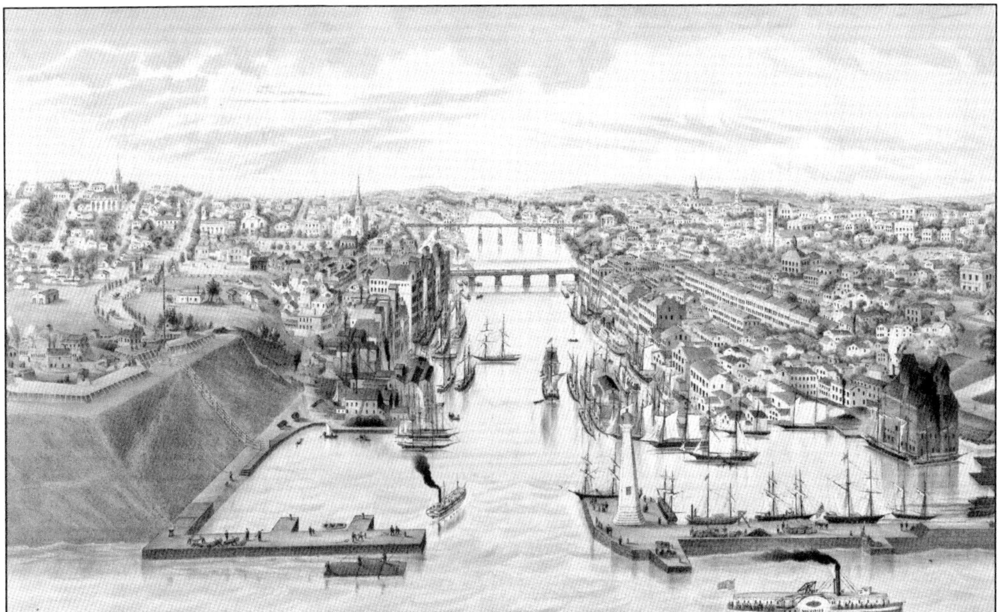

Between 1852 and 1855, a major US Army Corps of Engineers project upgraded Oswego Harbor, requiring an onsite officer to supervise the work. At the same time, following a push to improve all US lighthouses, the 1837 Oswego Harbor Lighthouse was converted to a fourth-order Fresnel lens, as illustrated in this 1855 Smith Brothers lithograph.

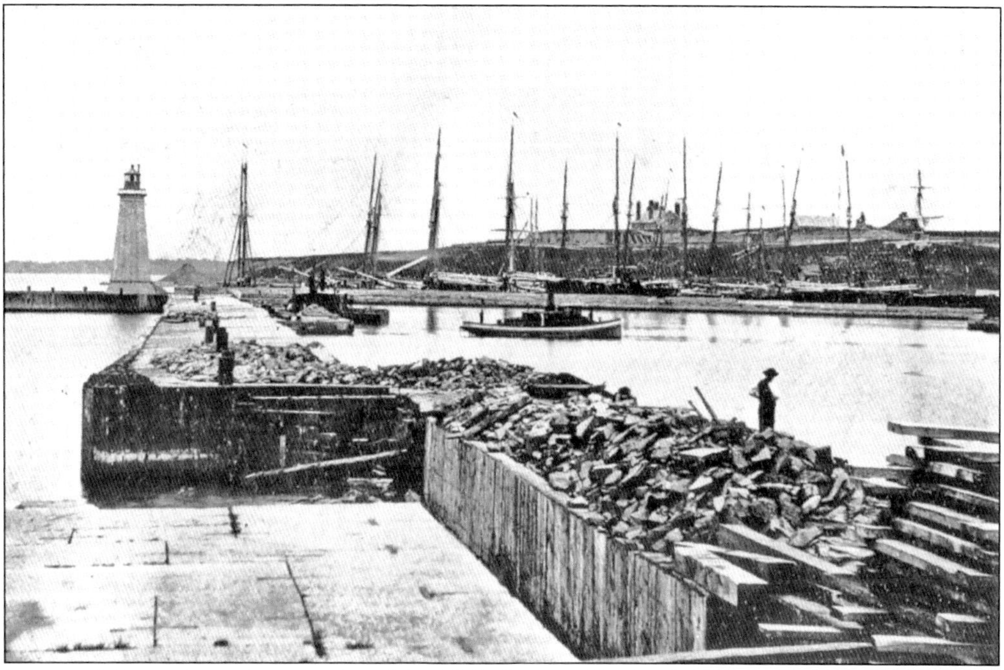

In one of the earliest photographs of the 1837 Oswego Harbor Lighthouse, the newly installed fourth-order Fresnel lens and the new lantern that housed it are clearly visible. The 1858 Light List confirms the lens was installed in 1855 with a visibility of 14 miles. Breakwater repair and upgrades were still ongoing on the west side of Oswego Harbor.

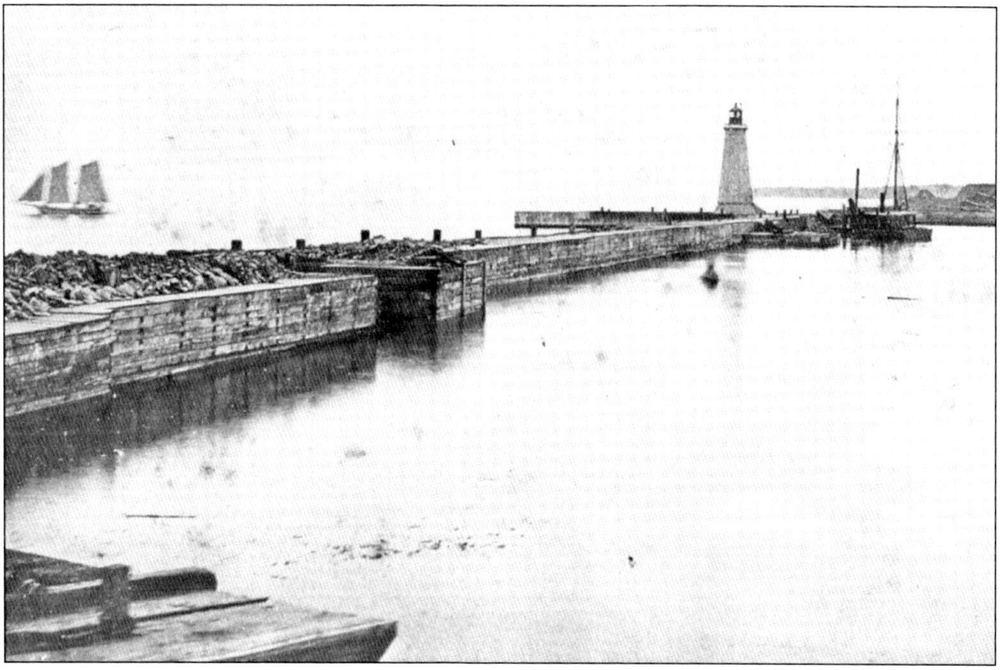

This c. 1855 photograph of the newly upgraded 1837 Oswego Harbor Lighthouse provides a different vantage point of the new fourth-order Fresnel lens. A schooner can be seen at left exiting the harbor under sail, and work on the west breakwater is still ongoing.

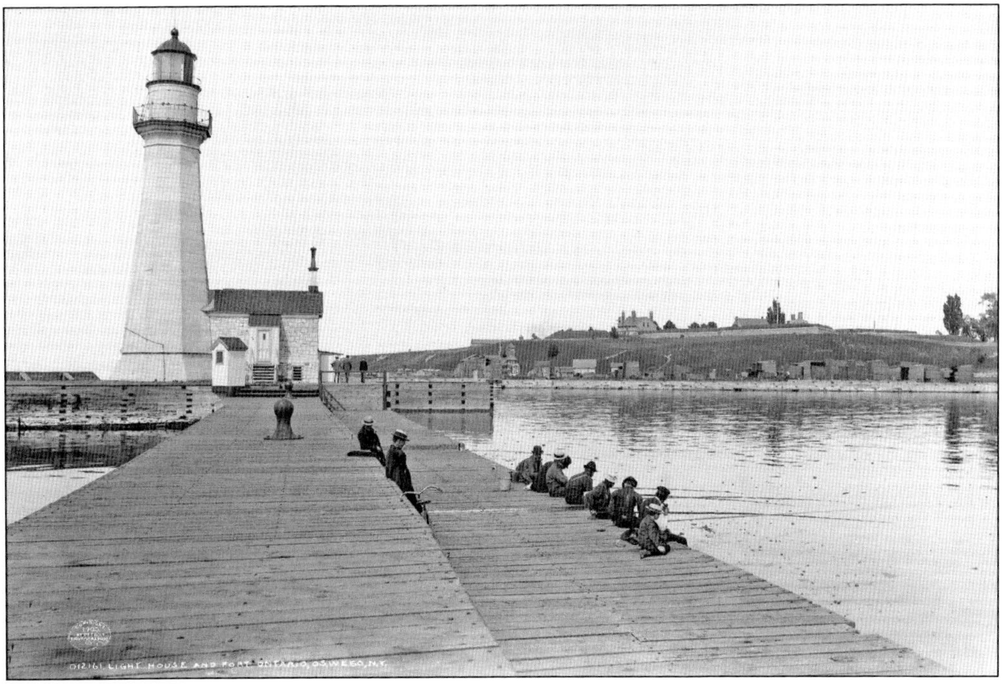

In 1869, the 1837 Oswego Harbor Lighthouse was again rebuilt to improve its visibility and extend it out into Lake Ontario. The height of the tower was extended 14 feet, and a larger third-order Fresnel lens was installed, which also required a new, larger lantern to house it. According to the 1914 Light List, when this light was still the principal Oswego lighthouse, it had a visibility of 16 miles. (Courtesy of the Library of Congress.)

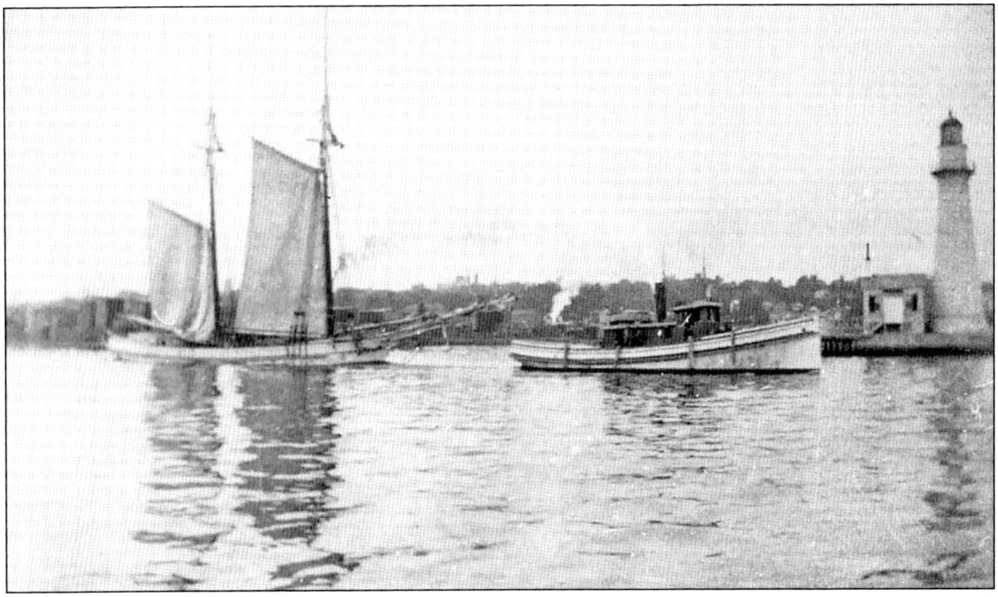

This photograph demonstrates the raised tower with the new, larger lantern and, on the small structure at the base of the tower, an entrance on the west side. This was a work area and, in case of stormy weather, a place for the keeper on duty to shelter until the storm was over. (Courtesy of Mark Slosek, City of Oswego historian.)

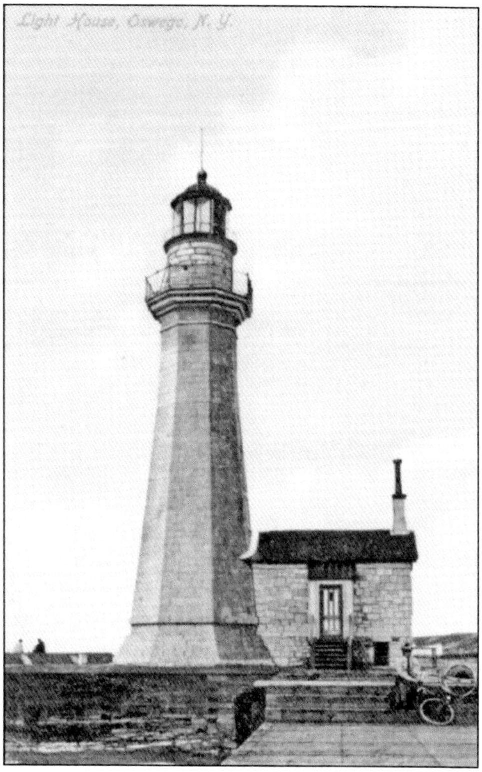

The 1837 Oswego Harbor Lighthouse was a favorite amongst locals, and a young lady (right) rode her bicycle along the breakwater to pose for a photograph. There are no additional structures at the base of the tower. Later (below), three young men walked out onto the breakwater to pose for a photograph with the two additional structures at the base of the lighthouse tower. A brown cast-iron oil house at left was added to the station in 1906 for safe storage of the kerosene fuel, and the small white structure at right is the necessary facility. (Below, courtesy of the Oswego County Historical Society.)

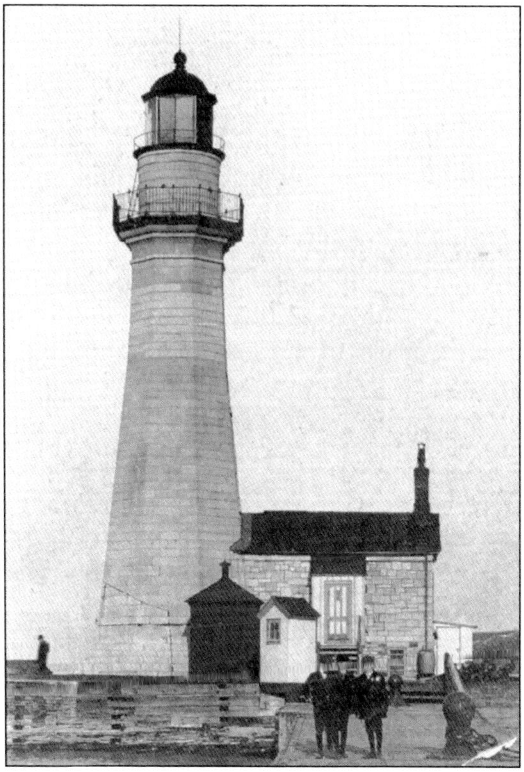

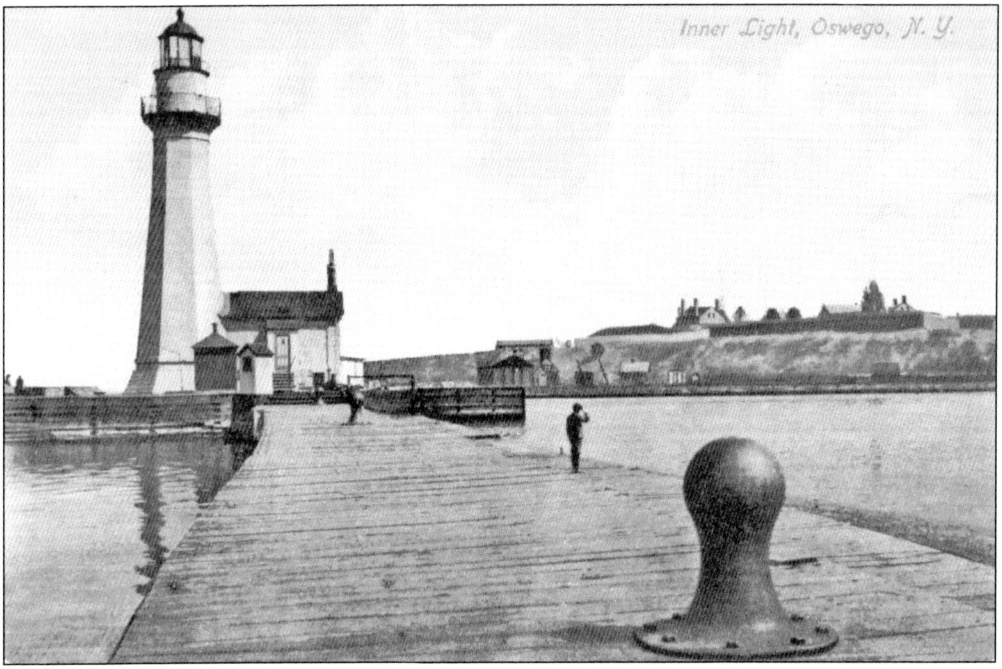

These two photographs were taken from approximately the same location. In the image above, a young man looks across the Oswego River toward Fort Ontario. Below, lighthouse keeper Charles H. Tucker in his uniform and overcoat rests against a bollard on the breakwater. Tucker assumed duties at the 1837 Oswego Harbor Lighthouse on June 1, 1904, and remained there until it was decommissioned in 1917. The oil house at the base of the tower was added during his tour of duty. (Below, courtesy of the Oswego County Historical Society.)

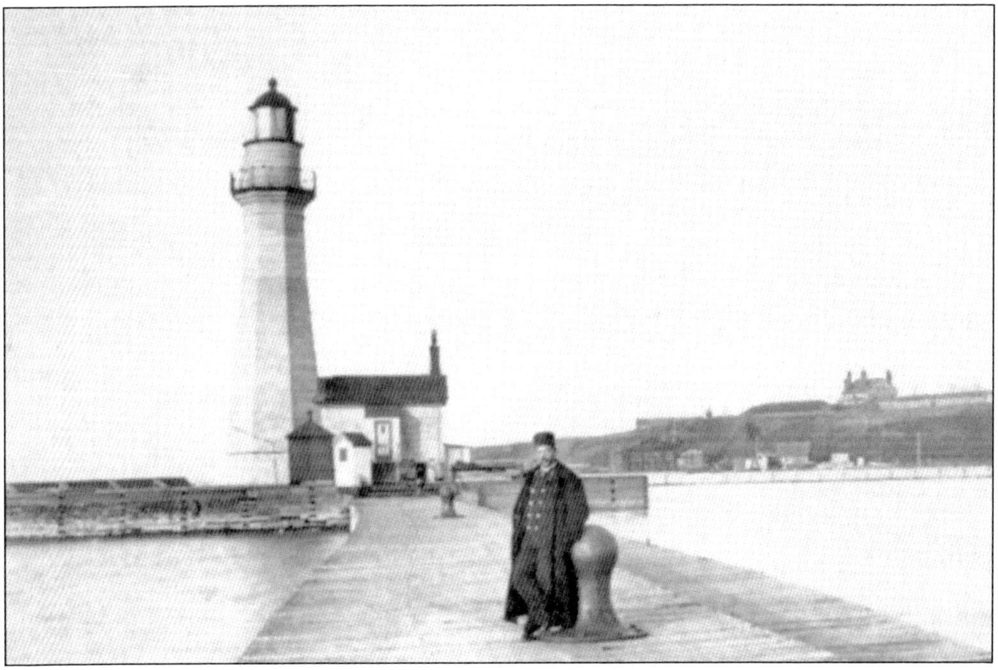

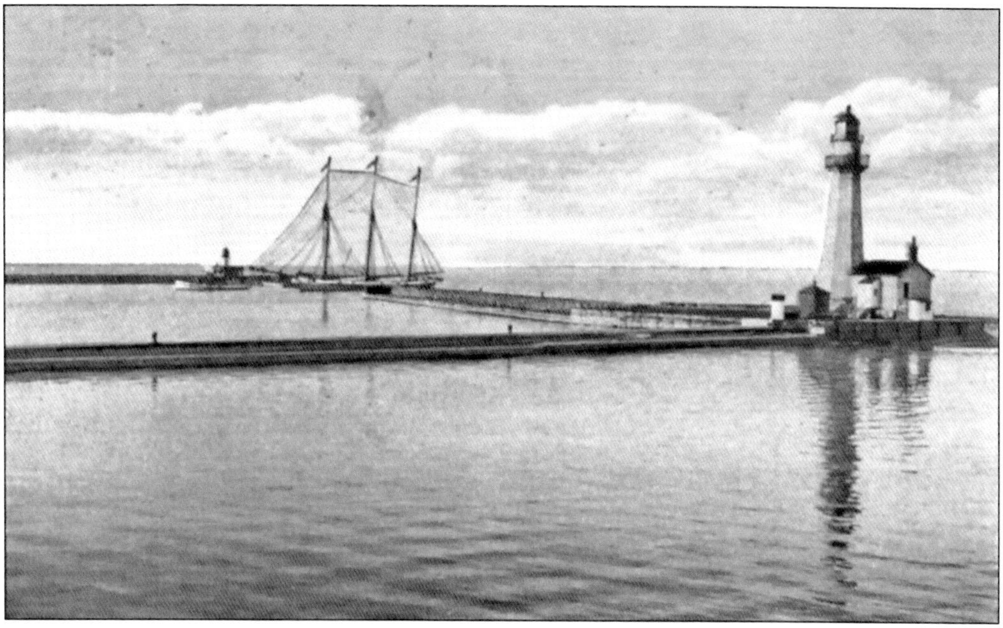

These are two postcards made from the same photograph depicting a three-masted schooner being towed by a tug through the gap between the outer and inner west breakwater. The oil house at the base of the 1837 Oswego Harbor Lighthouse tower dates them after 1906. The postcard below has been retouched to depict a night scene, with the lighthouse beam and lights in windows. Included is a window in the oil house, though one never existed there. These lighthouse night scene postcards were very popular in the early postcard era in the United States.

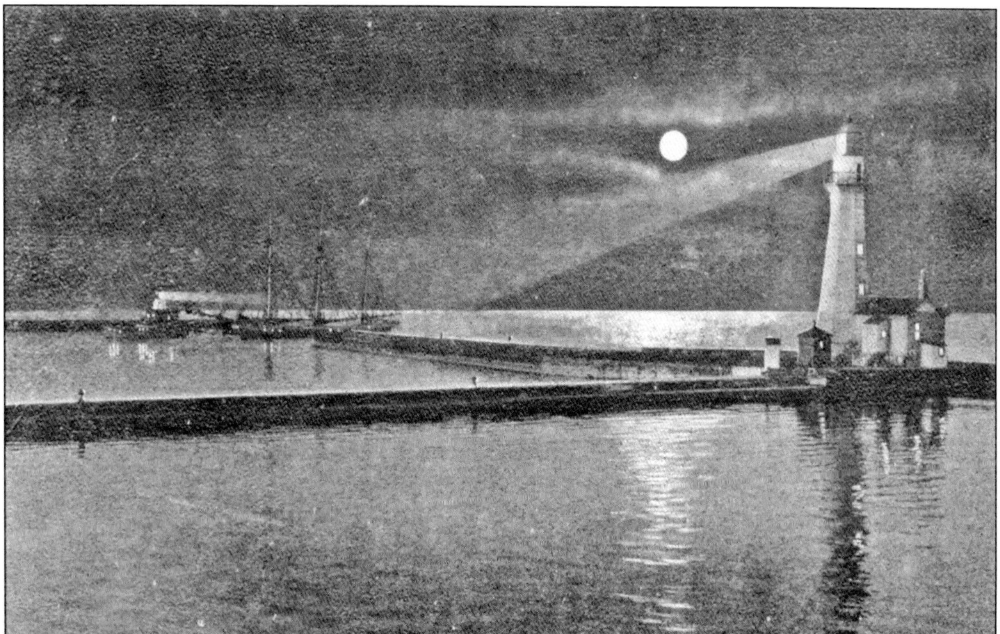

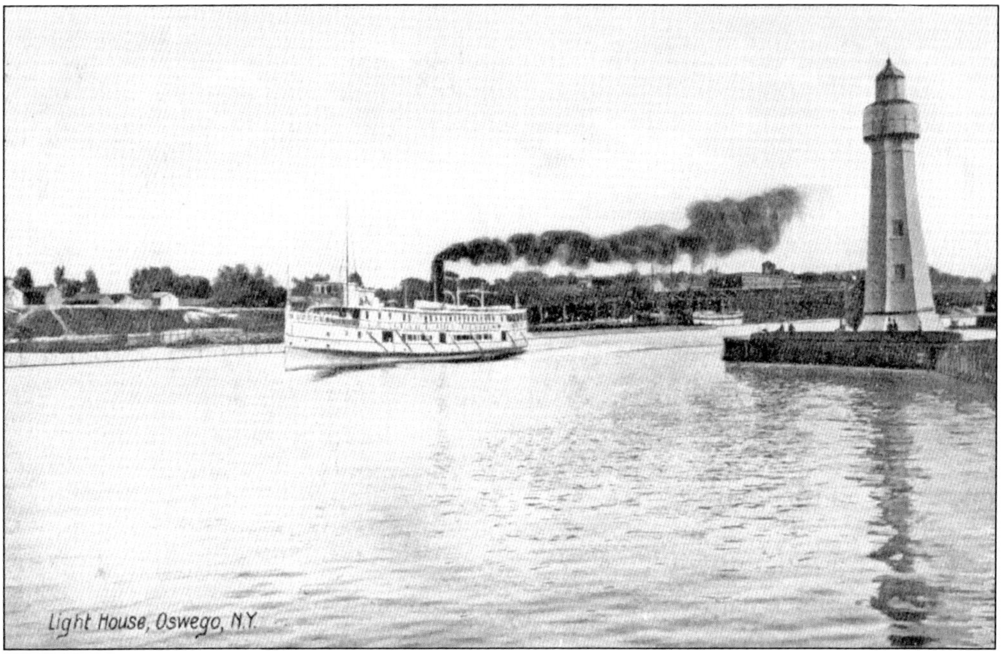

These postcards depict two passenger steamers departing Oswego Harbor and passing the 1837 Oswego Harbor Lighthouse. The SS *Arundell* (above) before 1906 and the SS *Iroquois* (below) after 1906 are seen from roughly opposite vantage points. The *Arundell* was built in Buffalo in 1878 and sailed on the Great Lakes until it sank in 1922. The *Iroquois* was built in Toledo in 1901 and sailed on the Great Lakes until 1907, when it was purchased by a shipping company in Seattle and sailed around Cape Horn to operate in Puget Sound.

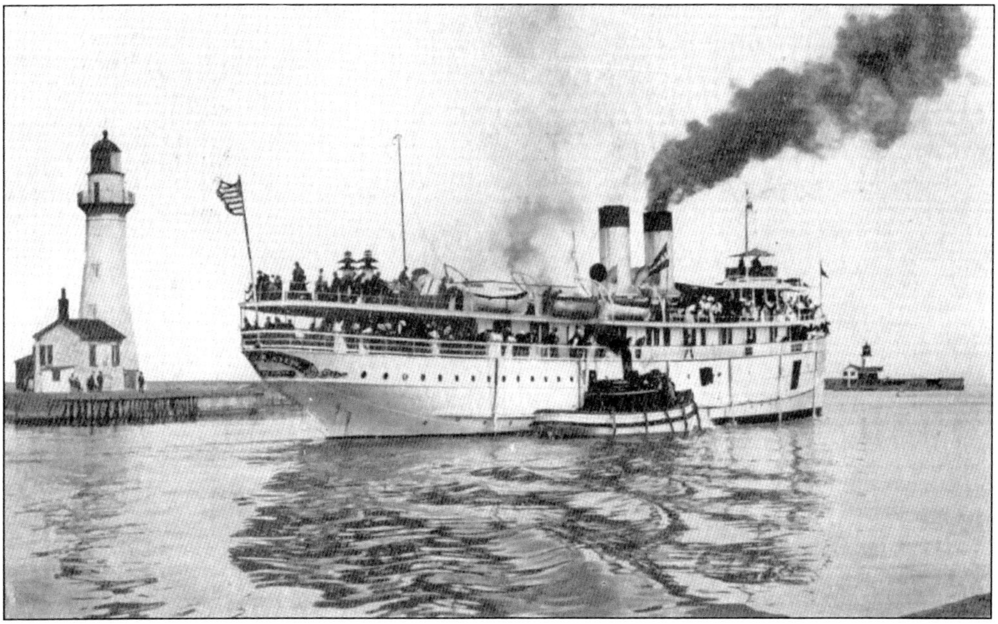

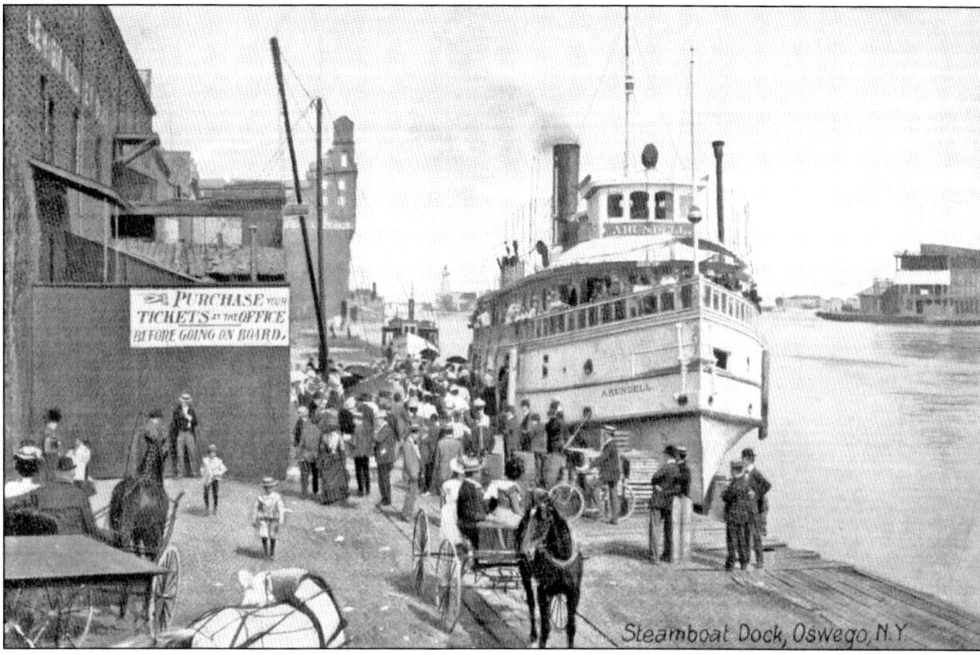

Maritime commerce in Oswego was facilitated by the efficient system of lighthouses and other lighted aids to navigation along the New York State Barge Canal and Lake Ontario. Further, the US Revenue Cutter Service and Life-Saving Service aided mariners and passengers. Steamboats like the *Arundell* were a vital part of that system. The US Coast Guard inherited those responsibilities and maintains them today. (Courtesy of Mark Slosek, City of Oswego historian.)

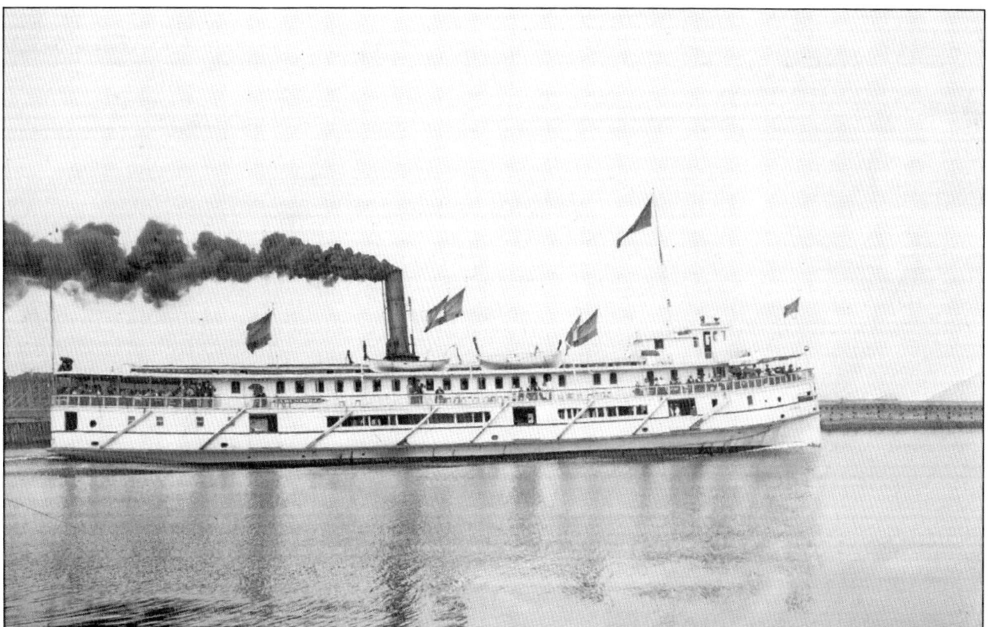

The *Arundell* is underway departing Oswego Harbor. It was an iron-hulled vessel built in Buffalo in 1878 that sailed between Buffalo, Rochester, and the Thousand Islands. (Courtesy of Mark Slosek, City of Oswego historian.)

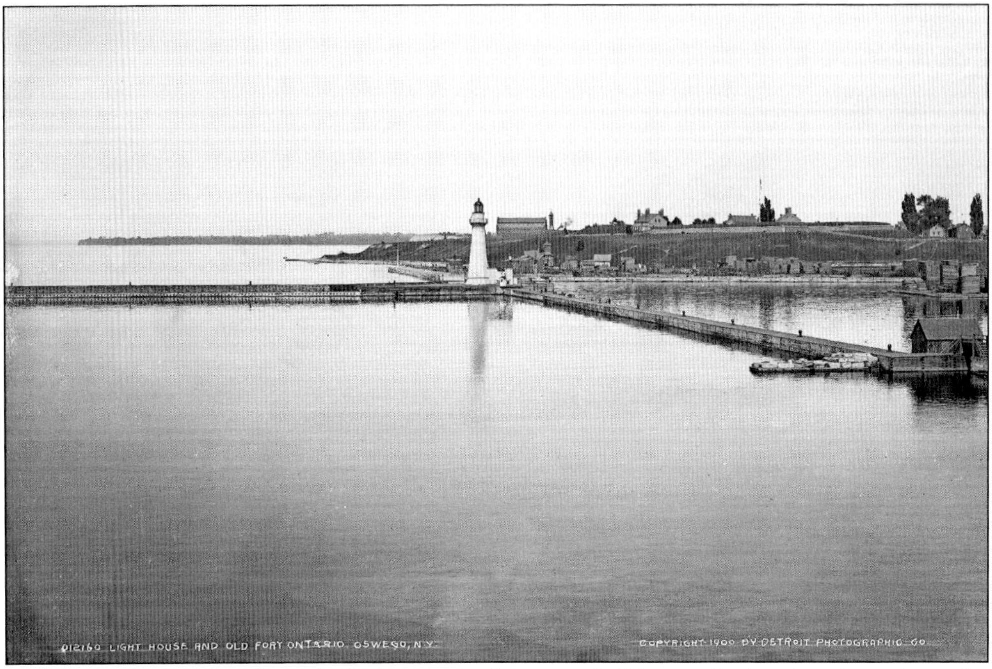

This photograph, taken from the Delaware, Lackawanna & Western Railroad coal trestle on the west side of Oswego Harbor, looks east at the 1837 Oswego Harbor Lighthouse with a view of Fort Ontario and the US Life-Saving station at Oswego in the background. The absence of the oil house dates it to before 1906, and the light station boathouse is viewed at the corner of the breakwater to the right. (Courtesy of the National Archives and Records Administration.)

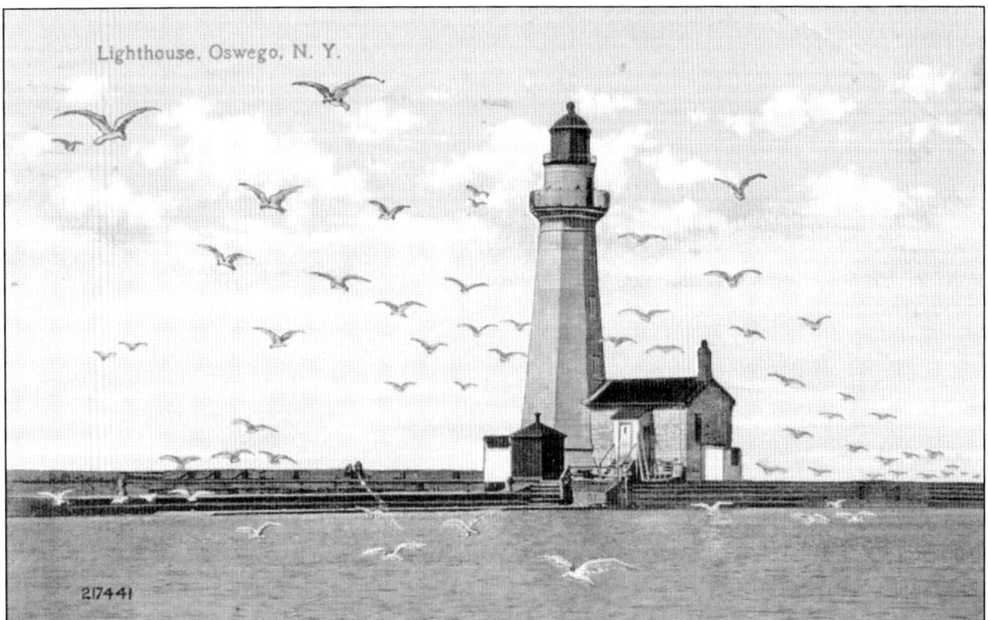

This postcard shows the 1837 Oswego Harbor Lighthouse with the iron oil house installed. These iron oil houses, which could be either round or square, were common at Great Lakes lighthouses during this period.

In 1917, the US Lighthouse Service designated the 1881 Oswego Breakwater Beacon (Oswego's third lighthouse) as the primary Oswego Harbor aid to navigation and decommissioned the 1837 Oswego Harbor Lighthouse. The 1837 lighthouse was replaced with a red lens lantern on a pole that sat next to the base of the disused tower. This post-1917 photograph shows that lens lantern, which would have been maintained by the keeper and assistant keeper assigned to the 1881 Oswego Breakwater Beacon.

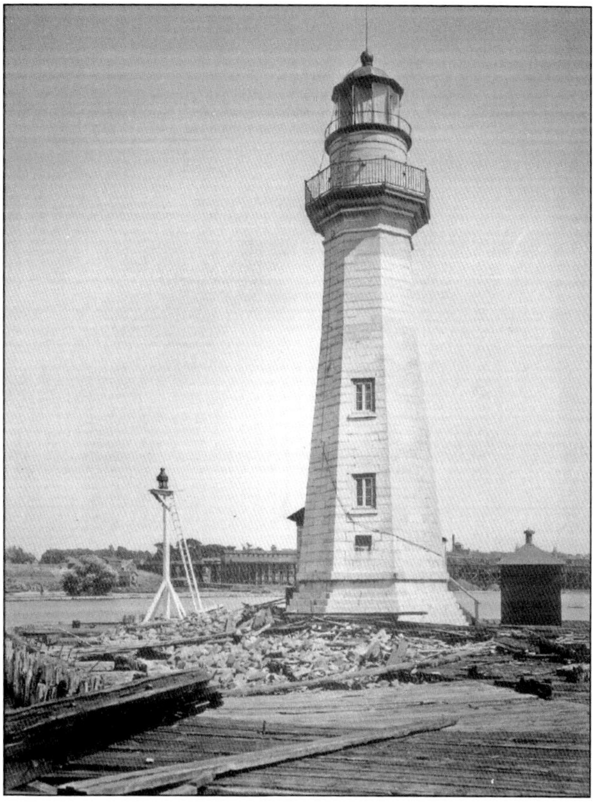

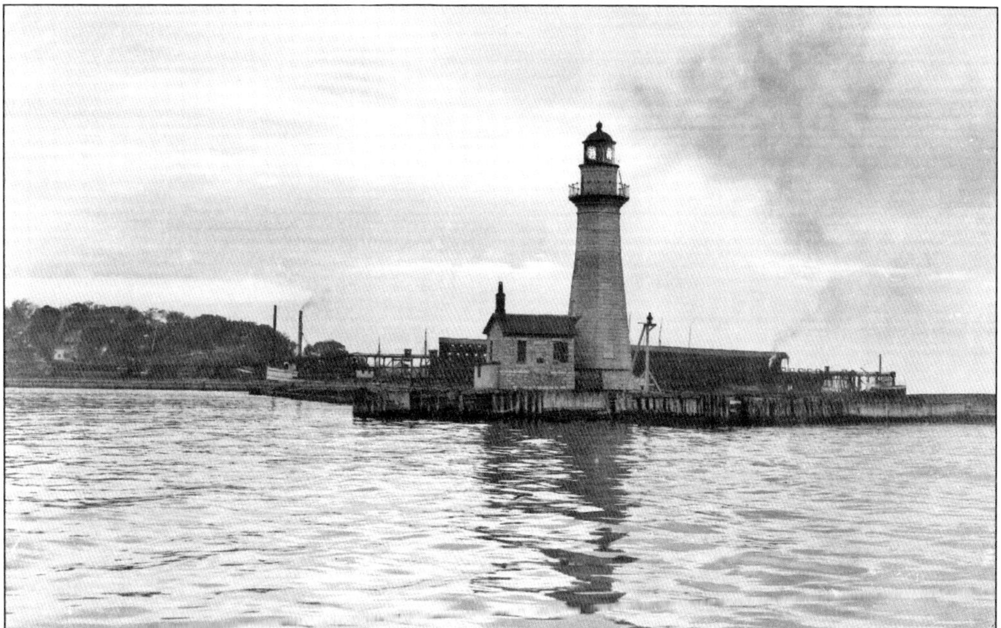

This photograph shows the 1837 Oswego Harbor Lighthouse and lantern pole from the east side of the Oswego River. The unused 1837 lighthouse rests along the deteriorating inner harbor breakwater prior to being dismantled. (Courtesy of Mark Slosek, City of Oswego historian.)

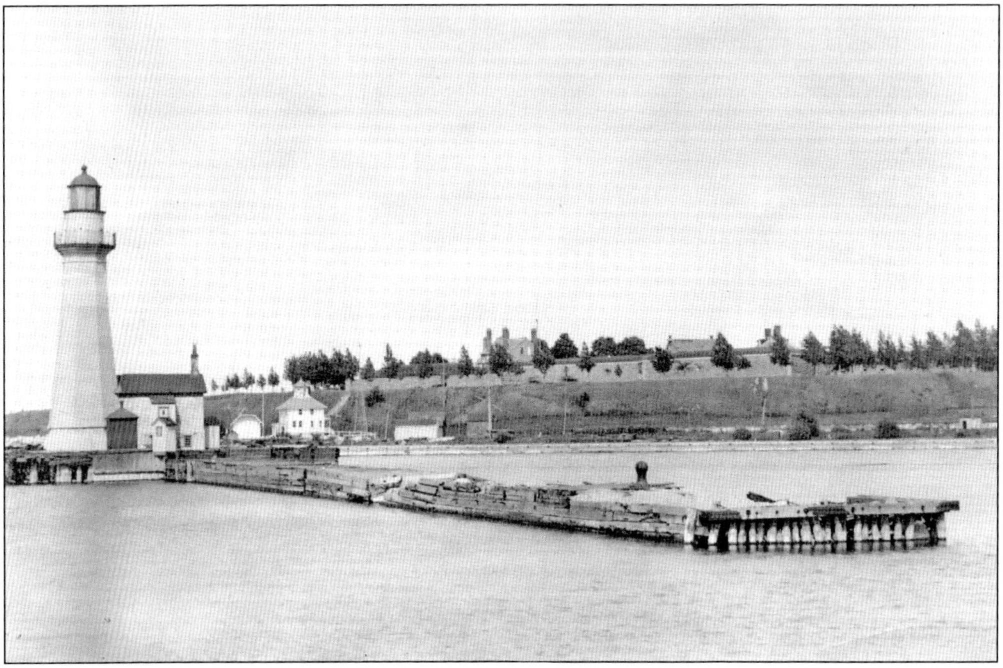

In 1920, New York State developed plans to construct a new one-million-bushel grain elevator in Oswego. The elevator was to be on the west side of Oswego Harbor and required a new pier on which to build it. The pier was constructed just west of the inner harbor breakwater and the 1837 Oswego Harbor Lighthouse tower. This required the removal of a section of that breakwater. This photograph, taken from the new pier, shows the gap created in the old breakwater because of that station's removal. (Courtesy of the National Archives and Records Administration.)

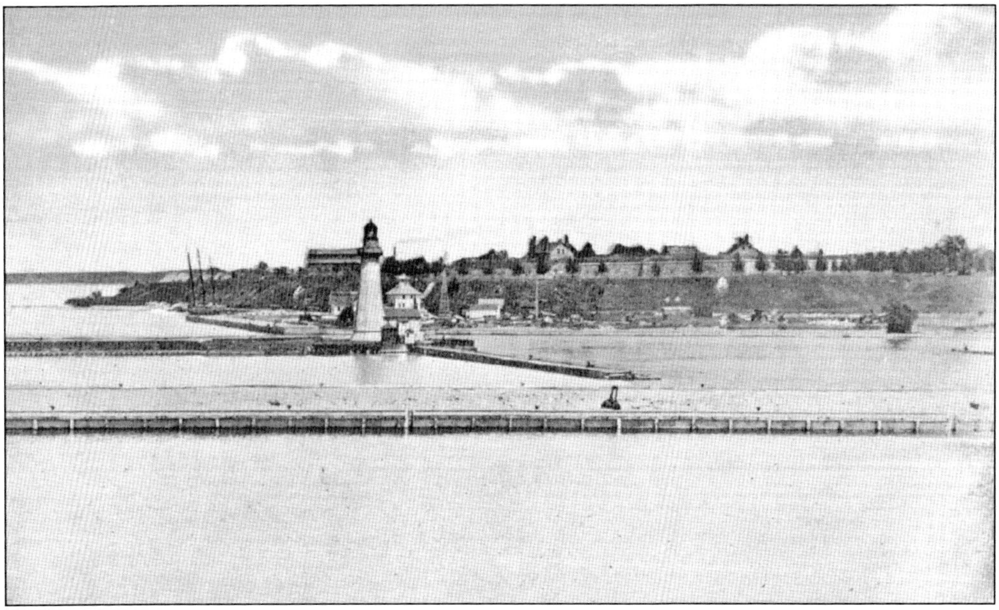

This postcard photograph, taken from the Delaware, Lackawanna & Western coal trestle, shows the new pier's position. Construction of the grain elevator, built in 1925, had not yet begun. The large grain elevator dominated Oswego Harbor until it was demolished in 1998.

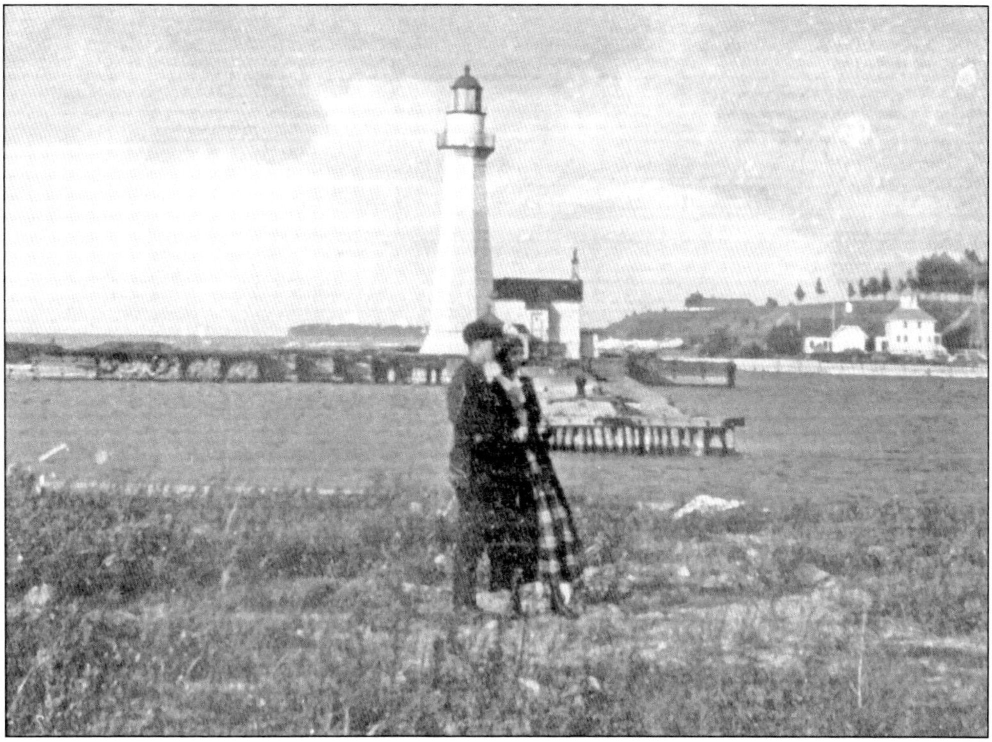

This photograph of a World War I–era soldier, probably attached to Fort Ontario, and his companion was taken on the new west-side pier where the grain elevator was built. The remainder of the inner breakwater is showing signs of increased decay.

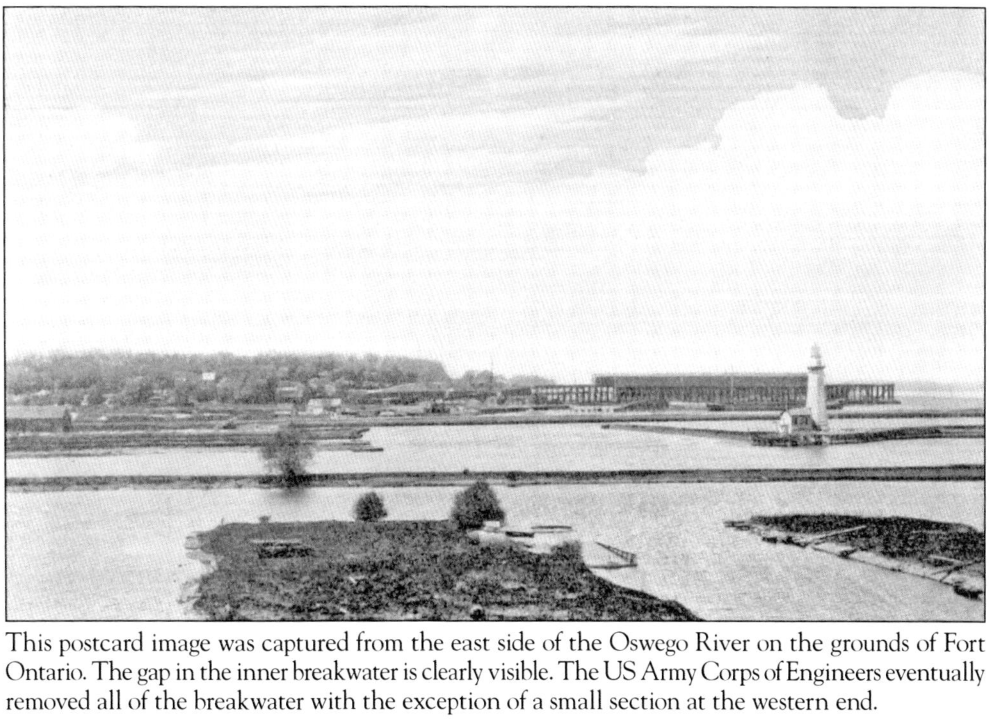

This postcard image was captured from the east side of the Oswego River on the grounds of Fort Ontario. The gap in the inner breakwater is clearly visible. The US Army Corps of Engineers eventually removed all of the breakwater with the exception of a small section at the western end.

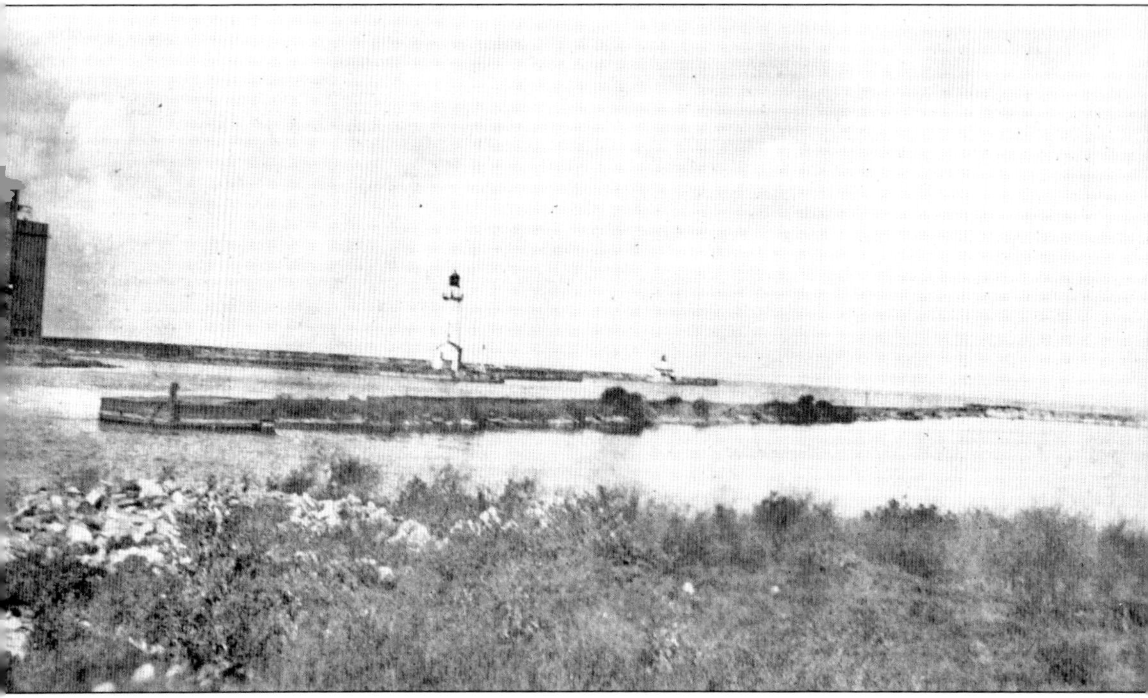

This photograph looks toward Lake Ontario and the west side of Oswego Harbor. The Oswego Breakwater Beacon, now the primary Oswego lighthouse, is visible, and so is the 1837 lighthouse tower, now discontinued. Next to the 1837 tower is the red lens lantern on a pole that replaced it in 1917. Both the old inner breakwaters on the east and west sides of the harbor are beginning to show signs of advanced deterioration. (Courtesy of the Oswego Coast Guard Station.)

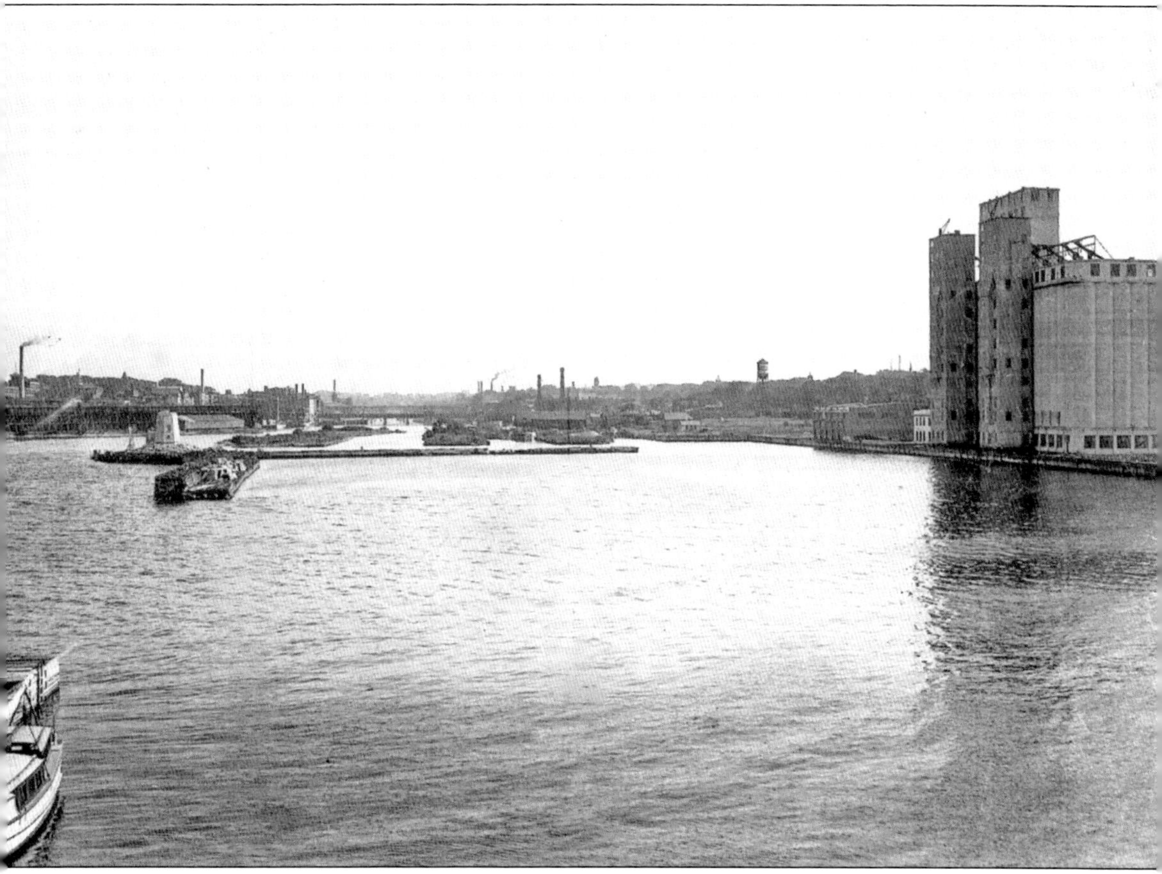

Bids to remove the 1837 Oswego Harbor Lighthouse tower opened on August 2, 1927, and the job was completed on October 8, 1927. The stone was used as riprap for a water intake elsewhere on Lake Ontario. This photograph shows the nearly completed removal of the stone tower. (Courtesy of the National Archives and Records Administration.)

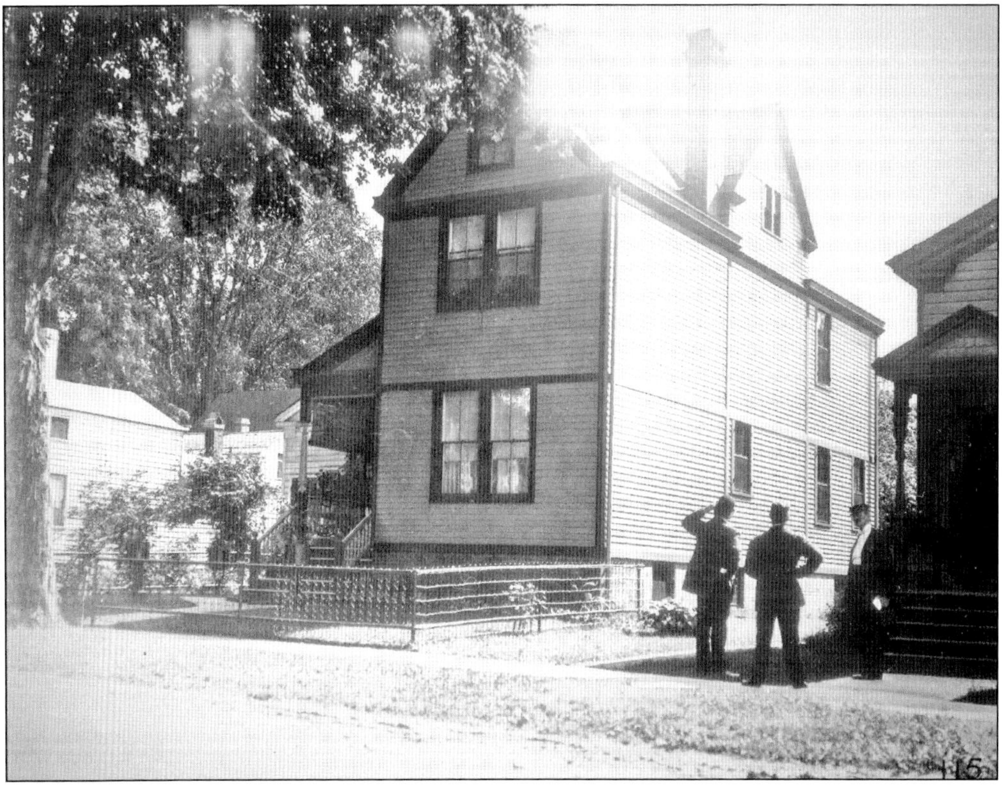

On September 10, 1846, the US Department of the Treasury, under which the Lighthouse Service functioned, purchased a plot of land in Oswego at what is now 22 West Third Street. A new keeper's dwelling was constructed there to replace the dwelling at Fort Ontario, which had passed to the US Army upon the decommissioning of the 1822 lighthouse. This post-1900 photograph was taken after the house underwent a major rebuild in 1897. (Courtesy of the National Archives and Records Administration.)

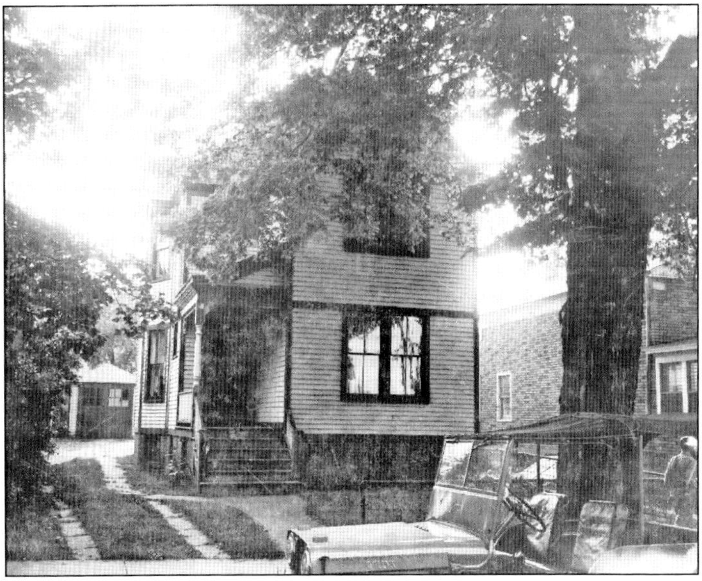

Although now privately owned, the keeper's dwelling was owned by the federal government until the mid-1950s. This photograph of the keeper's dwelling was taken in the late 1940s, before the structure was sold. (Courtesy of the National Archives and Records Administration.)

Three

Oswego Breakwater Beacon 1889–1931

In 1872, a two-decade-long expansion of Oswego Harbor began. A temporary beacon was placed at the end of the northern extension of the inner harbor breakwater, which stretched out toward Lake Ontario from the 1837 Oswego Harbor Lighthouse. Although new breakwaters were planned for both sides of Oswego Harbor, only the new outer breakwater on the west side was completed.

Construction of the new outer breakwater began roughly one mile west of the 1837 Oswego Harbor Lighthouse, and the outer end of the inner harbor's northern extension was exposed. To mitigate this exposure, a unique solution was devised by the US Lighthouse Service. In 1872, a wooden tower was constructed at the exposed location with glass panes on the three sides at the top. A trolley system ran from the upper window of the 1837 Oswego Harbor Lighthouse tower to the top of the new wooden tower. The trolley carried out a lens lantern that was displayed from the wooden tower, thus marking the end of the extension. This meant that the keeper did not have to carry the beacon out to the tower, a dangerous feat in inclement weather, when the light was needed most.

The trolley system worked for a number of years, but the breakwater kept expanding to accommodate increased shipping and commerce. Another solution was devised in 1877: a 27-foot cast-iron tower was built by the West Point Foundry in Cold Springs, New York, for $2,572 and was placed at the end of the extension showing a sixth-order Fresnel lens with a fixed red light. The tower's entry door was on the second level, and it was accessed by a keeper who walked along a raised walkway from the 1837 tower. Unlike the trolley system, this was a standard solution to an all-too-common problem on the Great Lakes and was used at many lighthouses.

In 1881, with the new outer breakwater complete, the cast-iron beacon was relocated to a caisson at the east end of the breakwater, and Oswego's first fog signal was added in 1882. In 1887, it was redesignated as a light station with its own keeper and assistant keeper. Thus Oswego Harbor's third lighthouse, the Oswego Breakwater Beacon, came into formal existence. Around this time, the light was upgraded to a fourth-order Fresnel lens with a fixed red light visible 12 miles out on Lake Ontario.

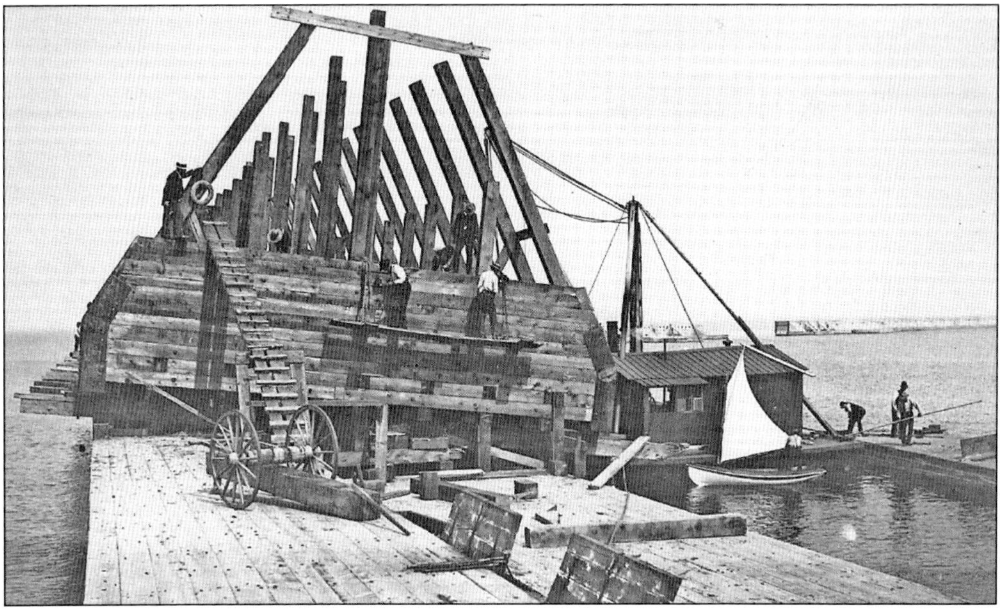

The new breakwater was constructed by combining a large number of timber cribs, which were sunk and then filled with stone. Here, one timber crib is under construction on top of an already completed section of the breakwater. It will then be launched into Oswego Harbor, floated into position, and filled with large stones. Later, the top of the breakwater was capped with concrete. The cold fresh water of Lake Ontario served to preserve the timbers, and much of this breakwater still exists today. (Courtesy of the Oswego County Historical Society.)

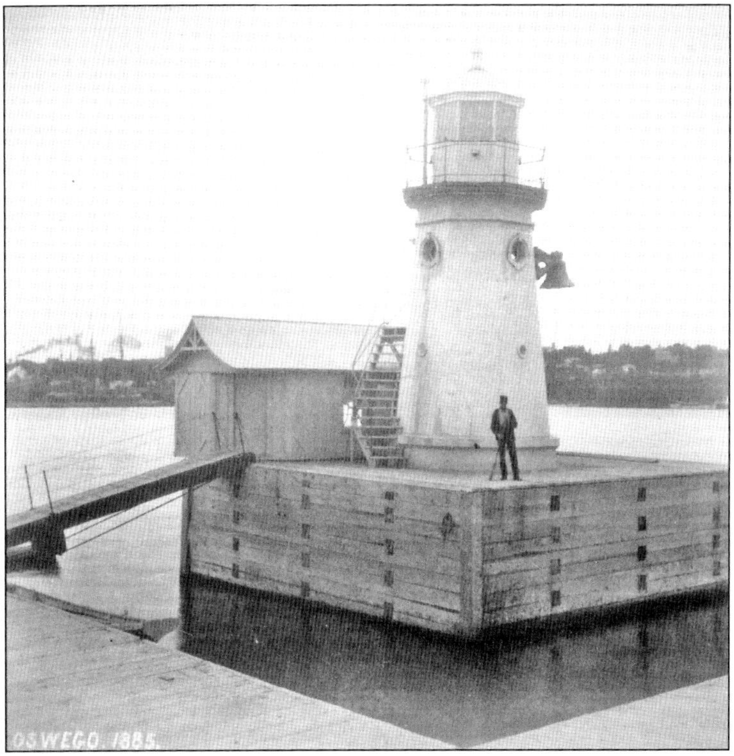

This photograph of the 1881 Oswego Breakwater Beacon was taken while it was still under construction. Although the 1882 fog bell is present, the tower remains unpainted, there are no railings on top of the caisson deck, and there is a set of stairs that accesses the tower's second-level entry door. (Courtesy of the National Archives and Records Administration.)

Taken just after construction was completed, this photograph of the Oswego Breakwater Beacon shows it painted in the standard US Lighthouse Service brown, with safety railings installed around the top of the caisson. The beacon's boathouse was added in 1882, as can be seen next to the tower. Although Oswego Harbor's outer breakwater was attached to shore, that was over one mile west, making a boat the preferred means of access. (Courtesy of Mark Slosek, City of Oswego historian.)

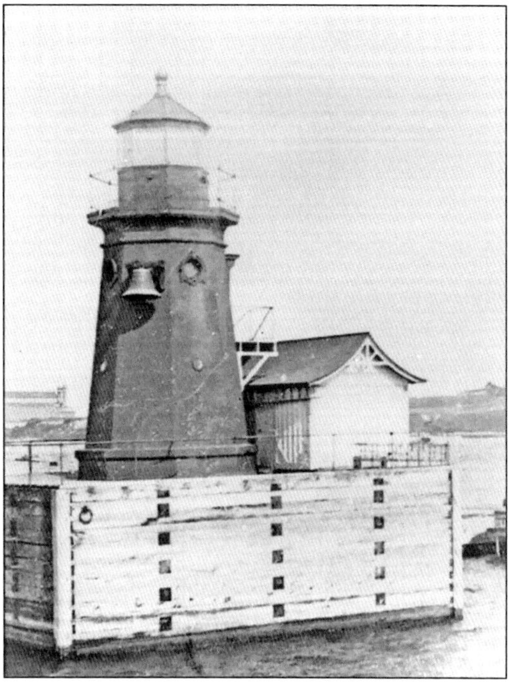

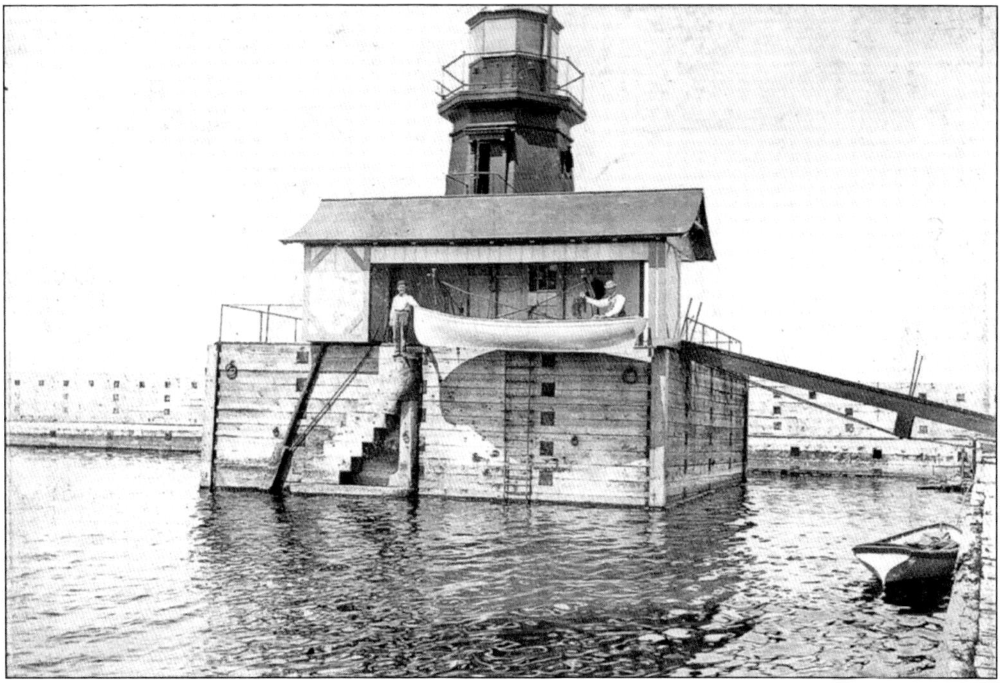

This photograph looks at the south side of the Oswego Breakwater Beacon as the station's boat is prepared for lowering into Lake Ontario. The stairway to the water level can be seen, as well as the privy at the end of the boathouse with its outflow pipe into Lake Ontario and the entry door to the tower above the roof of the boathouse. In its original location, the Oswego Breakwater Beacon's entry door was only reached by the long raised walkway along the breakwater extension from the 1837 Oswego Harbor Lighthouse tower.

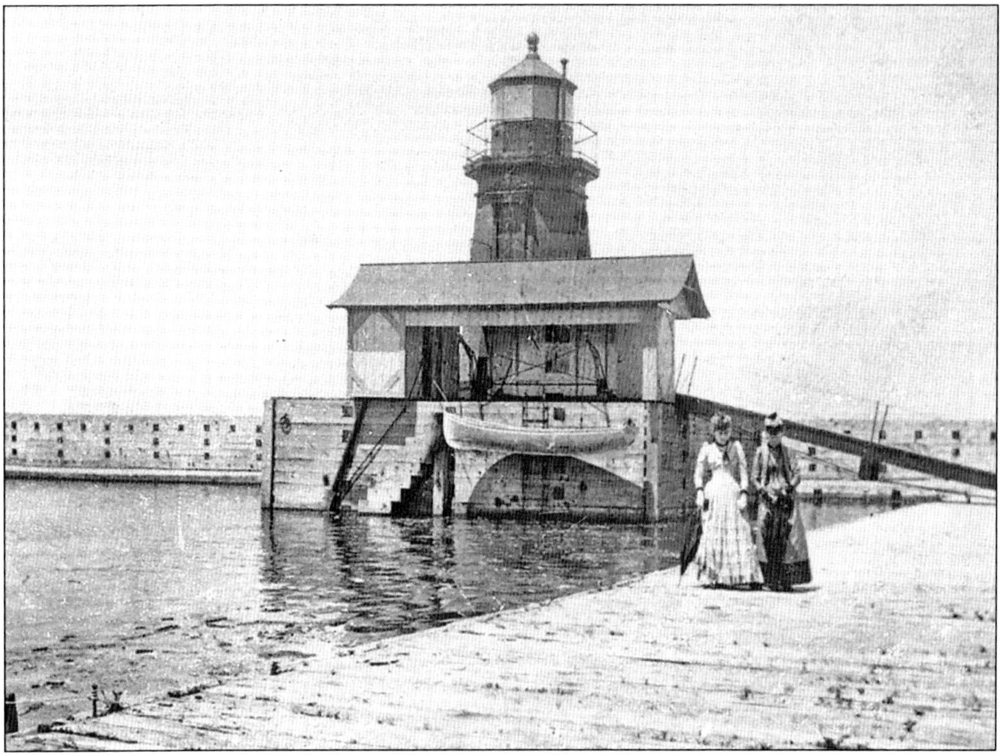

Mrs. G.M. Plumb (left) and Rosie Hamilton are visiting the new Oswego Breakwater Beacon. One can only assume that they arrived by boat, as the walk from shore over one mile away would have been difficult in their long dresses. (Courtesy of the Oswego County Historical Society.)

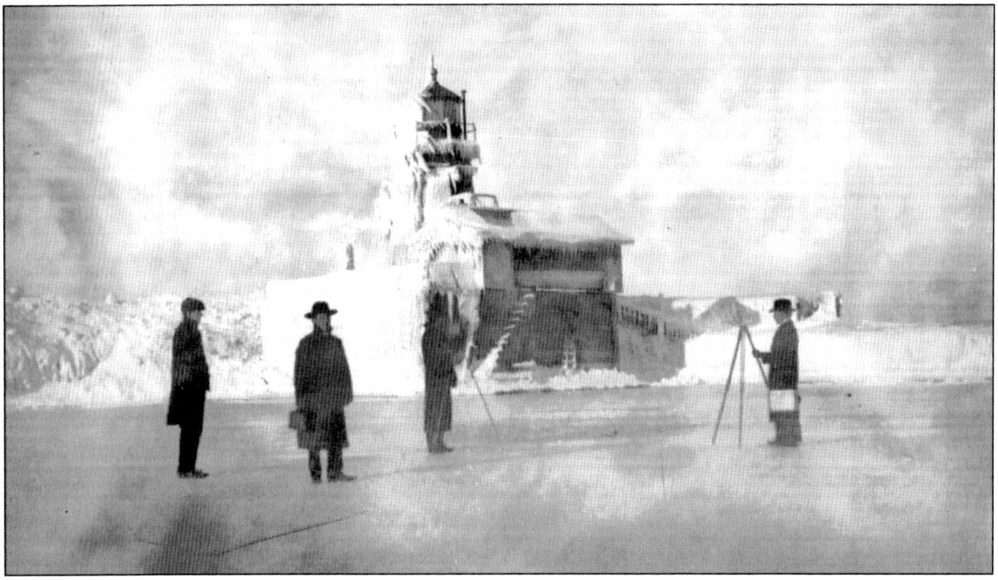

During a brutally cold winter—typical for the eastern shore of Lake Ontario—Oswego Harbor can freeze solid. Here, winds blowing from the west piled up ice in spectacular formations along the shoreline and breakwaters of Oswego. These photographers, and the one photographing them, are recording the spectacle from the ice. (Courtesy of Mark Slosek, City of Oswego historian.)

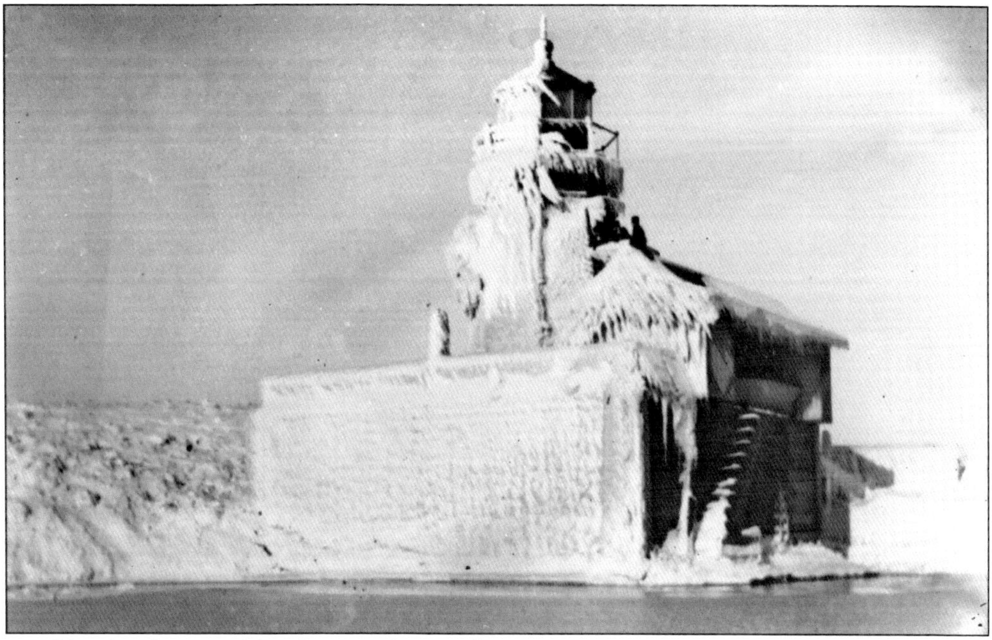

Possibly taken by one of the photographers in the previous image, this picture shows an individual near the door to the tower of the Oswego Breakwater Beacon. He may be a keeper attempting to gain access to the tower. In the winter, the Great Lakes aids to navigation were shut down, but keepers had to try to keep them maintained. (Courtesy of Mark Slosek, City of Oswego historian.)

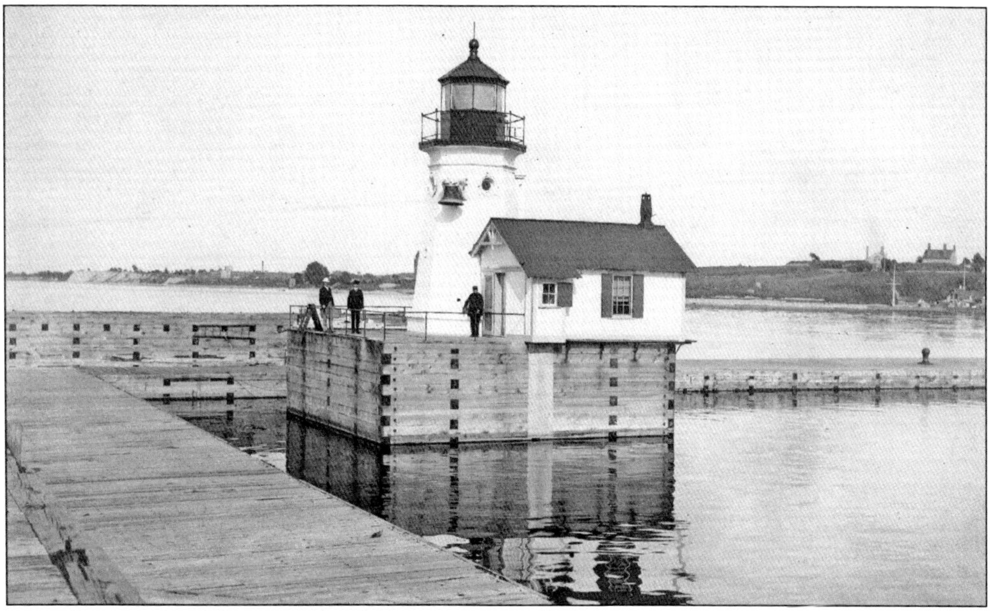

This photograph of the west side of the Oswego Breakwater Beacon was taken after the addition of the keeper's quarters in 1898. Those quarters were on the southwest side of the 35-square-foot timber and stone caisson. The beacon's tower is painted white, dating it after 1900. The water closet has been moved from the boathouse to the new quarters, which were also equipped with a stove for heat and cooking, storage space, and a bed in case the keeper on duty was not able to get to shore due to bad weather. (Courtesy of the National Archives and Records Administration.)

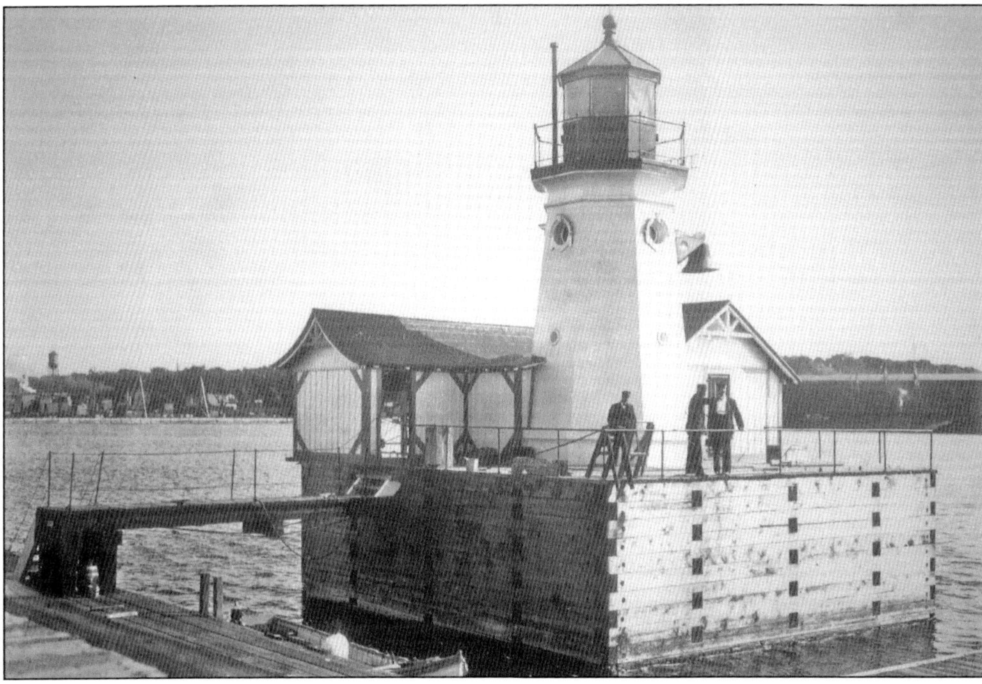

This post-1900 photograph of the northeast corner of the newly painted Oswego Breakwater Beacon also features the new keeper's quarters. The bridge from the caisson deck to the breakwater has been leveled and was likely safer during slippery conditions. The entrance to the tower has been further modified to eliminate the external stairs to the second level. (Courtesy of the National Archives and Records Administration.)

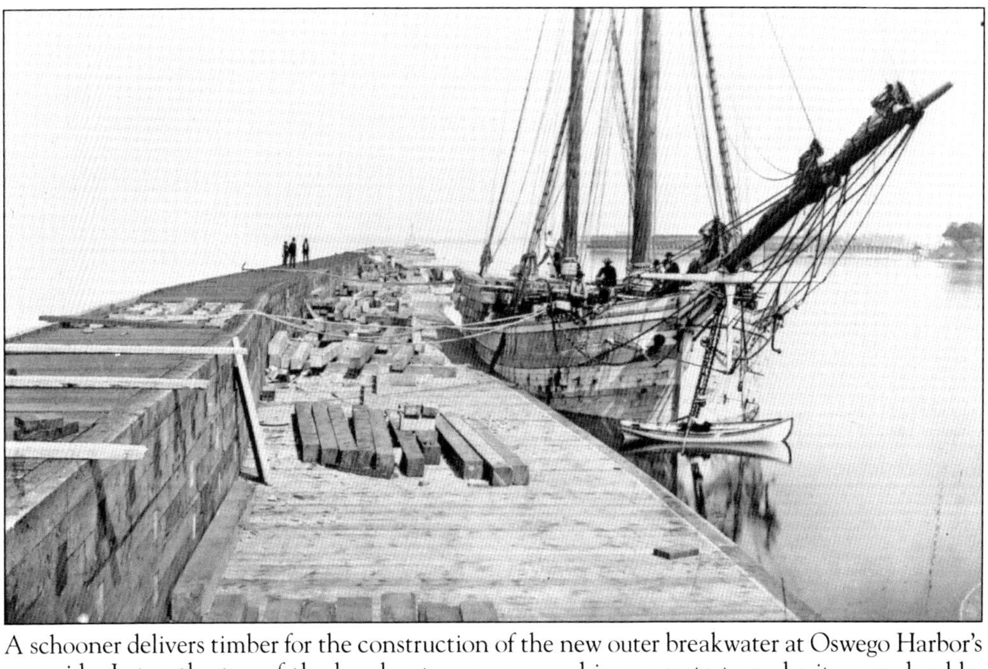

A schooner delivers timber for the construction of the new outer breakwater at Oswego Harbor's west side. Later, the top of the breakwater was covered in concrete to make it more durable. (Courtesy of Mark Slosek, City of Oswego historian.)

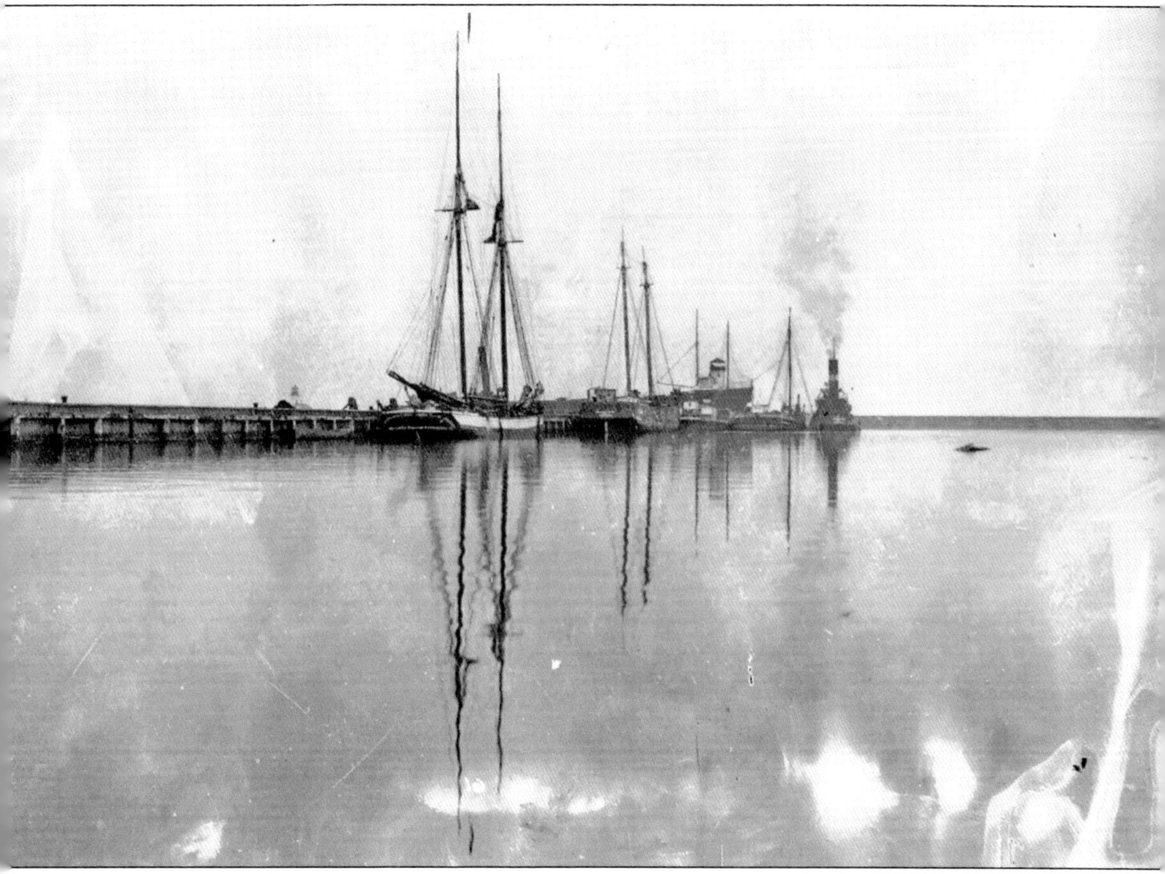

This photograph demonstrates the continuing construction of the west outer breakwater as schooners and tugboats are moored along the west side of the Oswego Breakwater Beacon. Construction is taking form on the final concrete-capped timber breakwater. (Courtesy of Mark Slosek, City of Oswego historian.)

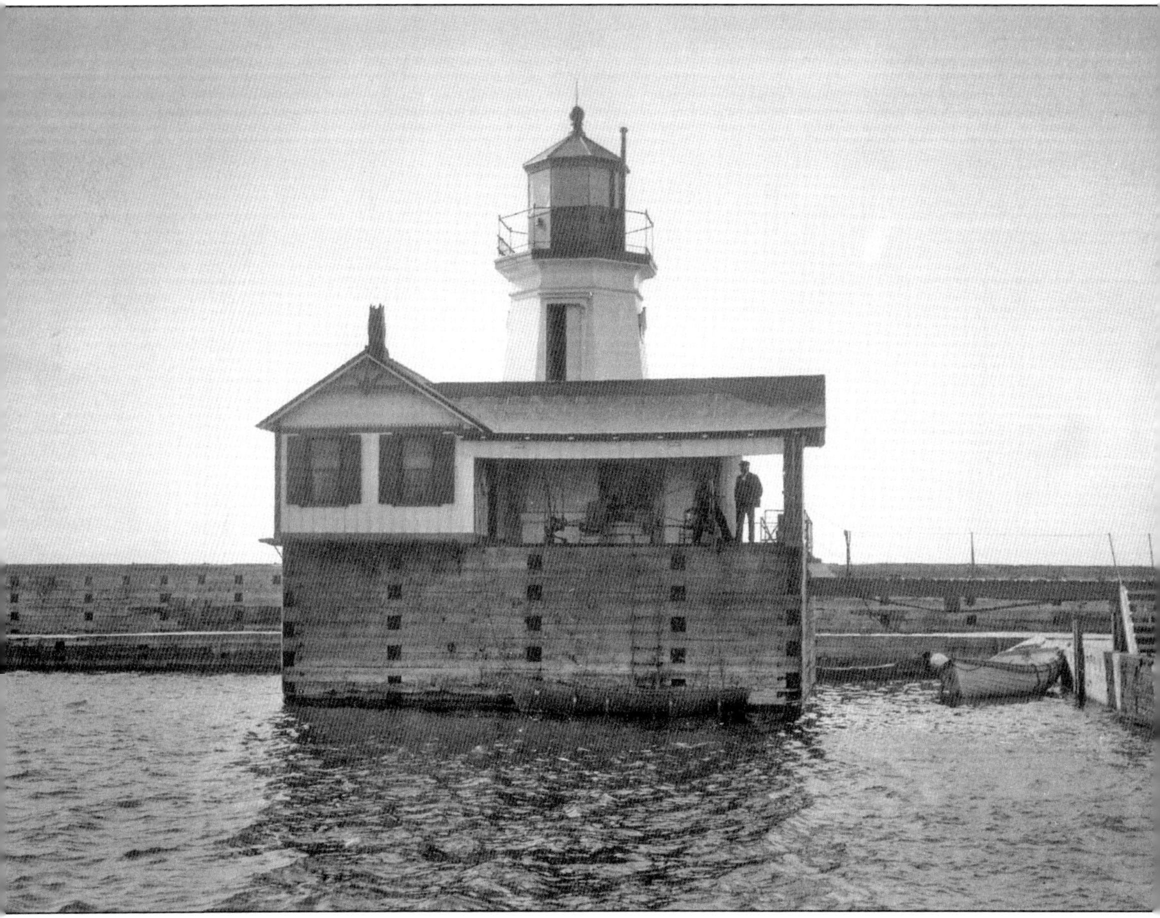

This post-expansion view of the south side of the Oswego Breakwater Beacon shows the structures on the caisson and the freshly painted white tower. Drawings of the expansion dated February 28, 1898, illustrate what may have been a caisson-level entry to the tower. Note that the original entry door on the tower's second level is open, most likely for ventilation. (Courtesy of the National Archives and Records Administration.)

Another view of the west side of the new keeper's quarters shows the fog bell. It is next to the window just above the keeper's structure that provided access to the light tower.

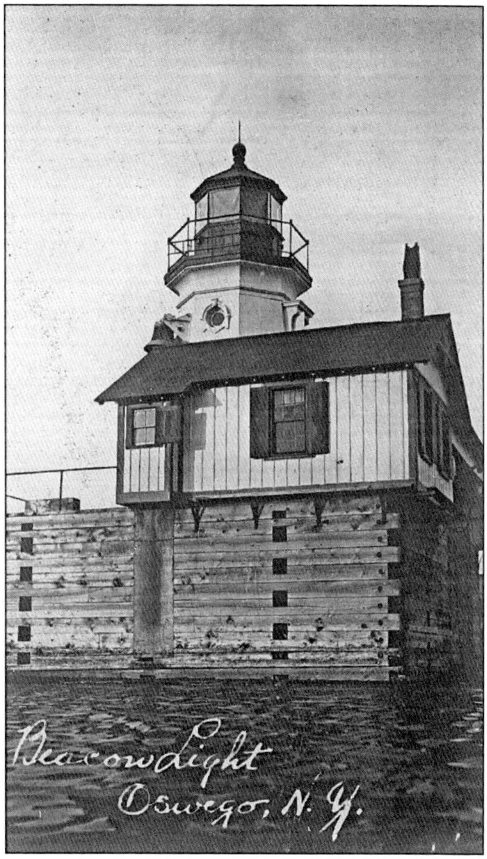

Powerful steam tugs were an absolute necessity if sailing vessels were to safely enter or depart Oswego Harbor in weather with high winds from the west or northwest. Here, five of Oswego's tugboat fleet are standing by, moored alongside the outer west breakwater with steam blowing, ready to assist any sailing vessels. It is often said that tugboat crews would race to capture the business of incoming vessels. (Courtesy of Mark Slosek, City of Oswego historian.)

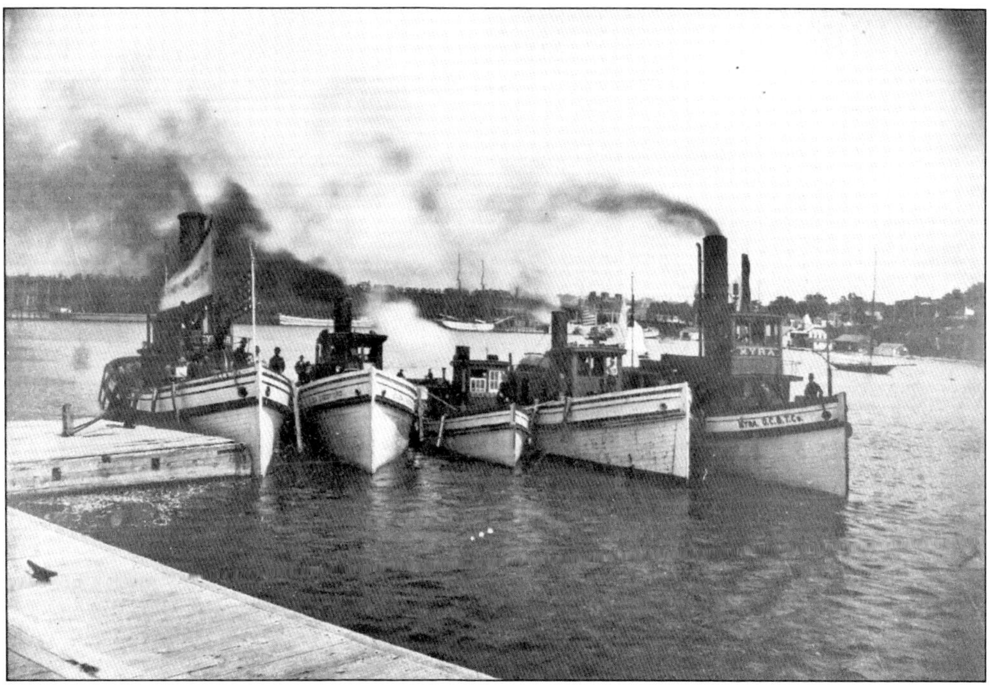

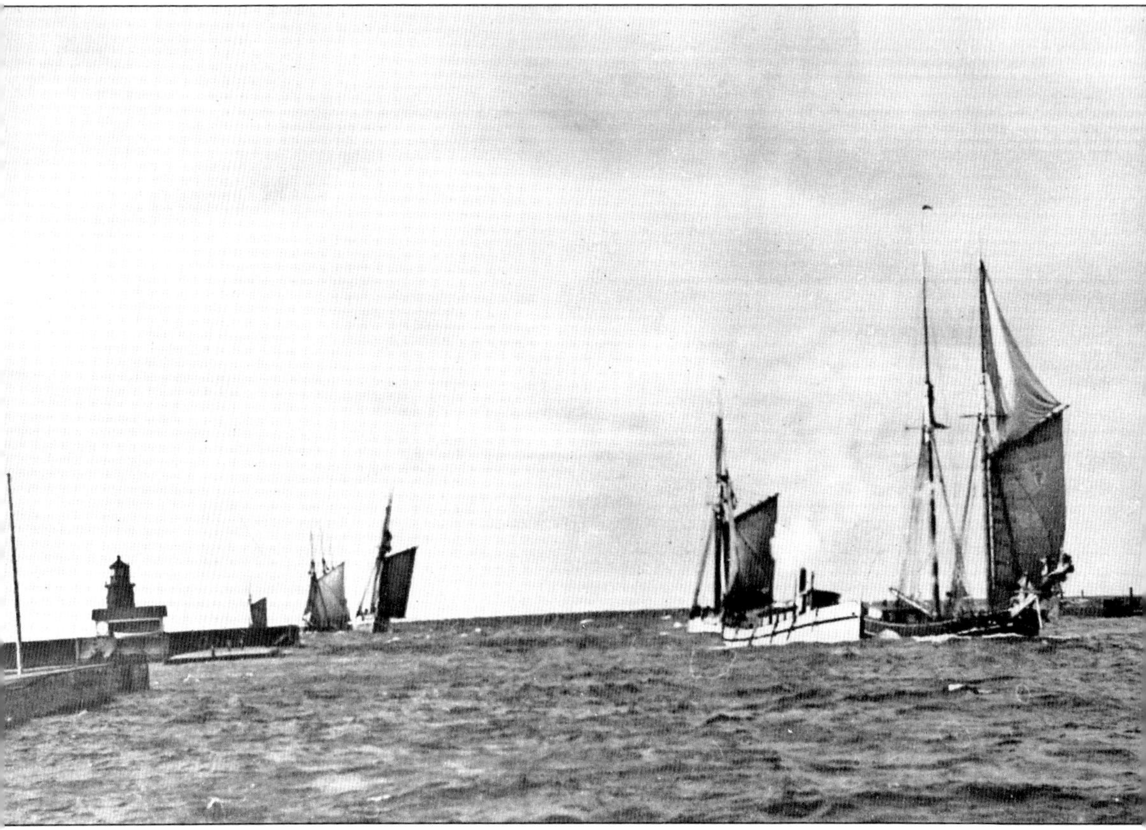

This photograph amply illustrates the assistance of the Oswego tugboats to schooners entering Oswego Harbor. West winds gave the five schooners difficulty, and the tug in the foreground has taken a line from the first schooner to help it safely enter the harbor. (Courtesy of Mark Slosek, City of Oswego historian.)

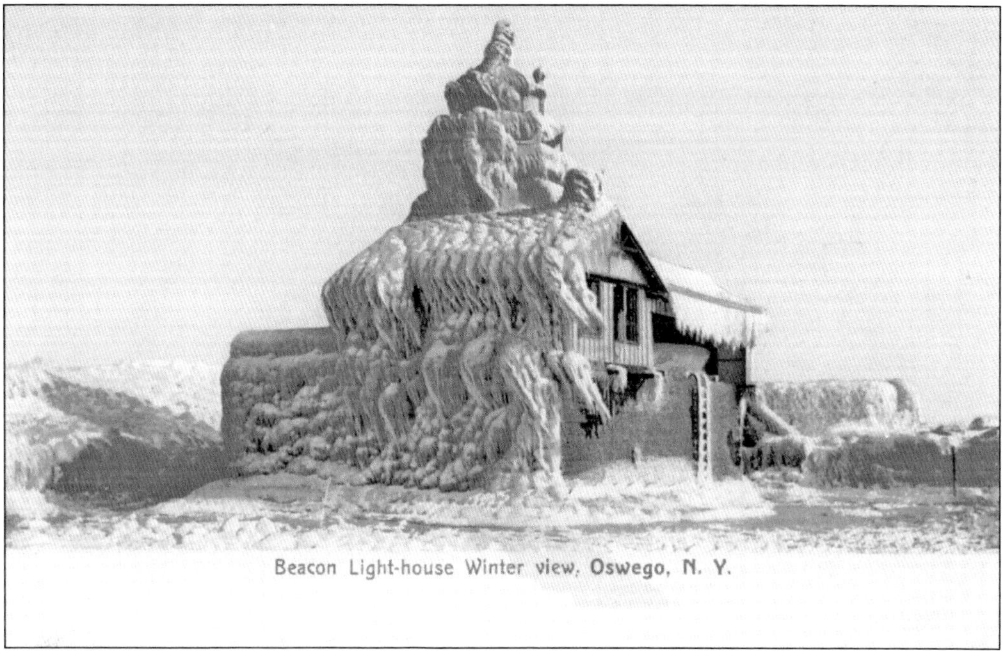

The Oswego Breakwater Beacon was especially vulnerable to extreme weather and was often covered with ice during the winter storms that typically came from the west or northwest along Lake Ontario. This photograph, taken at the southwest corner of the structure, features the iconic ice formations of eastern Lake Ontario.

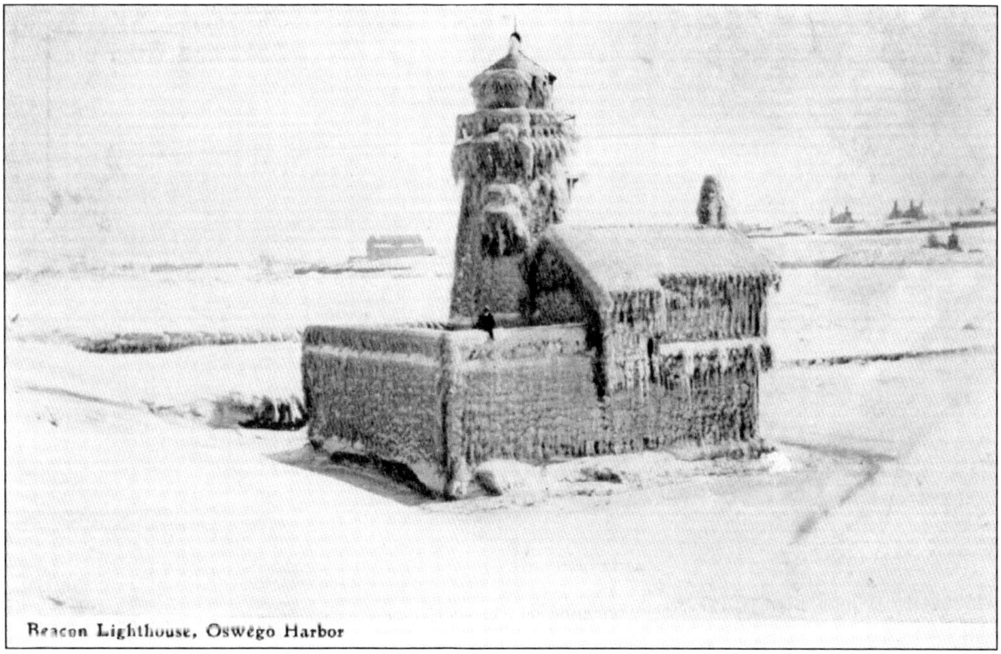

This is a postcard view of the northwest corner of the Oswego Breakwater Beacon. The original photograph must have been taken from the breakwater, a difficult feat at this time of the year. Note the visitor perched on the ice-covered railing.

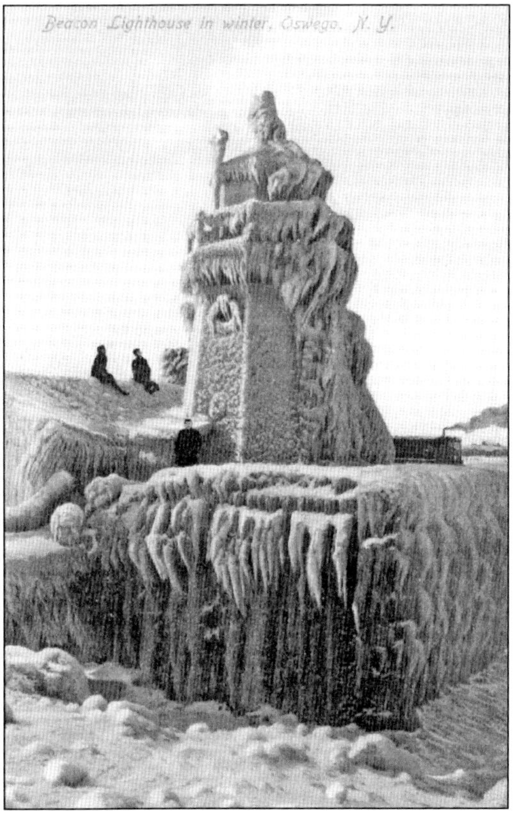

In spite of the obvious danger, the ice-covered Oswego Breakwater Beacon attracted adventurous Oswegonians. Many walked out to it and climbed the ice-covered structures. There always seemed to be a handy photographer ready to capture the event.

This post-1900 photograph aptly summarizes the value of the lighthouse keeper's hard work and exposure to danger. A passenger steamer loaded with travelers and a cargo schooner loaded with raw materials pass the Oswego Breakwater Beacon outbound into Lake Ontario. (Courtesy of Mark Slosek, City of Oswego historian.)

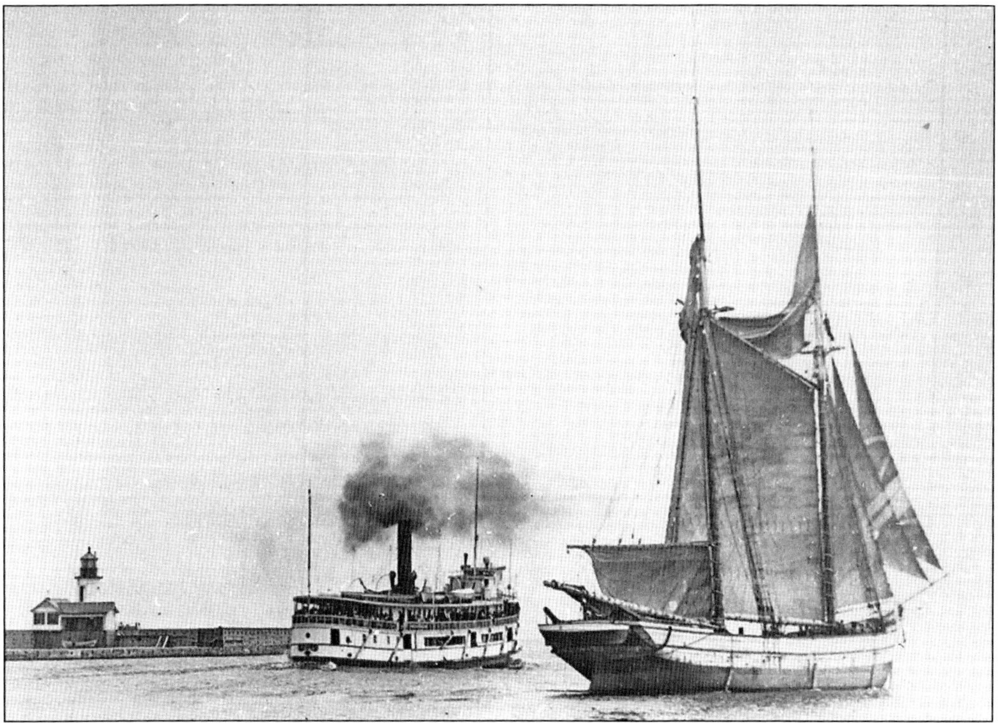

Four

West Pierhead Lighthouse 1931–2017

The project to build Oswego's fourth lighthouse began in 1930 and was part of a larger port of Oswego expansion necessitated by increased commercial opportunity and larger, deeper-draft vessels now entering Lake Ontario via the fourth, and current, Welland Canal. In order to accommodate the larger commercial freighters of the upper Great Lakes, the Port of Oswego reconfigured the entire harbor to its current form. This required removing the eastern third of the outer west breakwater and replacing it with an arrowhead breakwater. A matching arrowhead breakwater was placed on the east side, and the old east breakwater was removed.

To accomplish this feat, the Oswego Breakwater Beacon was removed and replaced with a new lighthouse known as the Oswego West Pierhead Lighthouse at the end of the new west arrowhead breakwater. The red lens lantern on a post that replaced the 1837 Oswego Harbor Lighthouse was discontinued, and all remaining parts of the inner breakwater were removed as well. Further, a beacon was placed atop the 147-foot New York State Grain Elevator known as the Oswego Elevator Light, which became the principal Oswego Harbor aid to navigation.

The Oswego Breakwater Beacon officially went dark in August 1931 and was replaced by the Oswego Elevator Light as the only active aid to navigation in Oswego until 1934. As part of the west arrowhead breakwater construction, the US Army Corps of Engineers built a stone and timber crib with a concrete cap to begin construction of the Oswego West Pierhead Lighthouse at its east end. In 1933, the US Lighthouse Service completed the concrete caisson, and in 1934, the new Oswego West Pierhead Lighthouse was activated. The new lighthouse included a powerful compressed-air foghorn, and in 1936, a new radio beacon and distance finding system were added. Also in 1934, a new duplex keeper's dwelling was built at 31–33 West Fifth Street in Oswego to house the keeper and first assistant keeper.

Resident civilian keepers of the US Lighthouse Service staffed the Oswego West Pierhead Lighthouse until 1939, when the US Coast Guard acquired all federal lighthouses. Coastguardsmen keepers staffed the lighthouse until 1968, when the station was fully automated. In 2009, the lighthouse was transferred to the City of Oswego under the auspices of the National Historic Lighthouse Preservation Act, and in 2014, it was leased to the H. Lee White Maritime Museum, which has since assumed responsibility for its restoration and public interpretation.

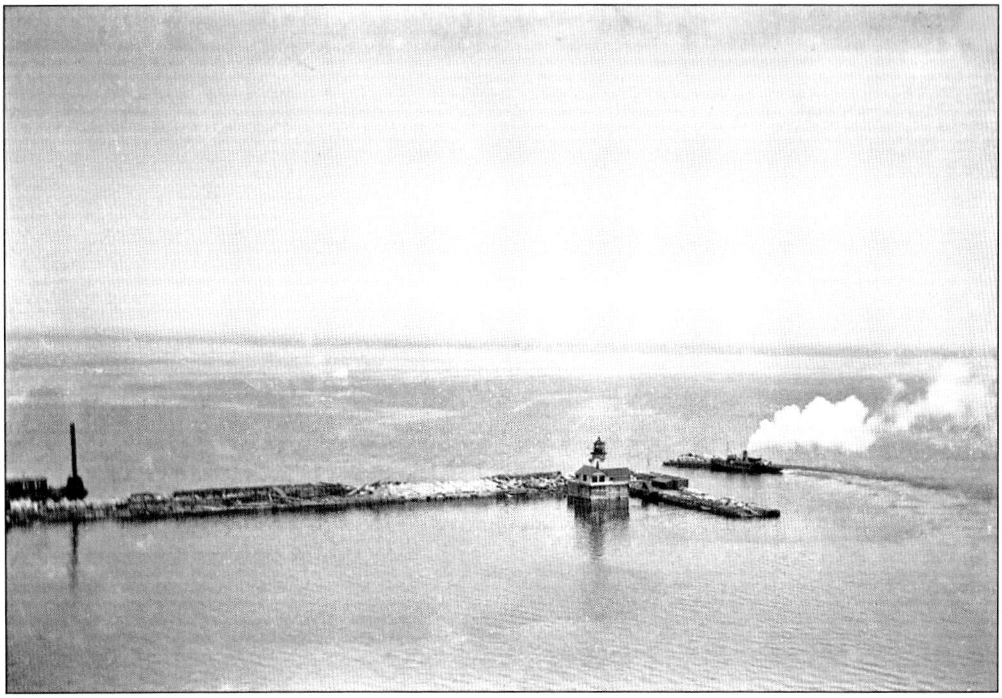

When the project to build Oswego Harbor's new arrowhead breakwater began, the old outer breakwater had to be dismantled first. Here, the east end of the outer breakwater is being dismantled in 1931, and the Oswego Breakwater Beacon was removed shortly thereafter in August 1931. (Courtesy of Mark Slosek, City of Oswego historian.)

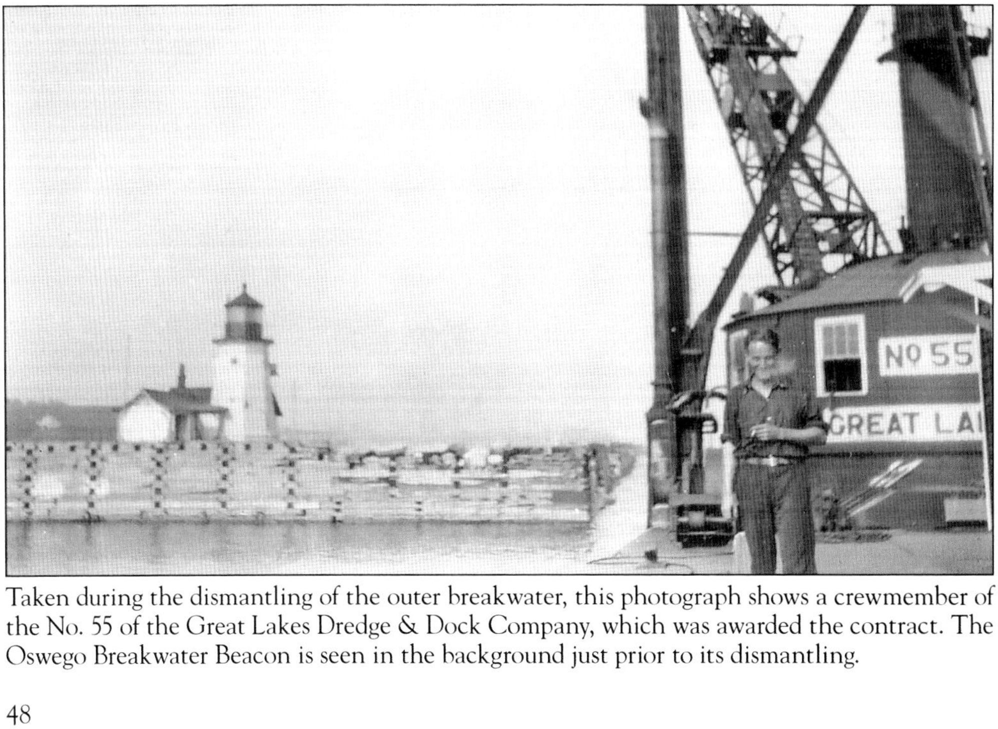

Taken during the dismantling of the outer breakwater, this photograph shows a crewmember of the No. 55 of the Great Lakes Dredge & Dock Company, which was awarded the contract. The Oswego Breakwater Beacon is seen in the background just prior to its dismantling.

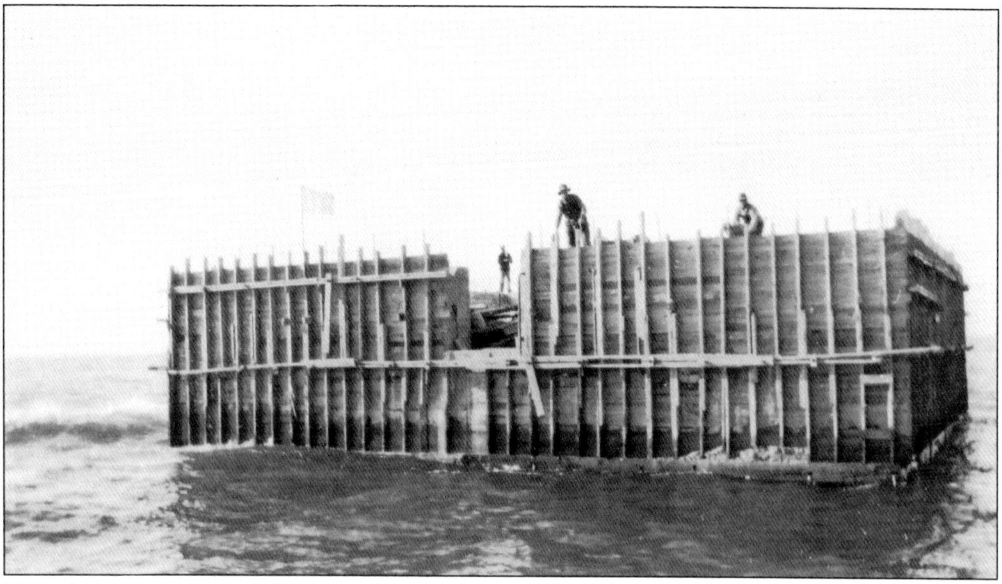

This timber crib formed the base of the caisson for the Oswego West Pierhead Lighthouse. It is seen being towed to its location at the east end of the new west arrowhead breakwater in Oswego Harbor.

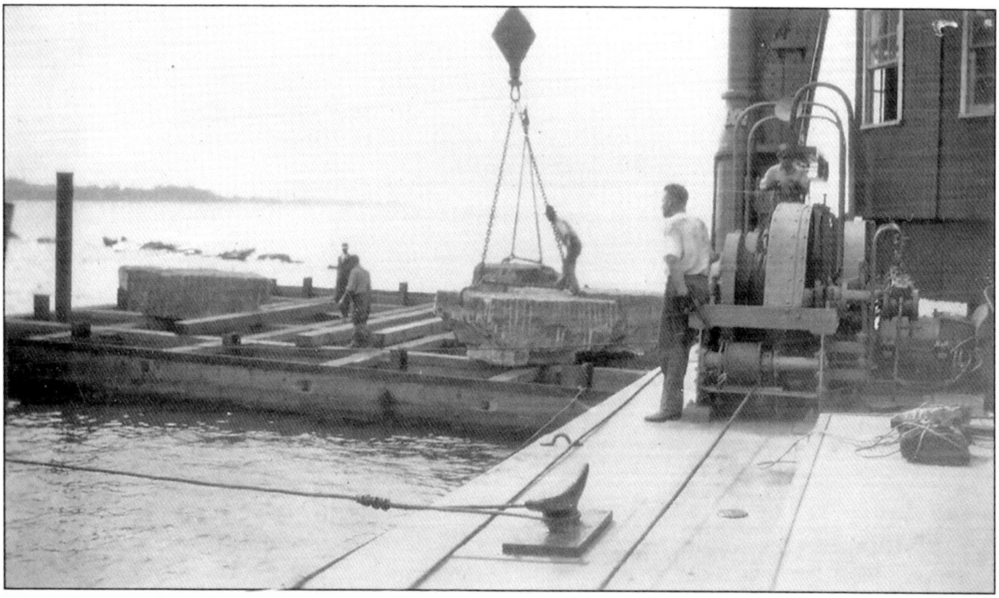

The timber crib for the lighthouse caisson was filled with large stones after it was placed in its proper location. Great Lakes Dredge & Dock Company, which was contracted by the US Army Corps of Engineers out of Buffalo, performed much of this phase of the project.

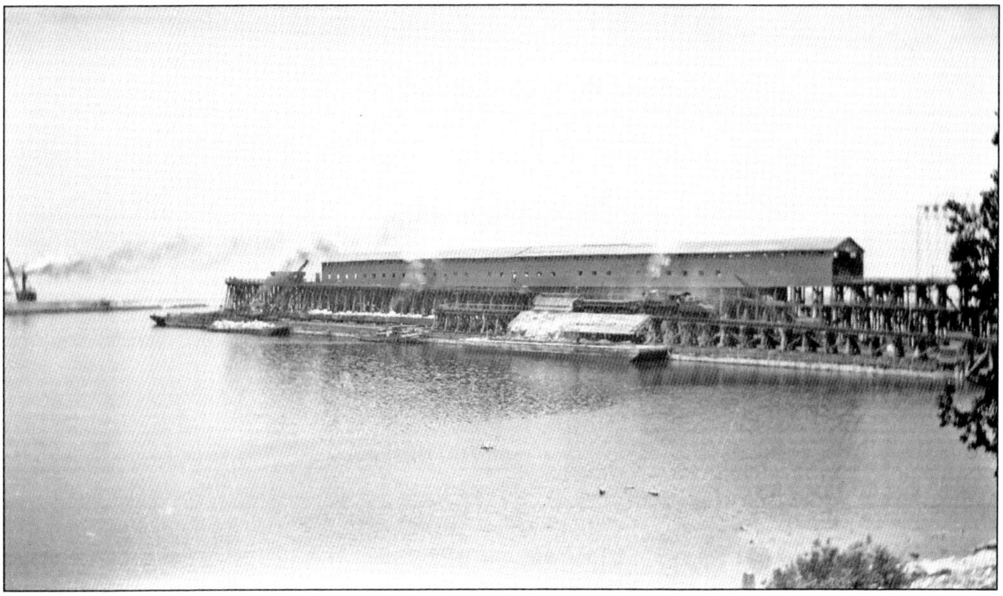

This c. 1930s photograph shows the west side of the Delaware, Lackawanna & Western Railroad coal trestle with several barges alongside it. Some appear to be loading stone rather than coal. Work on the Oswego Harbor expansion is underway, as is evidenced by the steam crane at left working on the west arrowhead breakwater. (Courtesy of Mark Slosek, City of Oswego historian.)

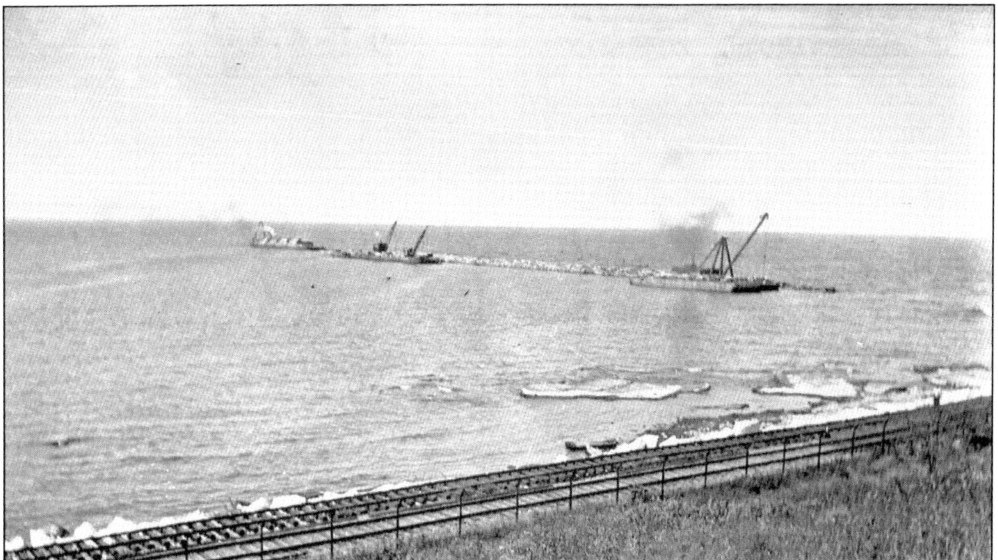

This c. 1934 photograph of the east side of Oswego Harbor chronicles the work on the new east arrowhead breakwater. This was the first east-side breakwater construction since the 1820s. (Courtesy of Mark Slosek, City of Oswego historian.)

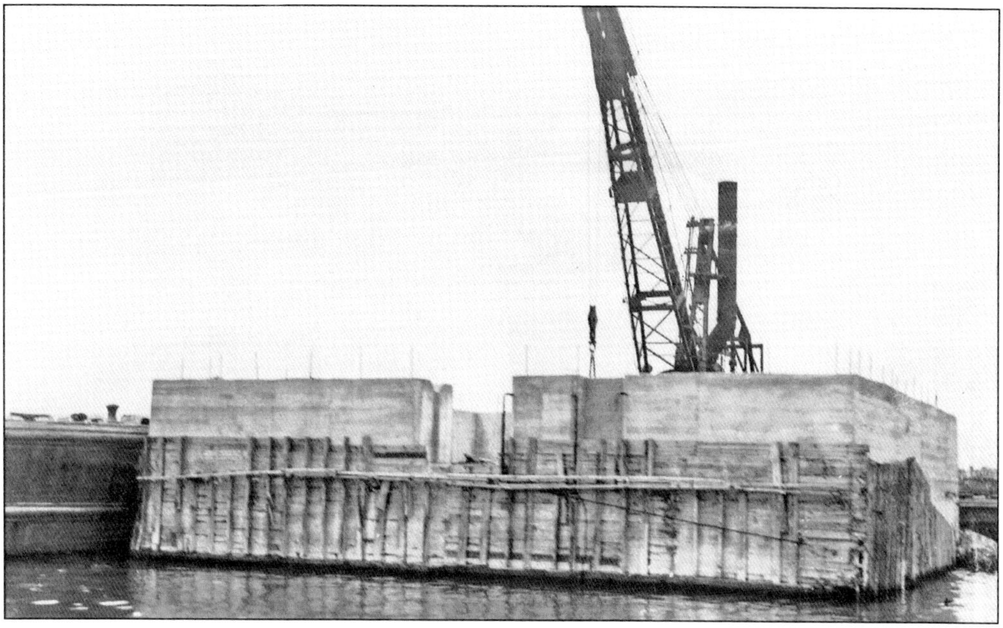

These photographs show the concrete-capped and stone-filled timber crib that formed the base of the caisson upon which the Oswego West Pierhead was constructed. Pictured above is the south side of the caisson with the bottom half of the central equipment door visible. Below is the northeast corner of the new structure. This was the extent of the US Army Corps of Engineers project, and it retains ownership of this portion of the structure. Today, the City of Oswego and the H. Lee White Maritime Museum leases and subleases respectively this part of the structure.

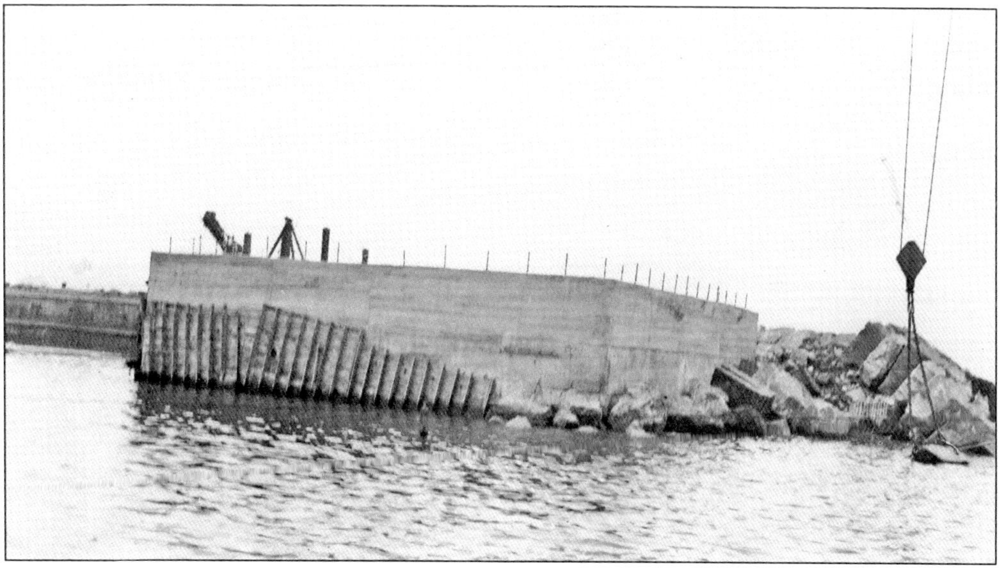

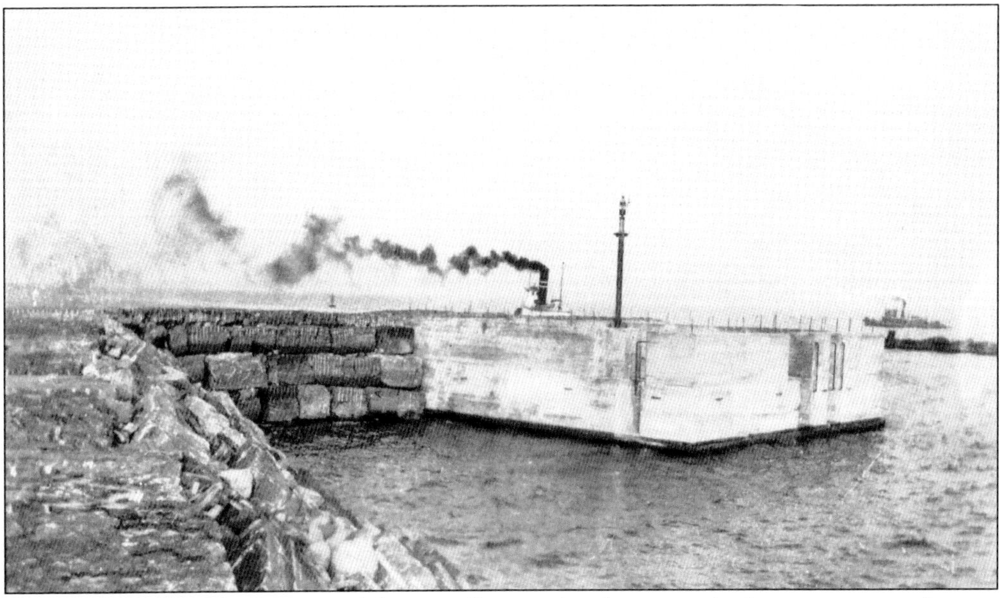

Looking at the southwest corner of the partially completed caisson, the large equipment door on the south side and the smaller personnel door on the west side can be seen. Ladders and handrails are already installed at the doors, and an additional approximately five feet of caisson has yet to be added to the top to complete the bottom of the structure. A temporary beacon was placed on the pole (center) to warn vessels entering Oswego Harbor.

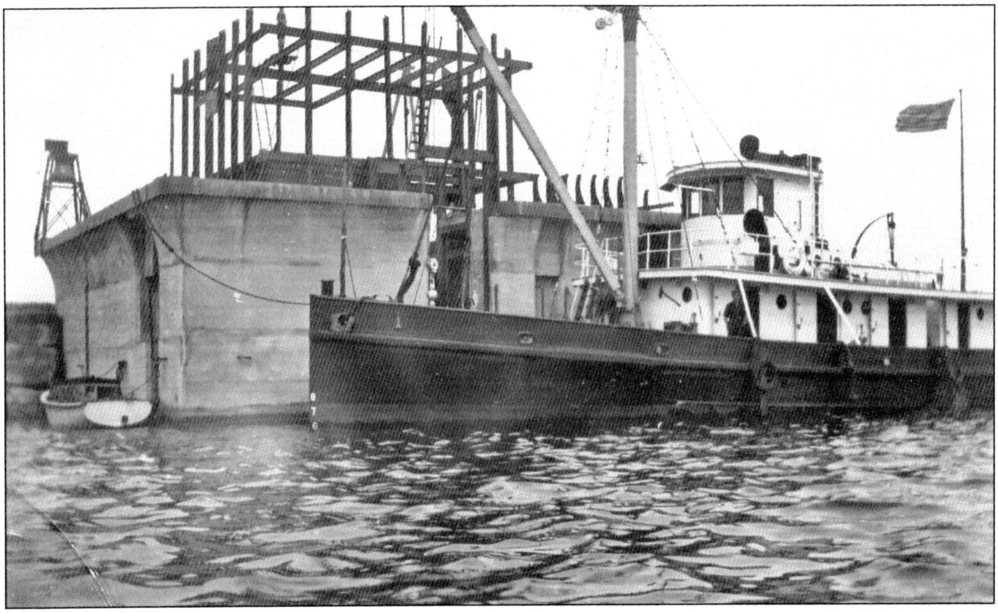

When the US Army Corps of Engineers completed its portion of the project, the 10th District of the US Lighthouse Service out of Buffalo began construction of the superstructure. The US Lighthouse tender *Cherry* is seen alongside the now-complete concrete caisson, and a temporary electrically operated fog bell has been installed on the northwest corner of the caisson.

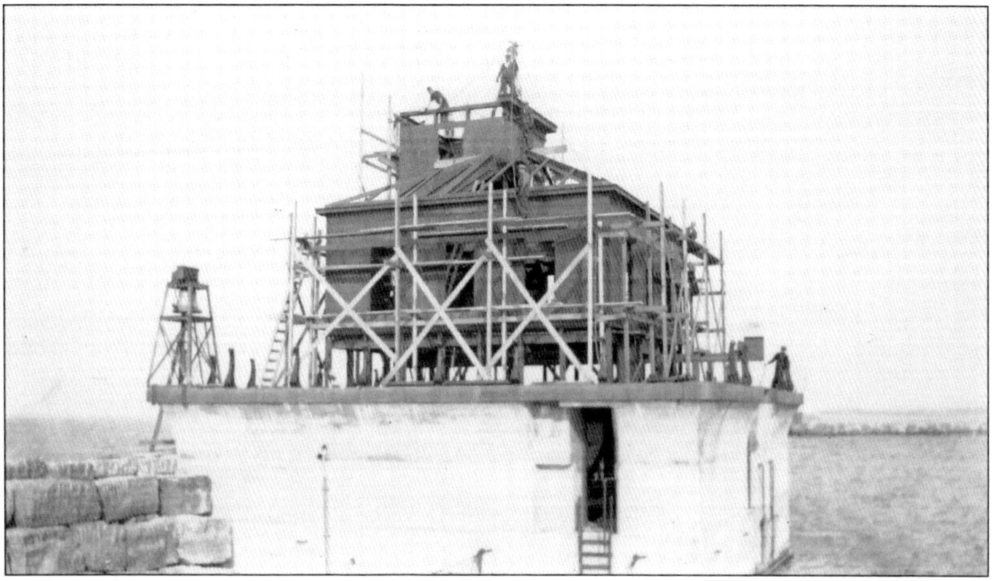

The steel frame and outer steel skin of the lighthouse tower and structure are beginning to take shape in this 1933 photograph of the West Pierhead Lighthouse. The west-side personnel door appears to be active, and the temporary fog bell can be seen on the northwest corner. The concrete parapet wall, which was constructed between the base of the steel skin and the top of the concrete caisson, has yet to be completed.

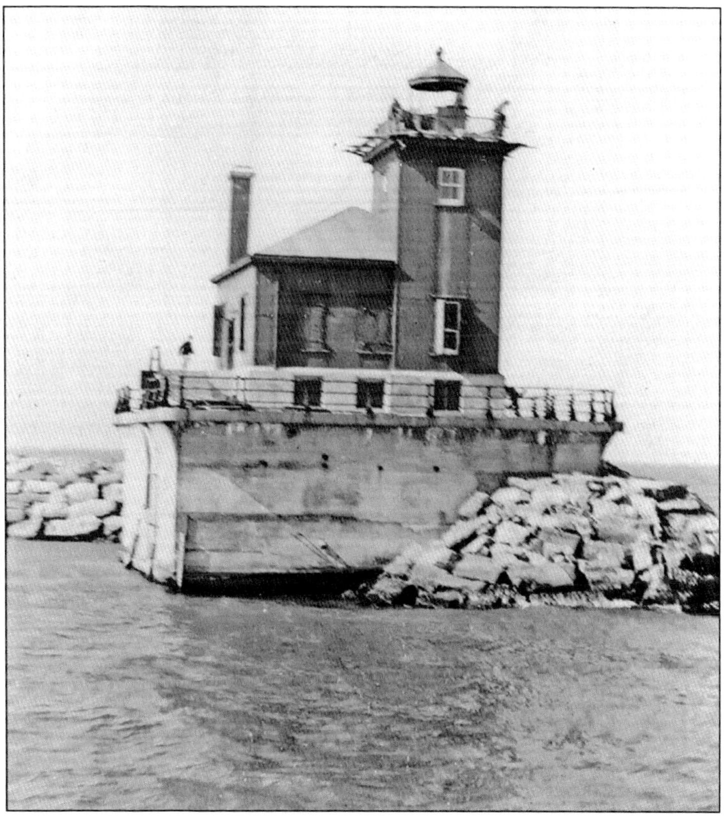

Construction of the Oswego West Pierhead Lighthouse was nearing completion when this photograph was taken in 1934. The superstructure appears nearly complete with the exception of a new paint job. The lantern at the top of the tower was being assembled from standard US Lighthouse Service components provided by the 10th District in Buffalo to be assembled onsite.

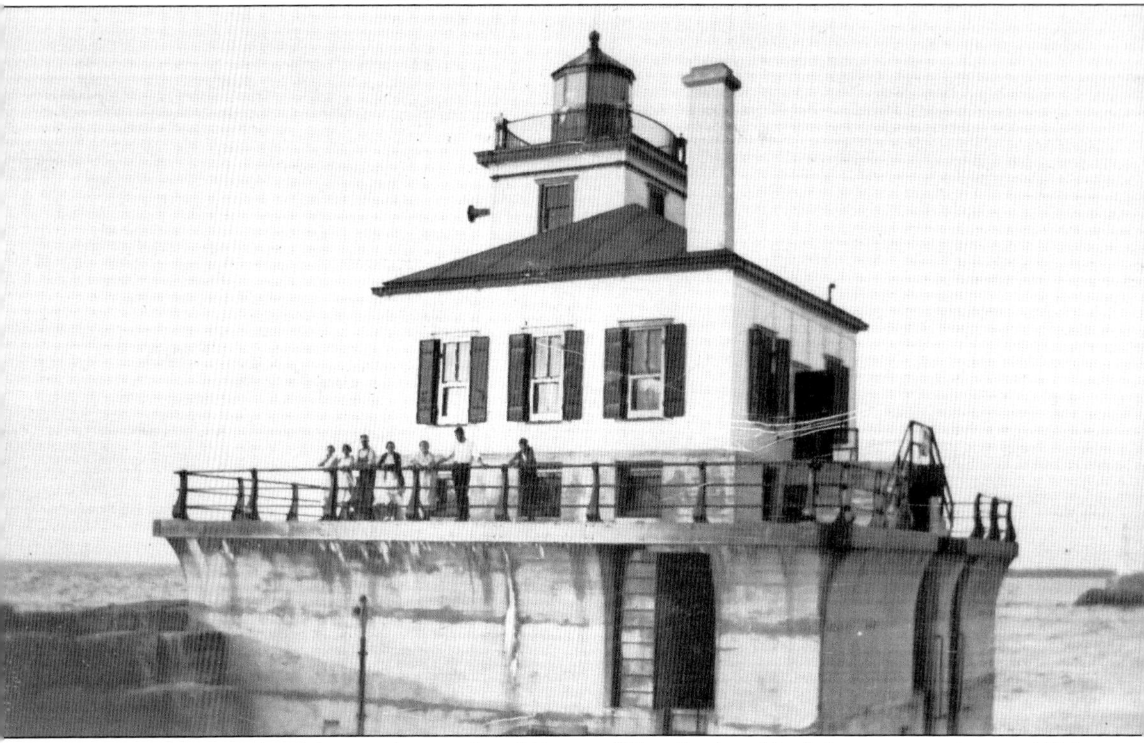

This photograph of the nearly completed Oswego West Pierhead Lighthouse was taken in 1934. Bert Egelston, the new lighthouse's first keeper, and his two assistants appear to have invited family members to visit their new station.

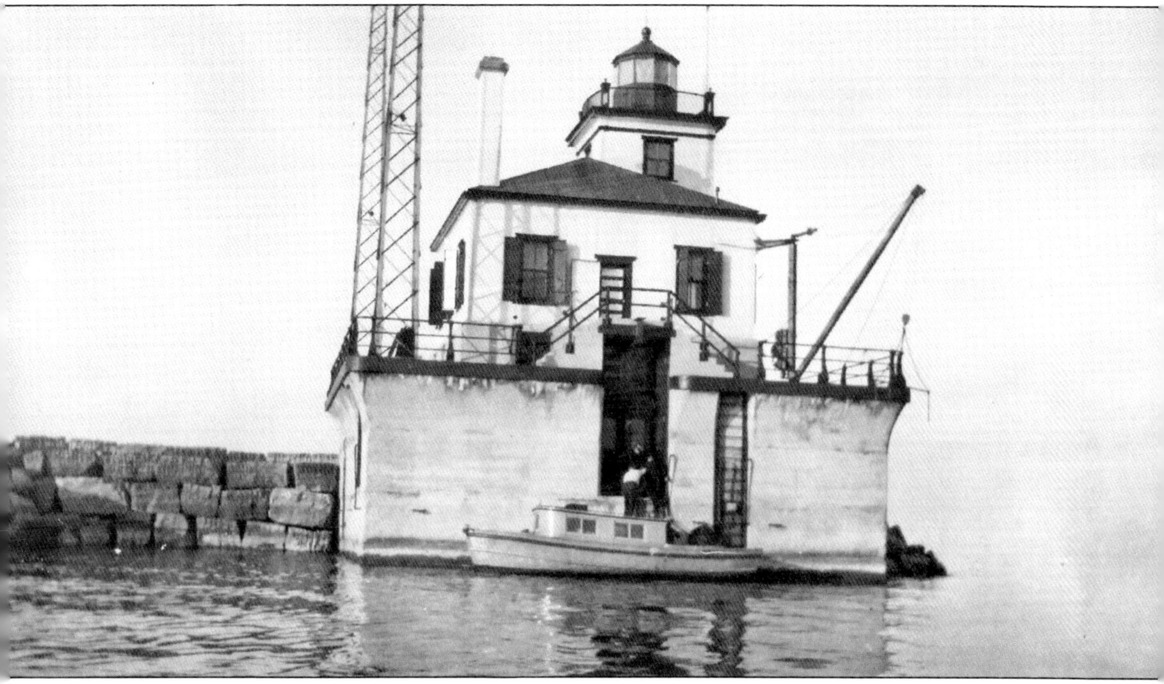

The Oswego West Pierhead Lighthouse began operation in 1934, and the radio beacon and distance-finding system shown here were added in 1936. The lighthouse's gray launch is moored at the south-side equipment door, which provided access to the machinery room in the basement inside the concrete caisson.

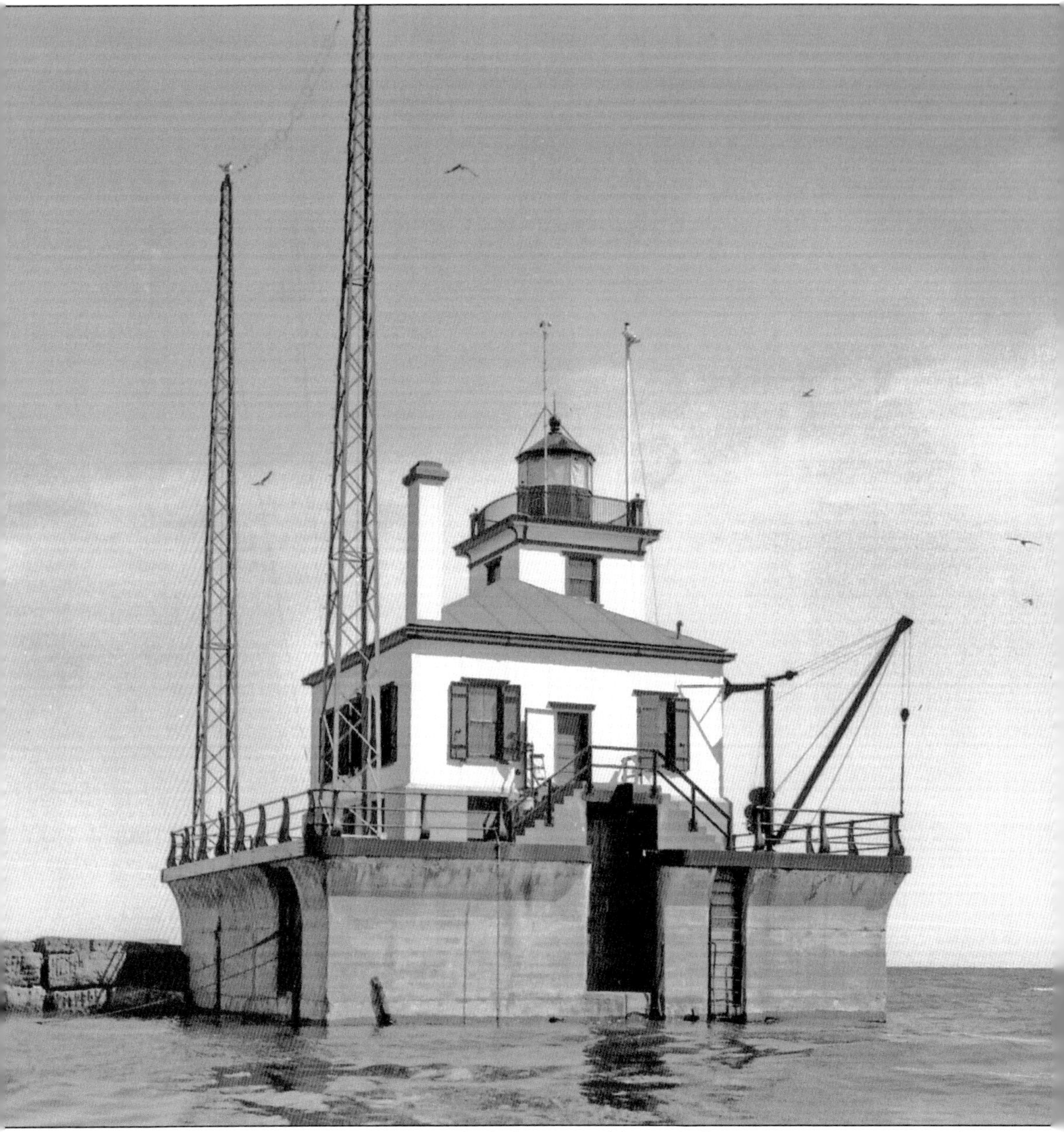

This photograph provides a glimpse at the full extent of the radio beacon antenna towers and the crane on the southeast corner of the caisson. A pole for weather instruments was added to the top of the tower, as the Oswego West Pierhead Lighthouse was also a weather station.

Bert Egelston is pictured standing on the west arrowhead breakwater next to the newly completed Oswego West Pierhead Lighthouse. He, with two assistant keepers, took command of the new light station upon its completion.

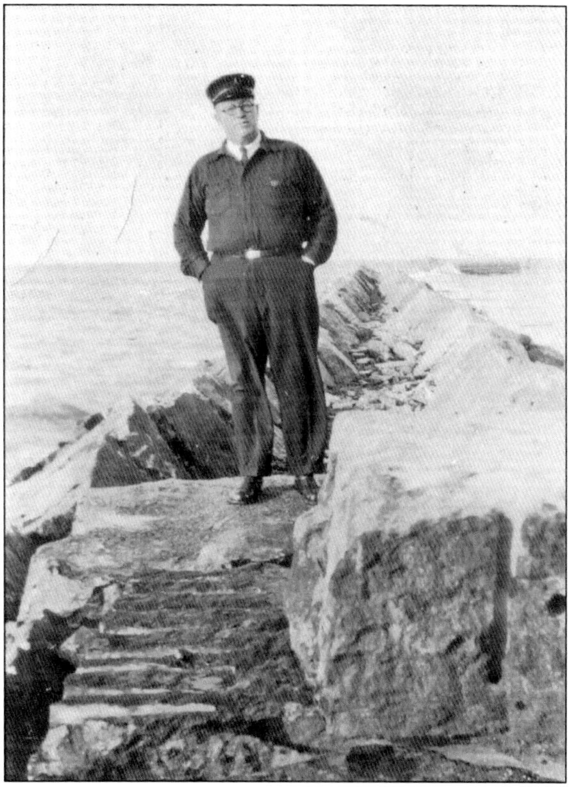

From left to right are First Assistant Keeper Karl Jackson, Keeper Bert Egelston, and Second Assistant Keeper Carl Sprague in the lighthouse's radio room near the radio beacon equipment. They are in their dress uniforms, which were used for special occasions. In this case, it was likely the start of the radio beacon operation in 1936.

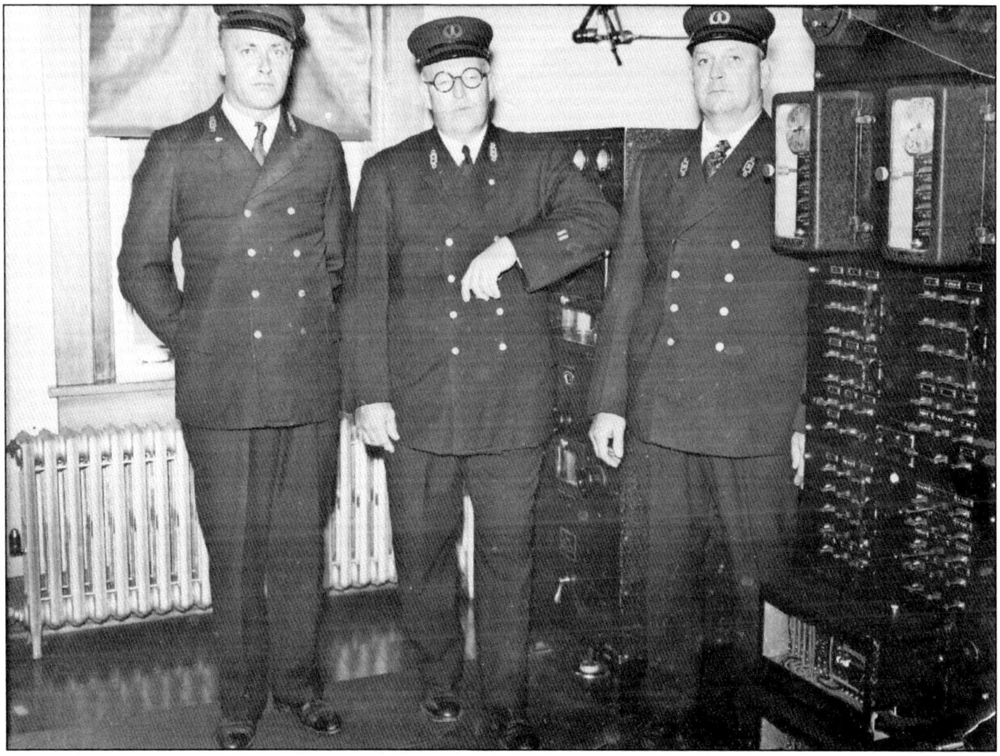

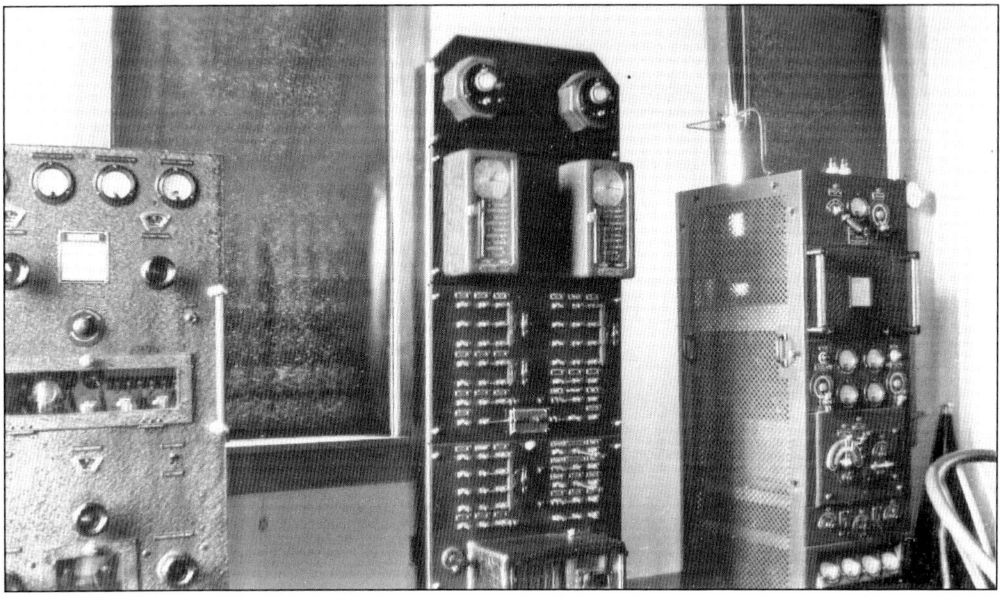

The radio beacon equipment was on the north wall of the radio room and consisted of two radio beacon transmitters flanked by a pair of timers in a central console. For reliability, this vital equipment was installed in pairs. The timers insured the radio beacon operated on a precise schedule and controlled the foghorn to operate the distance-finding system. This allowed a mariner to judge the distance from his ship to the lighthouse based on the time difference between the radio beacon signal and the foghorn sound signal.

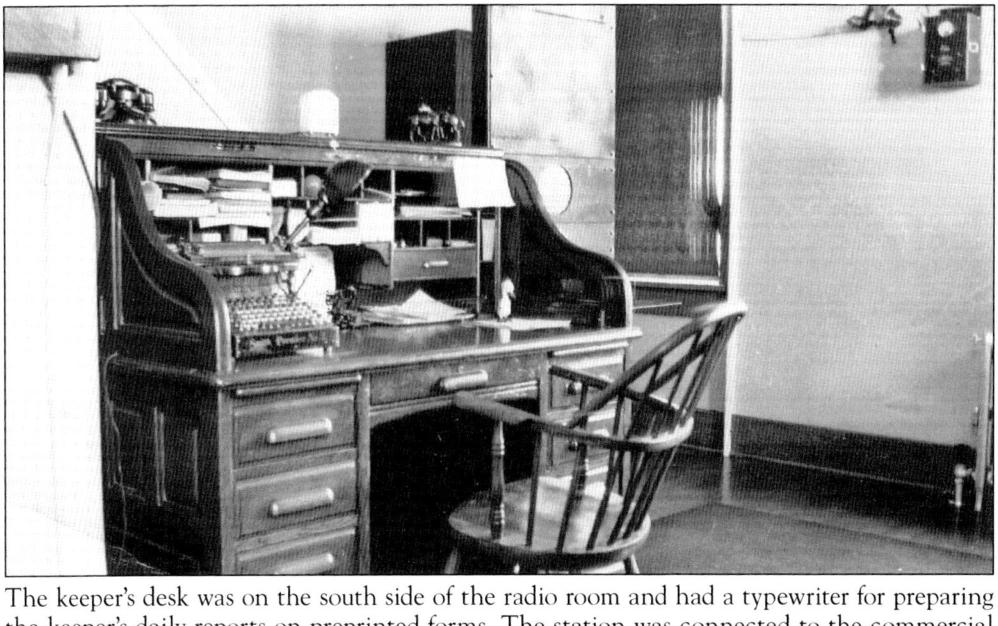

The keeper's desk was on the south side of the radio room and had a typewriter for preparing the keeper's daily reports on preprinted forms. The station was connected to the commercial telephone system by an underwater cable and was listed in the phone book. In the upper right corner, a meter can be seen that allowed the keeper to be sure the radio beacon transmitter was putting out the required signal power.

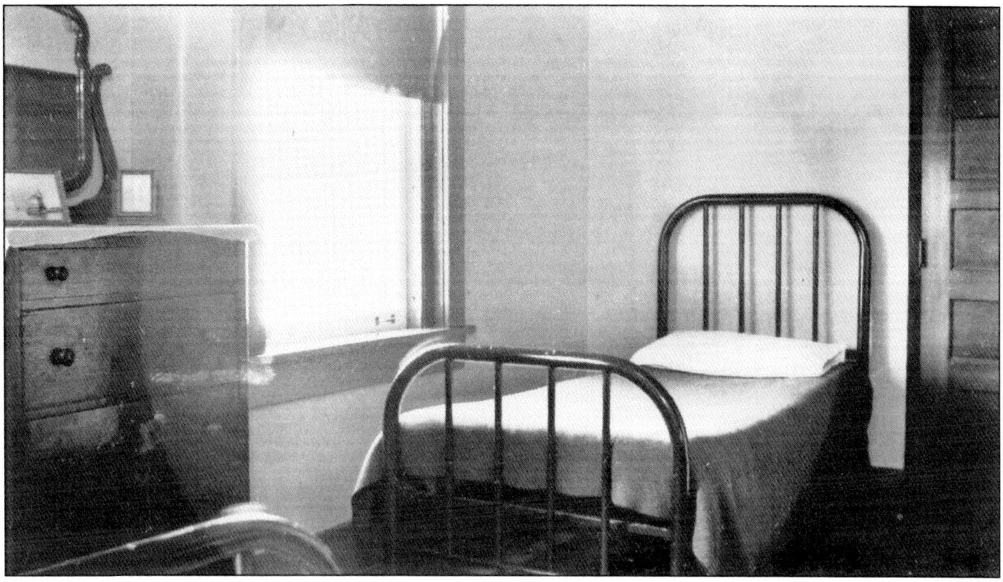

The keeper's bedroom was on the northeast corner of the building. There was one dresser and two closets. The framed photograph on the left of the dresser is of the breakwater lighthouse in Buffalo, where both Bert Egelston and Karl Jackson were stationed prior to Oswego.

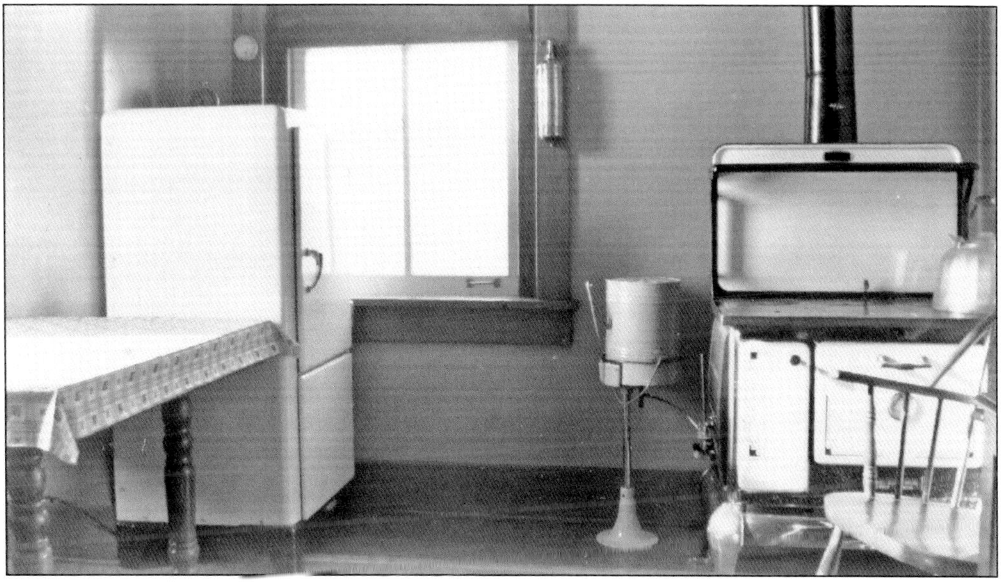

The lighthouse's kitchen was on the southwest corner of the building and had a refrigerator powered by commercial electricity fed by an underwater cable from shore. The stove (right) was fueled by kerosene initially, but was replaced by a propane stove in the 1950s.

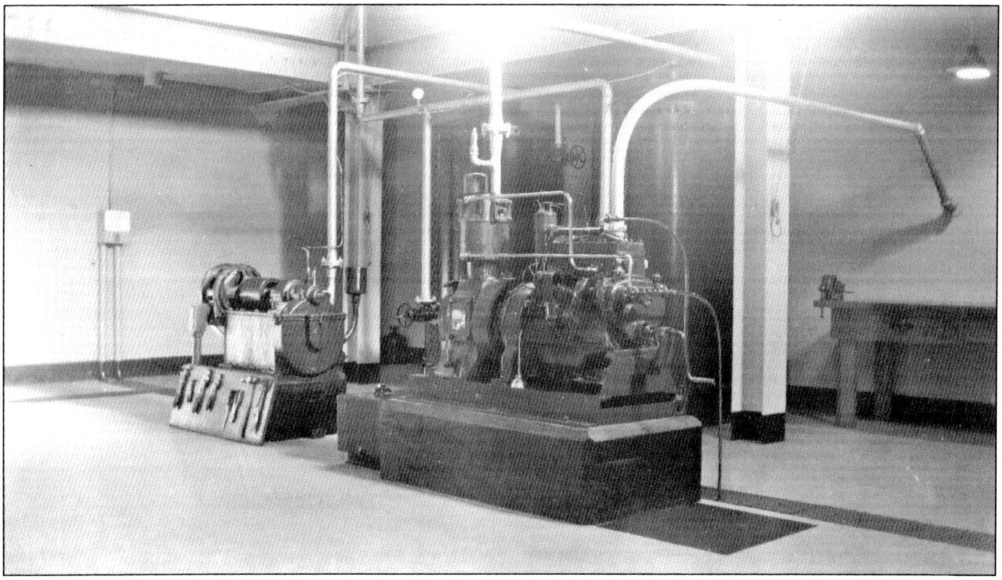

The lighthouse's machinery room was in the basement, safely contained within the concrete caisson. Seen here are the two compressors for the compressed-air foghorn system. The electric-powered one at left served as the primary compressor, while the diesel-powered one at right served as a backup in the event that shore-based power was lost. Behind the compressors are two large tanks that stored the compressed air.

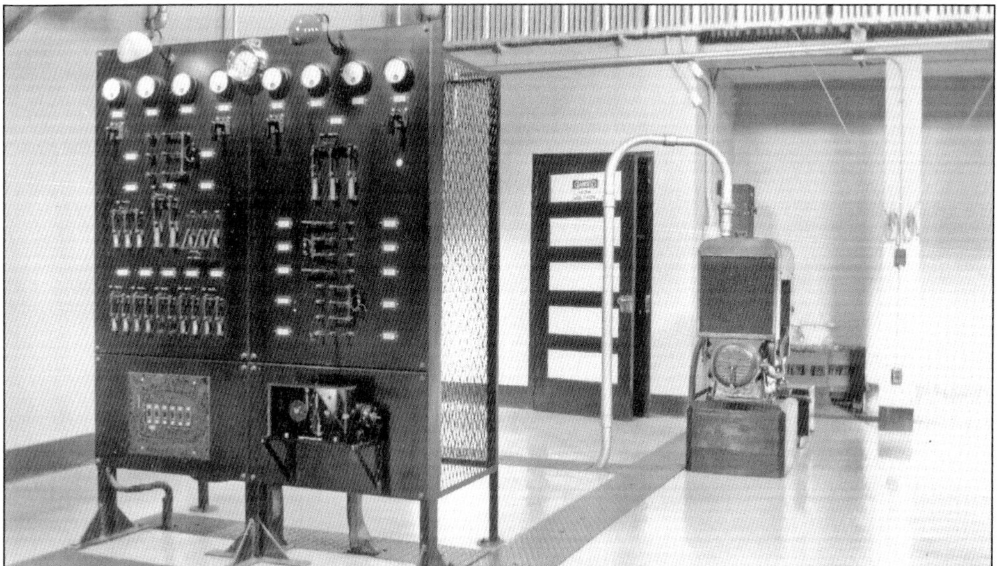

The west side of the machinery room contained the main power distribution panel (front) and the diesel-powered generator (rear). This generator handled most of the station's electrical requirements, with the exception of the electric compressor. Behind the generator was the transformer room, where the electric cable from shore entered the building. The lighthouse was heated by a coal-fired steam system in the basement, to the left of the power panel, as is evidenced by the large radiator at the top of the north wall. The furnace was later converted to oil.

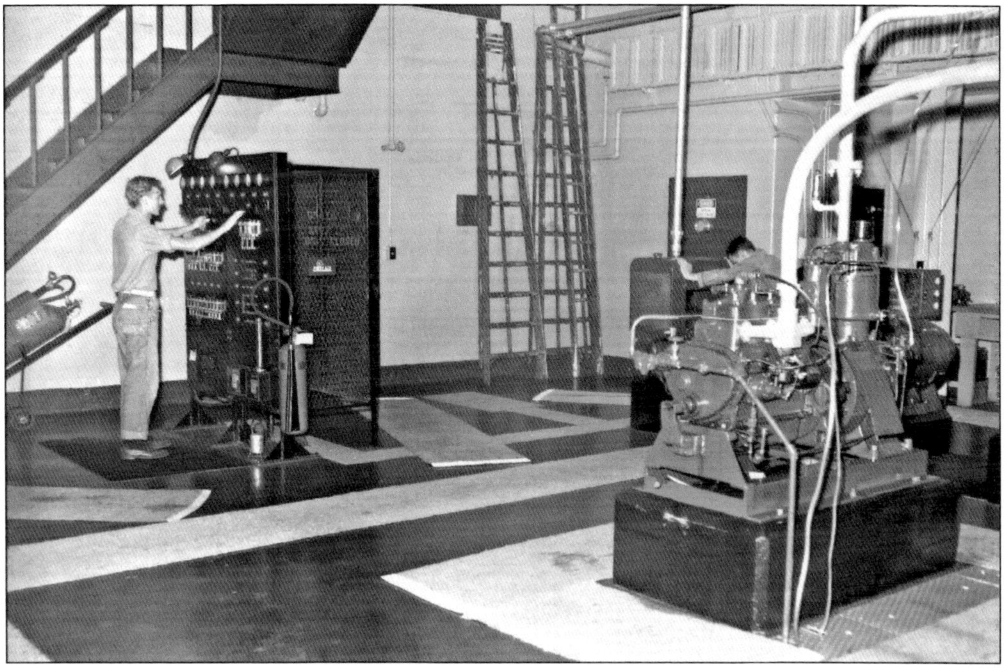

This c. 1950s photograph is also of the west side of the machinery room. SN. William H. Thomas is at the switchboard, and Engineman Richard E. Himes is inspecting the generator.

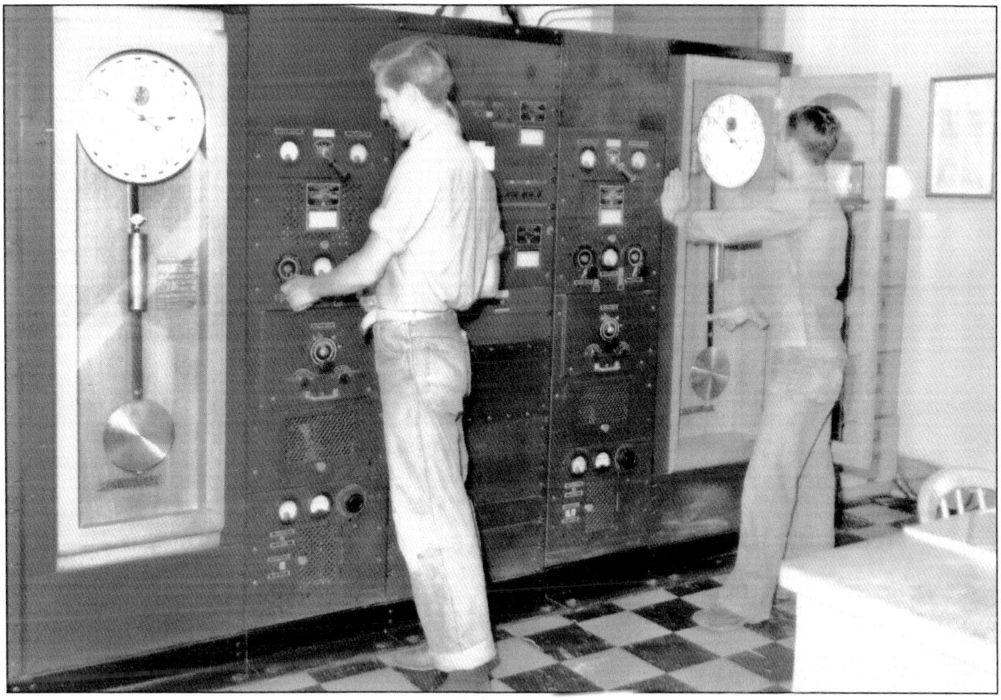

Taken at the same time, this photograph is of the new radio beacon equipment in the lighthouse's radio room. SN. William H. Thomas is checking the new transmitter, and Engineman Richard E. Himes is inspecting the timing clock. Flooring on the main level of the lighthouse was converted to red and black tile from hardwood in the 1950s.

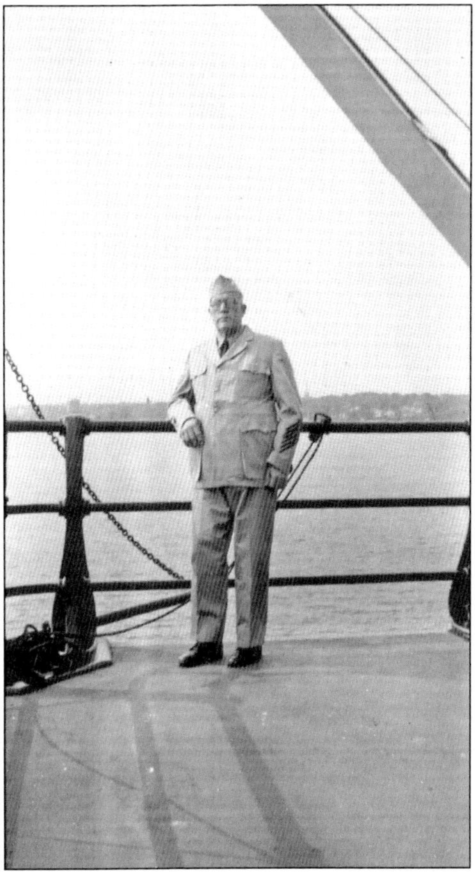

Keeper Bert Egelston is pictured in his uniform as a Coast Guard chief petty officer. He is pictured both at the Oswego West Pierhead Lighthouse (left) and at the shore-based dwelling (below) at 31–33 West Fifth Street in Oswego. The Coast Guard assumed responsibility for all US lighthouses in 1939, and Egelston and his two assistant keepers enlisted in the Coast Guard in August 1941. Bert Egelston retired in 1945 after roughly 30 years of service in the US Lighthouse Service and the Coast Guard.

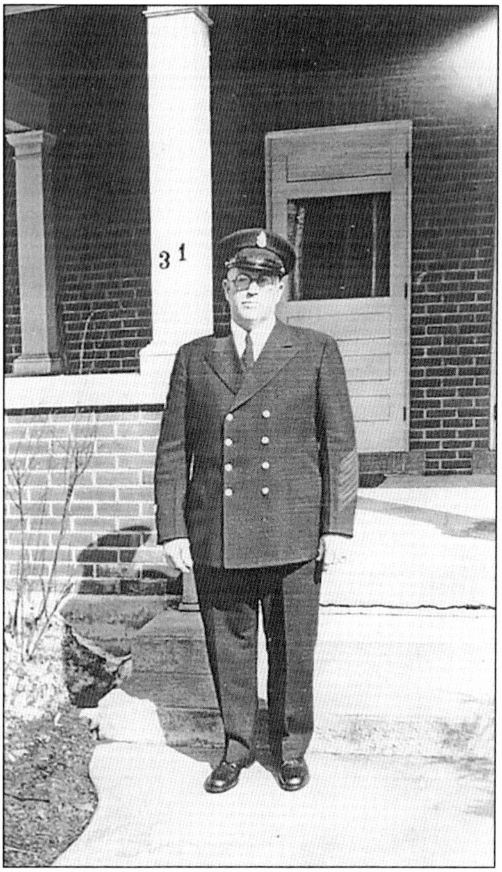

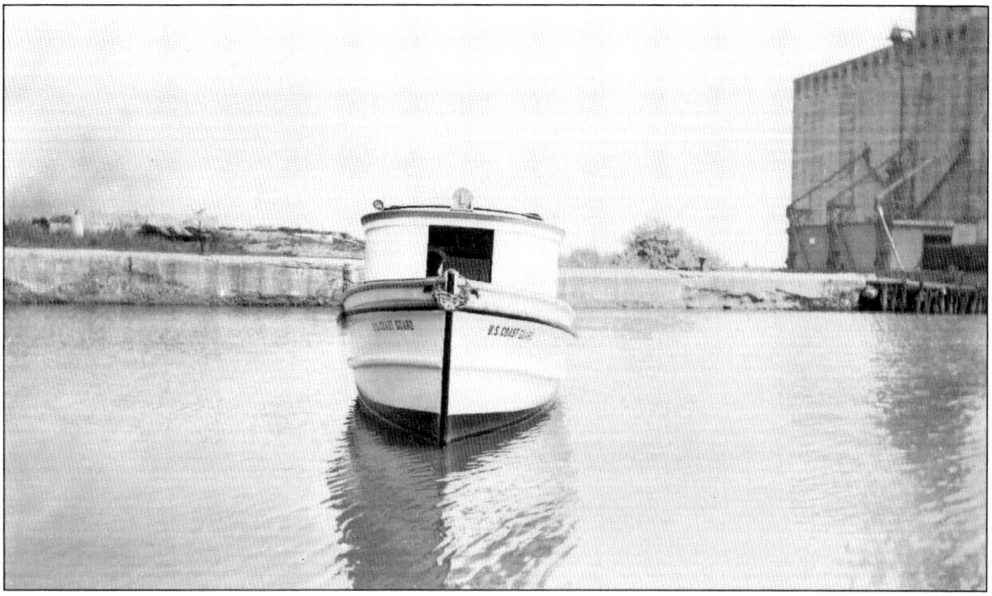

When the Coast Guard assumed responsibility for all lighthouses in 1939, it also acquired all the vessels, such as this light station launch, repainted white and properly identified as a Coast Guard vessel. The launch is in the basin on the west side of Oswego Harbor at what is now the Oswego Coast Guard Station, with the New York State Grain Elevator and the remains of the old inner breakwater in the background.

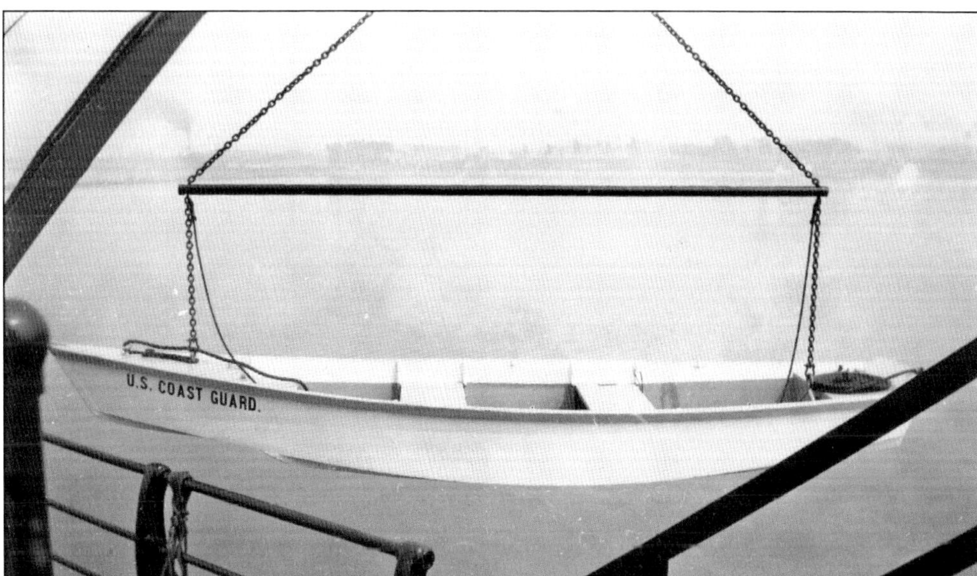

The light station was also equipped with a small skiff, which was hoisted up using the crane on the south side of the caisson deck, as shown here. Similar to the light station launch, the skiff was repainted white and identified as a Coast Guard vessel.

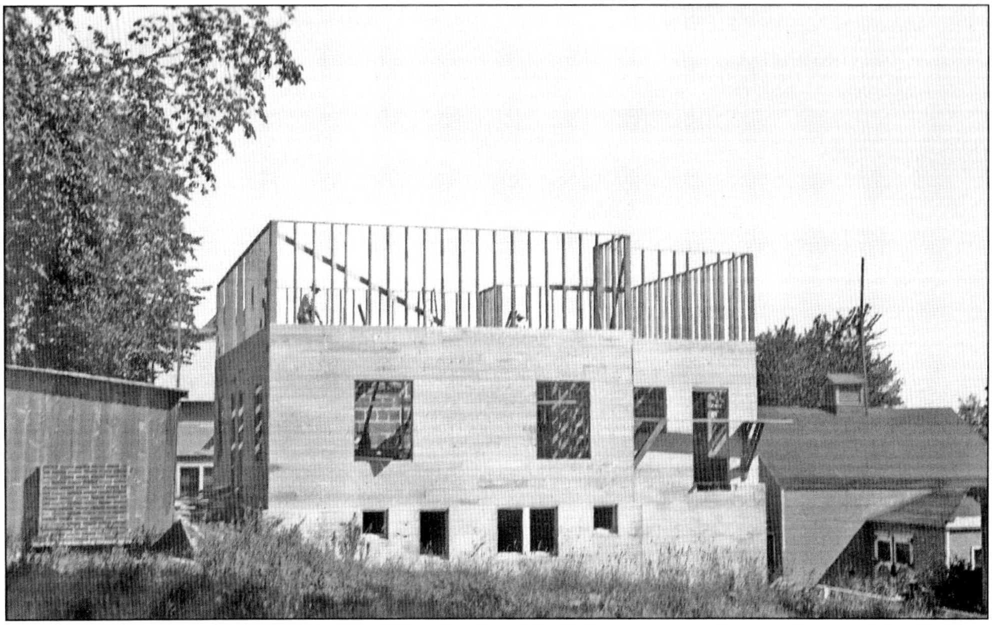

With the construction of the Oswego West Pierhead Lighthouse came the new keepers' dwelling at 31–33 West Fifth Street. This duplex served as the quarters for the keeper and the first assistant keeper. The previous dwelling at 22 West Third Street was retained for the second assistant keeper.

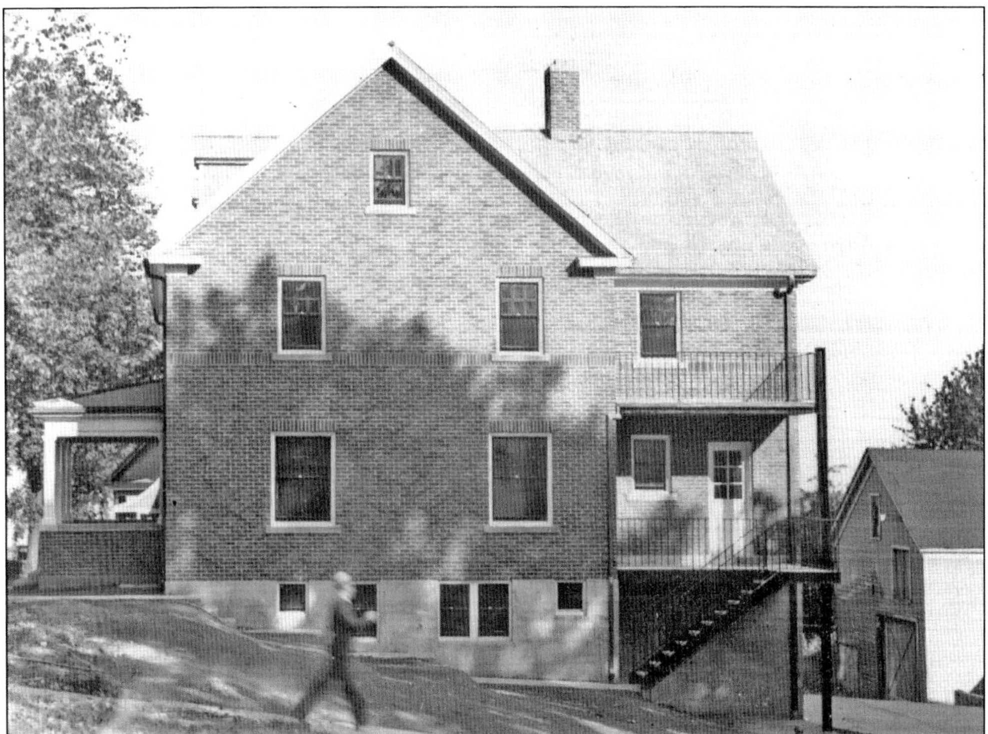

The Van Buren Street side of the new keepers' duplex is shown as it was nearing completion in the mid-1930s. A man can be seen walking down the steep Van Buren Street hill.

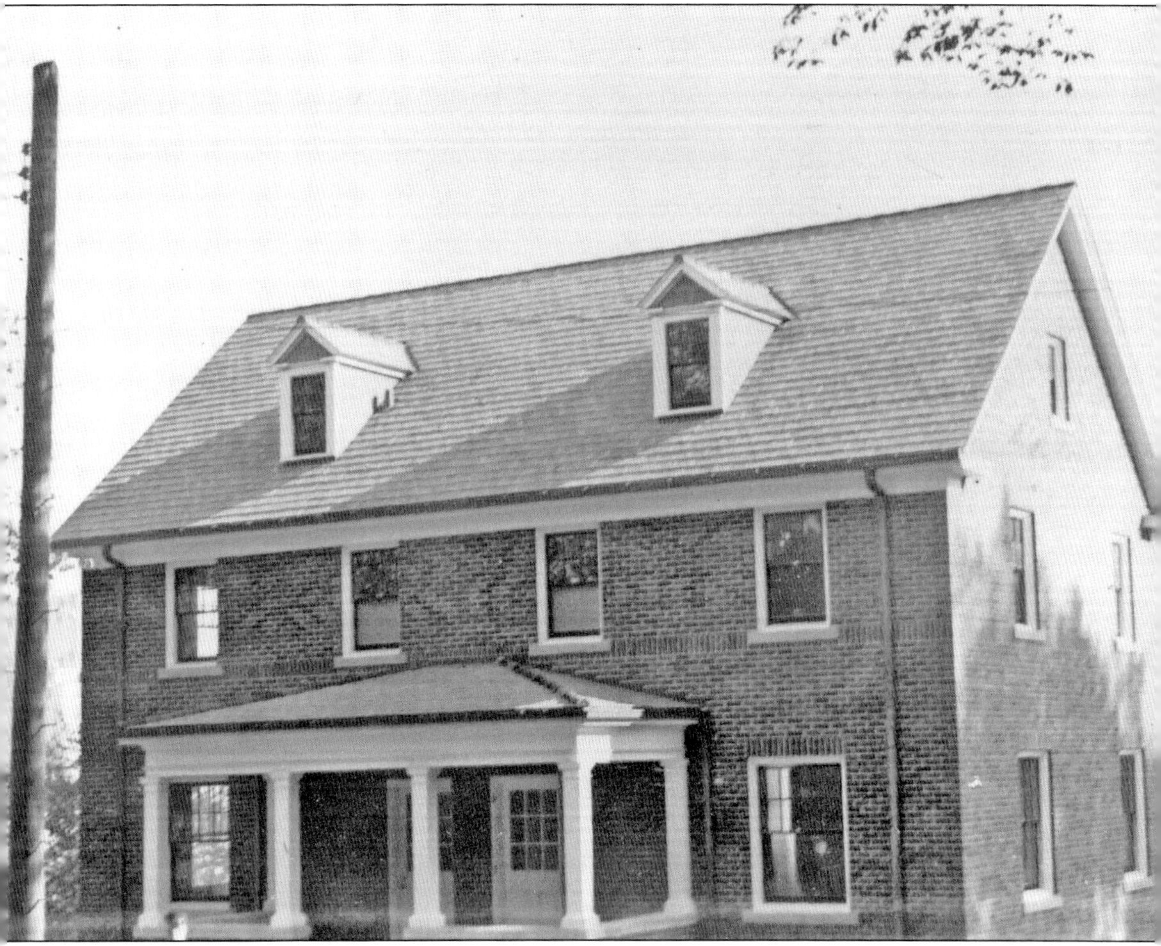

The keepers' duplex is seen here from the West Fifth Street, or front, side at the time it was completed. The duplex was sold to private owners in the mid-1950s. It retains many of its original features today.

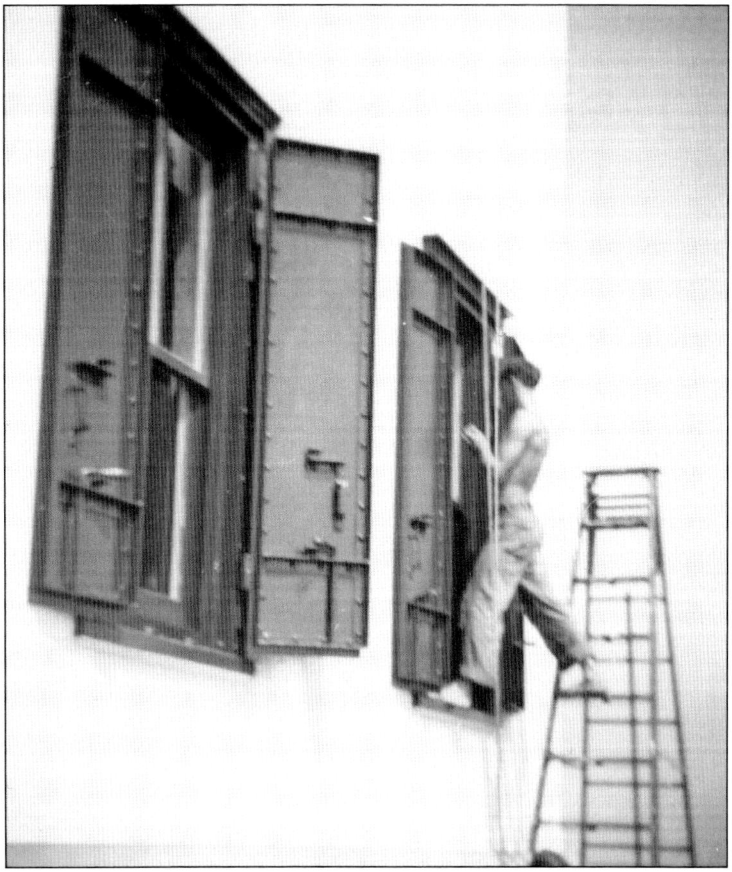

By the early 1950s, new Coast Guard personnel had assumed the keeper duties from the former US Lighthouse Service personnel. They worked to maintain the lighthouse, which included painting and clearing snow from the caisson in the winter, as seen in these late 1940s photographs. At left, Larry Stabnow performs maintenance on the exterior of a window at the Oswego West Pierhead Lighthouse in 1949. Below, three men are chipping ice after one of Oswego's infamously windy winter days.

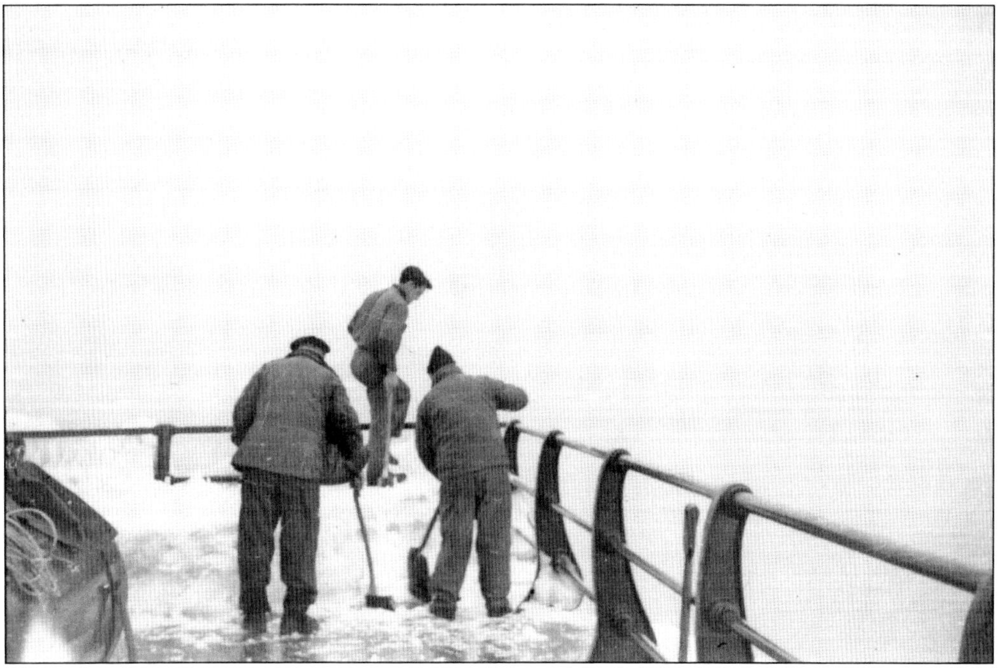

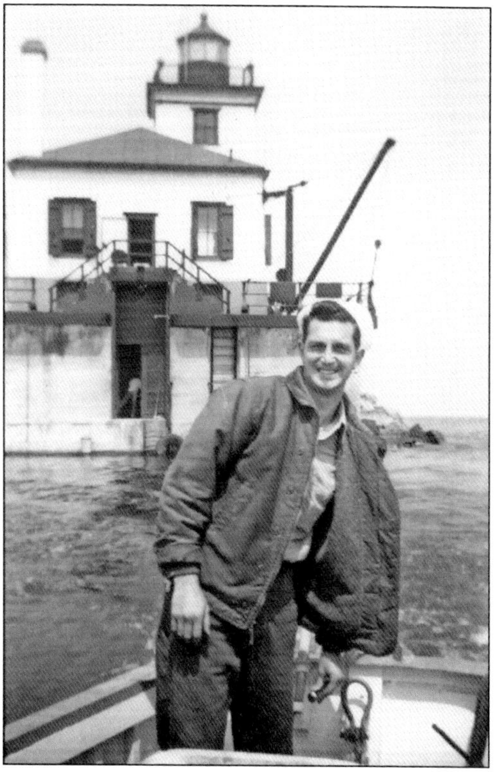

Occasionally, there was even time for enjoyable boat operations and relaxing on the caisson by the antenna tower. At right is Robert Boyor embarking at the Oswego West Pierhead Lighthouse, and below is Richard Himes relaxing on the deck during some downtime.

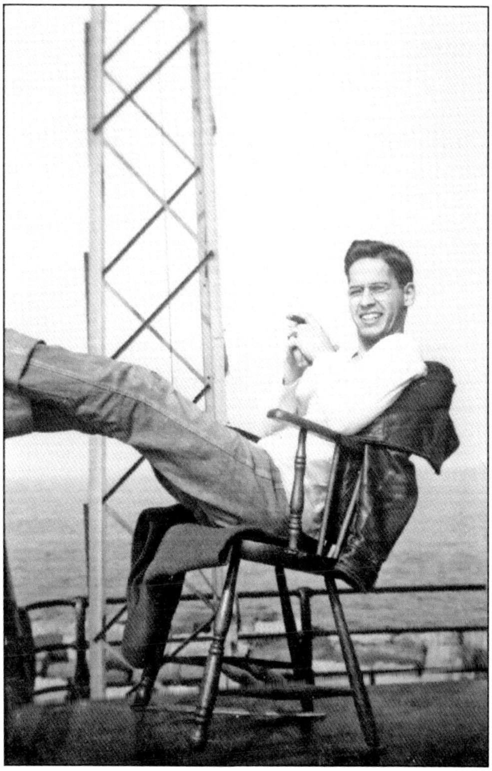

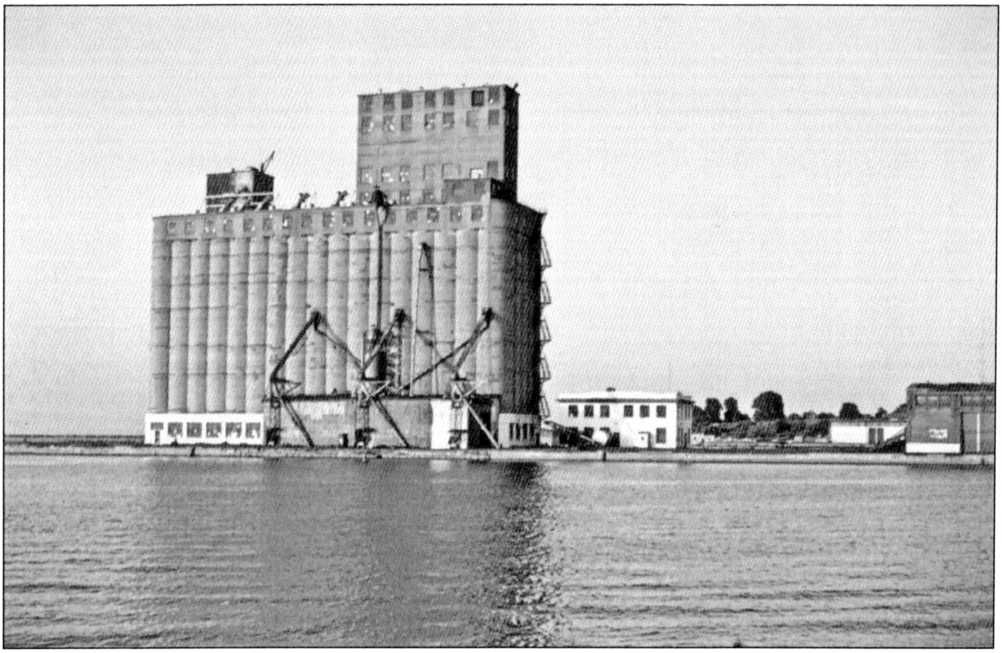

The Oswego Elevator Light was established in 1931, when the Oswego Breakwater Beacon was discontinued and removed as part of the Oswego Harbor expansion. The elevator's beacon, a 300-millimeter electric light visible for 16 miles, was placed on top of the New York State Grain Elevator, 147 feet above Lake Ontario. Although it was originally intended to be temporary, it remained in use as the primary Oswego light until 1968. The present H. Lee White Maritime Museum is housed in the grain elevator's support building, seen at the lower right.

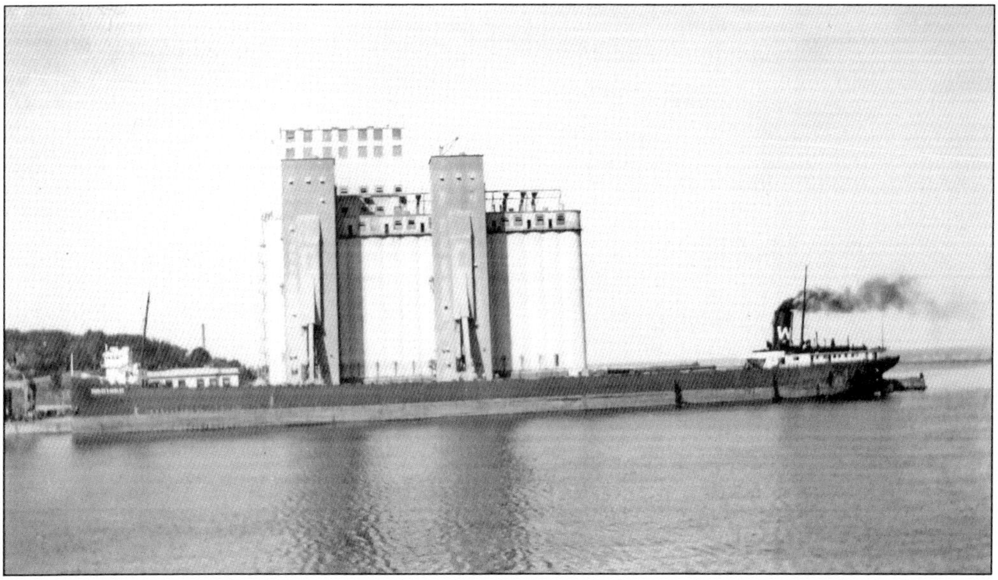

Taken from the east side of Oswego Harbor, this photograph shows a large Great Lakes bulk carrier moored alongside the grain elevator's east side. The vessel is unloading its cargo into the two large elevator units. These could move along the elevator building to access the vessel's holds.

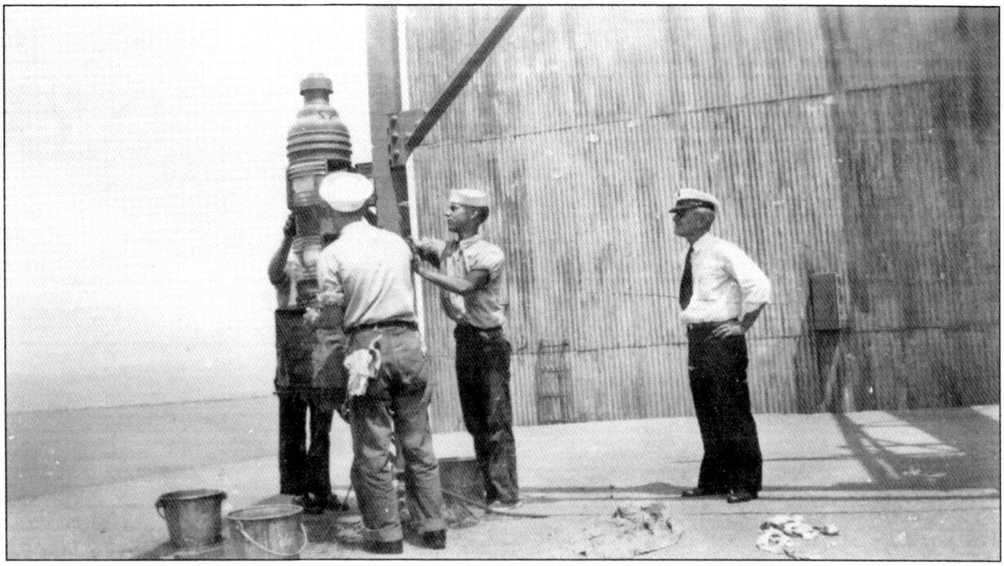

Maintaining the Oswego Elevator Light was the responsibility of the Oswego Coast Guard Station's crew. From left to right are Fireman Richard Himes, BM3 Conrad Brickman, and Chief Boatswain's Mate Kenneth Outten, the station's officer in charge, as they clean the 300-millimeter lantern in July 1949.

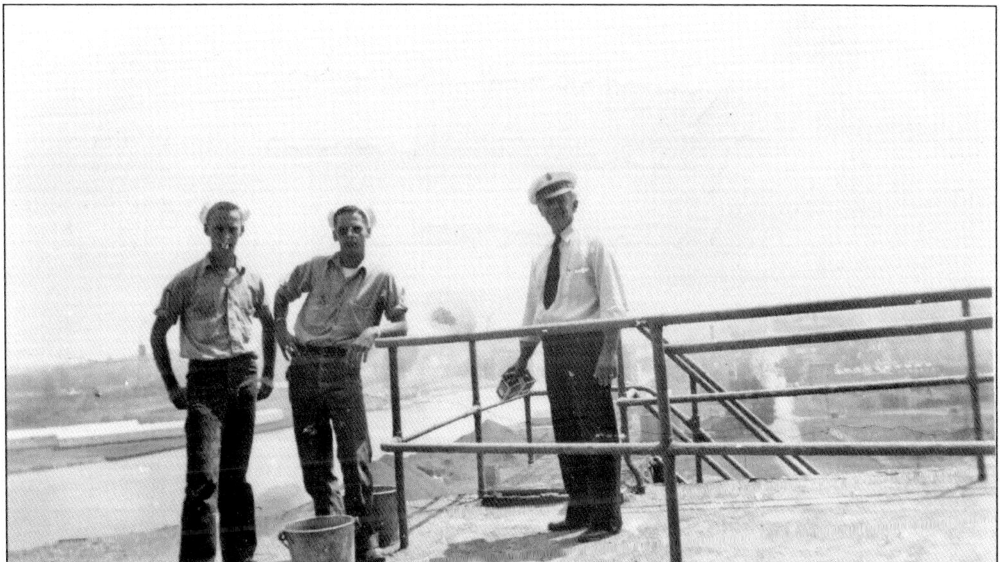

With their cleaning completed, two of the crew and Chief Outten prepare to descend the stairway on the south end of the grain elevator's light platform. With the prevalence of grain dust at the elevator, this cleaning job was likely a frequent one.

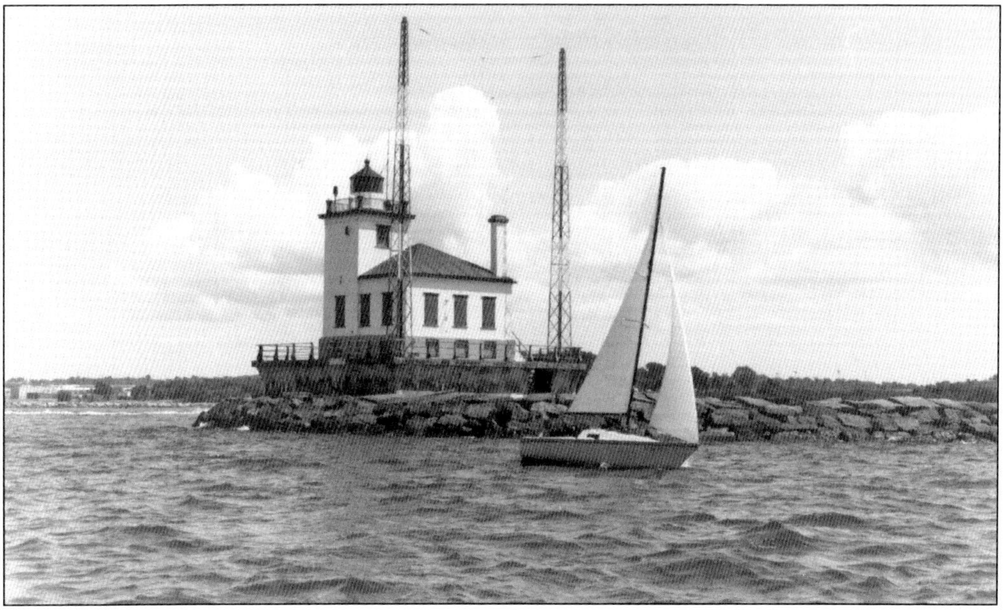

This photograph was taken in 1991 and originally featured in the *Palladium Times* on July 19, 1993. In 1968, the Oswego West Pierhead Lighthouse was automated, and the resident Coast Guard keepers from Station Oswego were removed from their duty. The compressed-air foghorn was replaced with an electric one, and an additional battery-powered standby light was added to take over if electrical power was lost. Both of these features were installed on the north side of the lantern gallery.

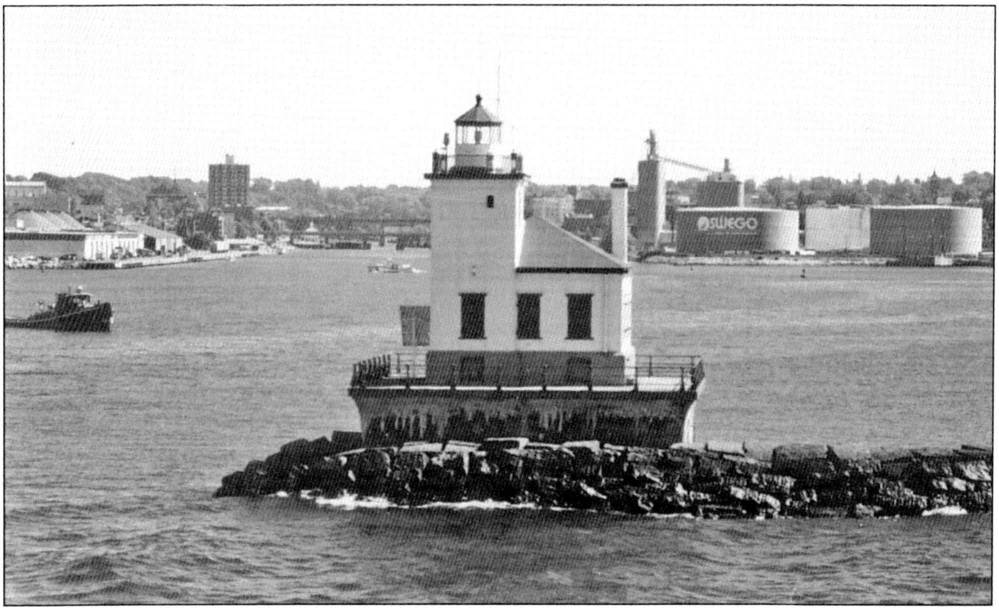

This post-1995 image of the Oswego West Pierhead Lighthouse shows the additional changes to the structure. That year, the lighthouse was converted to solar power, and the large solar array faced south, just visible to the left of the lighthouse on the caisson. The fourth-order Fresnel lens was replaced by a VRB-25 rotating light, and the original lens was loaned to the H. Lee White Maritime Museum, where it is exhibited today.

Five

Revenue Cutter Service 1809–1915

The US Revenue Cutter Service was created by an act of Congress on August 4, 1790. Its mission was to patrol the coast of the young American republic to suppress smuggling—a pressing need, as customs duties were a major source of income for the new government. Revenue cutters, fast and light with shallow drafts, cruised along the coast and, in addition to their primary mission, assisted mariners in distress. Initially, customs enforcement on the Great Lakes was handled by local collectors of customs employing launches crewed by volunteers who were possibly deputized members of local militia units. Prior to the War of 1812, the US Navy took on the task of customs enforcement on the Great Lakes, especially after the Embargo Act of 1807. The brig *Oneida*, built in Oswego, was one of the vessels employed in such work on the Great Lakes.

The first revenue cutter specifically associated with Oswego was *Jefferson*. This iron-hulled, steam-powered vessel was manufactured in Pittsburgh and assembled in Oswego in 1845. It proved unsatisfactory on the lake and was reassigned to Boston in 1848. In 1849, two new cutters were built in Erie, Pennsylvania: *Harrison* and *Cobb*. *Harrison* was stationed in Oswego until it was sold in 1856 and was replaced by *Cobb*, which was lost while sailing along the East Coast in 1861 at the start of the Civil War.

After the Civil War, a number of revenue cutters were based in Oswego, including *Salmon P. Chase* in 1866, *George M. Bibb* in 1883, and *Dallas* in 1903. Great Lakes revenue cutters were decommissioned at the end of the shipping season, the enlisted crew discharged, and the vessel laid up for winter. When spring rolled around, crews were reenlisted, and the vessels moved to their operating stations. *Dallas* was probably the last revenue cutter stationed at Oswego.

In January 1915, the US Revenue Cutter Service and the US Life-Saving Service merged, forming the US Coast Guard. This organization, with an expanded mission and increased personnel on hand, began a new era of Oswego's maritime history.

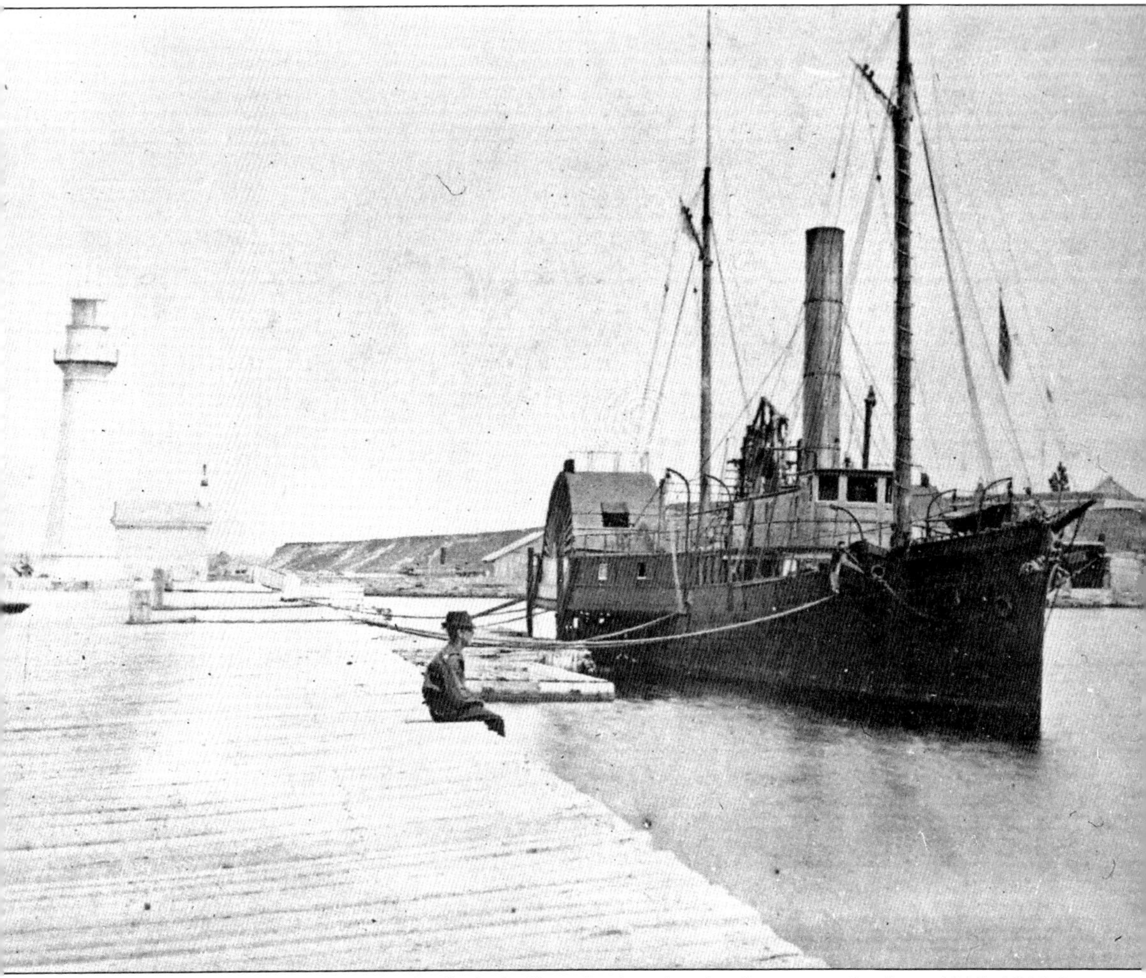

One of a class of five wooden-hulled, shallow-draft, side-wheel steamers built in 1865–1866 for service on the Great Lakes, the revenue cutter *Salmon P. Chase* is seen here moored along the inside of the west inner harbor breakwater at Oswego. *Chase* was built in Brooklyn and was stationed in Oswego until sold in 1875. (Courtesy of Mark Slosek, City of Oswego historian.)

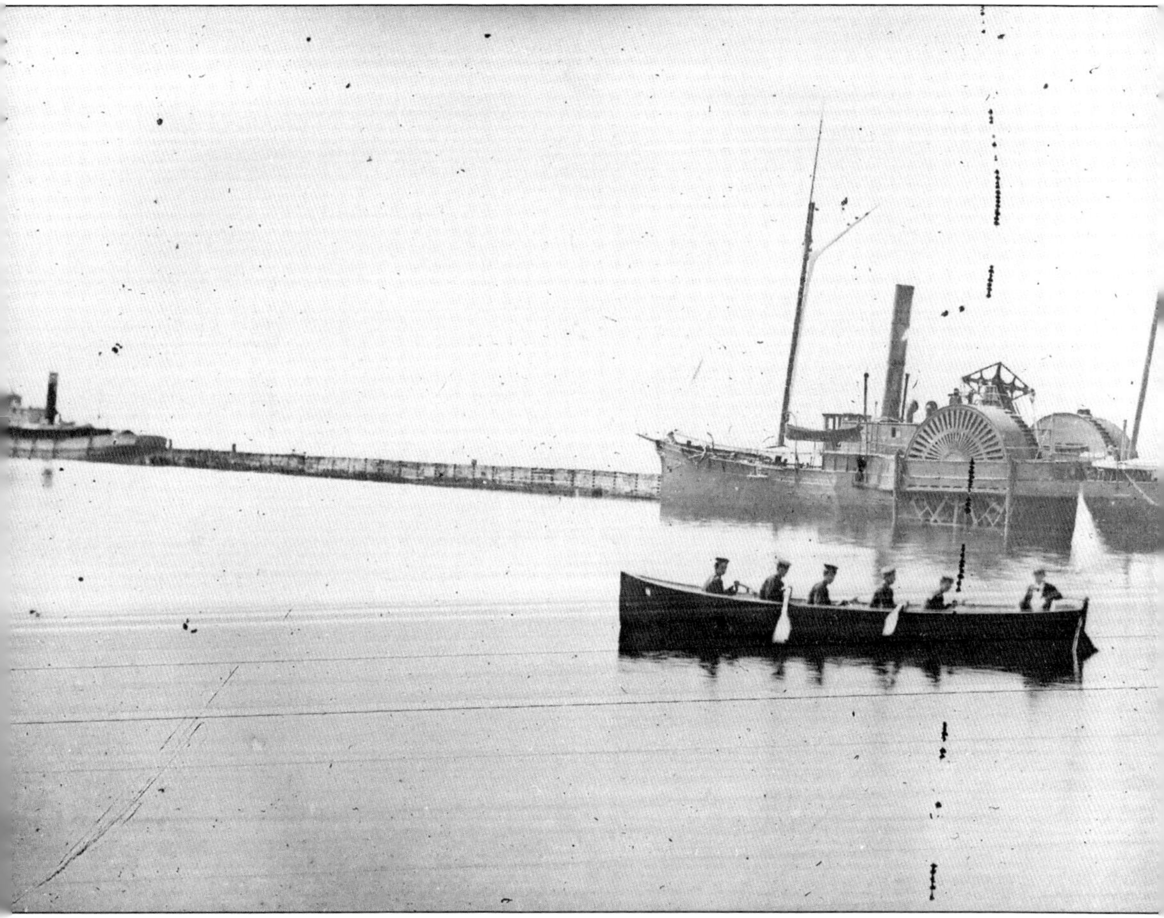

As crew members train in a small boat in the foreground, the revenue cutter *Salmon P. Chase* is moored alongside the west outer breakwater in the background. Pictured just prior to 1875, the outer breakwater is still under construction east of this location. (Courtesy of Mark Slosek, City of Oswego historian.)

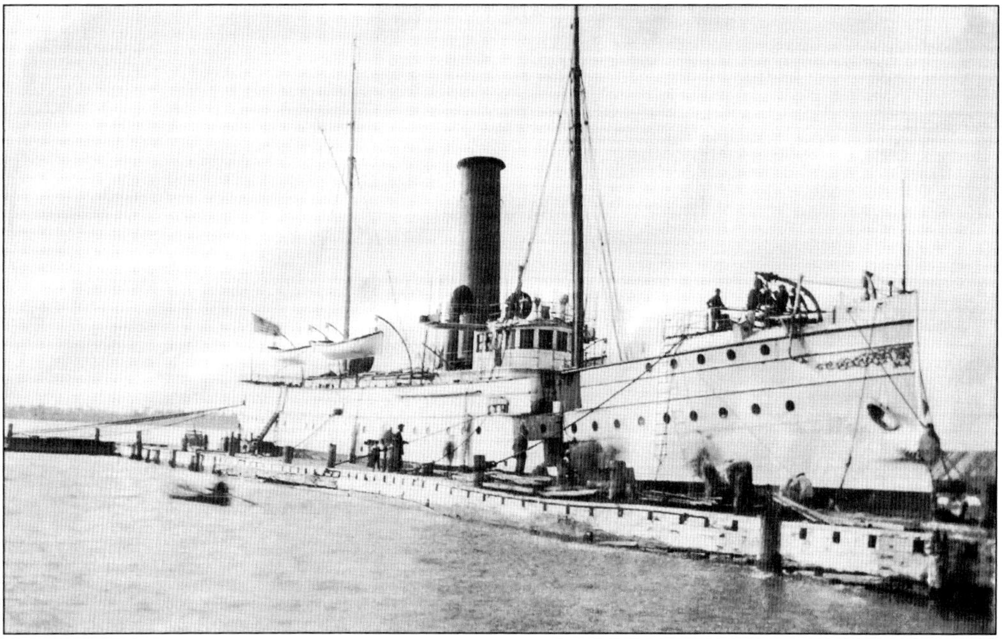

The revenue cutter *Gresham*, built by the Globe Iron Works in Cleveland, was commissioned on May 30, 1897. *Gresham*'s unique design anticipated naval service and included naval armament such as a torpedo tube at the bow. This armament resulted in protests over possible violation of the Webster-Ashburton Treaty with Canada, which limited naval armaments on the Great Lakes.

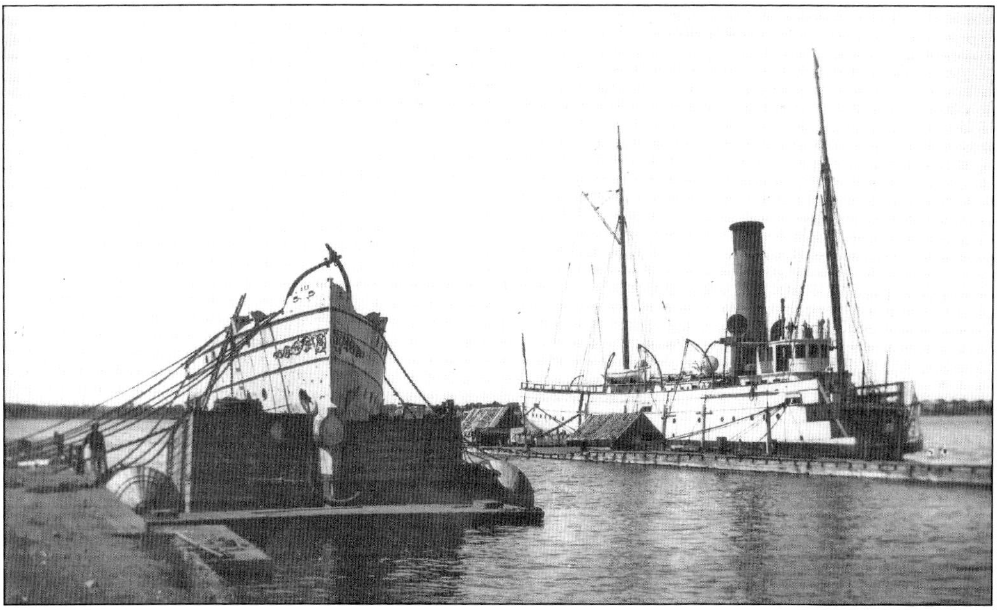

In March 1898, *Gresham* was ordered out of the Great Lakes so it could cooperate with the US Navy during the Spanish-American War. However, the vessel was too long to fit through the locks to go down the St. Lawrence River to the Atlantic Ocean. *Gresham* sailed to Ogdensburg, New York, where it was cut in half so it could go down the river. This photograph shows the vessel in two halves after being refloated from the dry dock where that was done. *Gresham* served in the Navy from 1935 to 1944 and did not return to the Great Lakes.

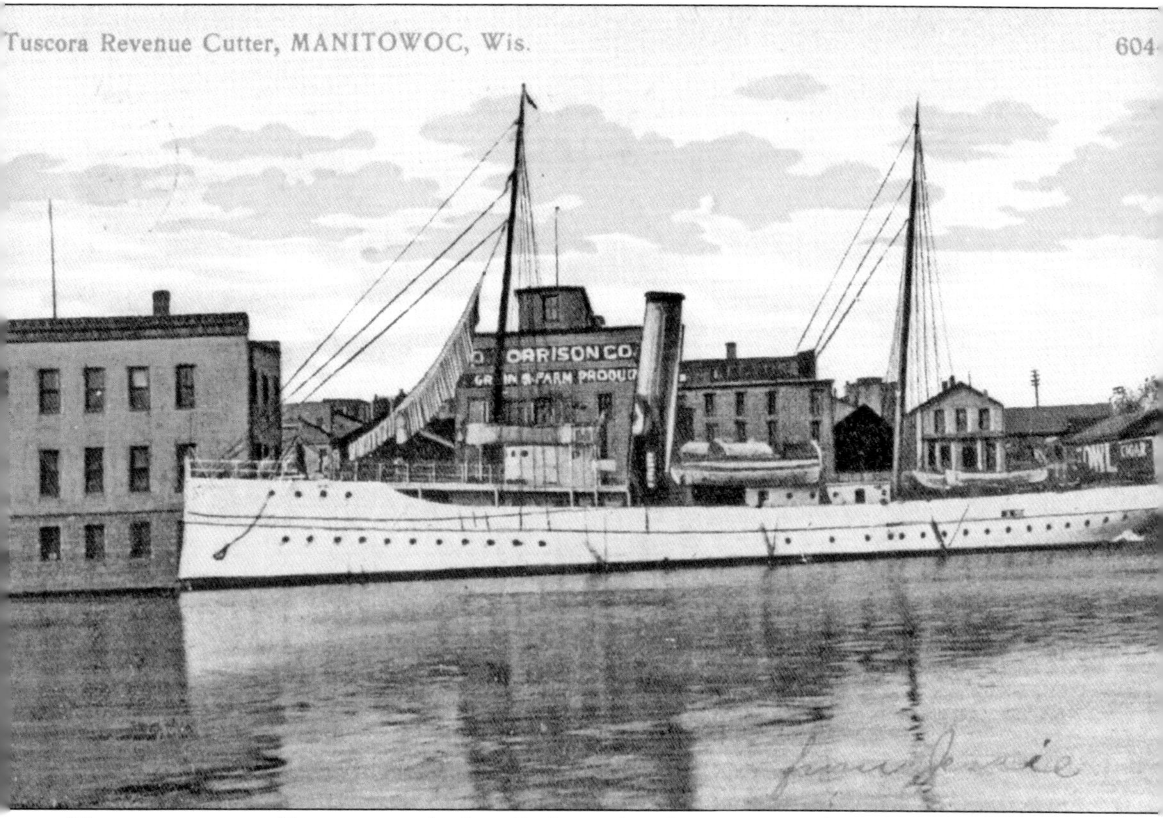

The revenue cutter *Tuscarora* was built in Richmond and commissioned in 1902. In 1904, the newly built revenue cutter was transferred to the Great Lakes and based in Milwaukee. As with the other revenue cutters on the Great Lakes, *Tuscarora* was laid up during the winter months, when the shipping season was closed due to ice. During World War I, *Tuscarora* cooperated with the Navy, first on the Great Lakes and later on the East Coast. In 1920, it returned to Milwaukee, but in 1926, *Tuscarora* was sent to Boston. In the 1930s, it was based in Florida.

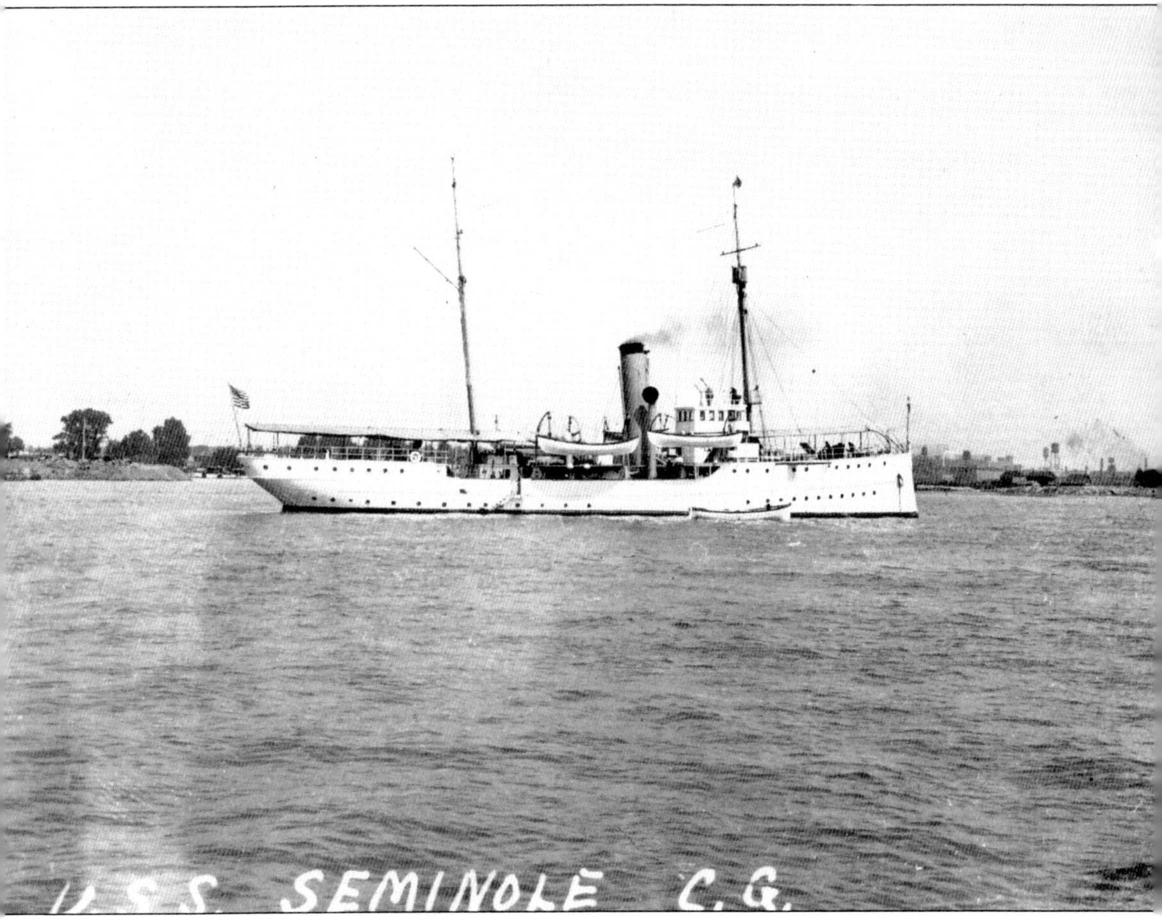

The revenue cutter *Seminole* was built in Baltimore and commissioned in 1900. It operated along the southern US coast and in the Caribbean as a Coast Guard cutter after 1915, until being transferred to the Great Lakes in 1929. It was decommissioned in 1934. (Courtesy of the Oswego Coast Guard Station.)

Six

Life-Saving Service 1875–1915

The US Life-Saving Service had its origins on the Atlantic coast, where shipwrecks were common occurrences despite lighthouses to guide mariners and warn of danger. Early attempts to provide aid to shipwrecked mariners were made by private organizations such as the Massachusetts Humane Society along Cape Cod and the federal government along the coast of New Jersey. Some, like the Massachusetts Humane Society, succeeded in some regards, but other attempts failed due to lack of funding and poor organization. Public pressure mounted in the early 1870s and prompted the US Department of the Treasury's Revenue Marine, under the supervision of Sumner Kimball, to organize the US Life-Saving Service. The service provided around 300 Life-Saving stations at its height along the coastal waterways and Great Lakes. Station Oswego was on the east side of the mouth of the Oswego River just below Fort Ontario and was completed in 1876.

Throughout the Great Lakes, stations were located at or near major harbors, where shipping tended to concentrate. Stations were led by a keeper, and six to eight civilian surfmen were hired to join him during the nine-month shipping season. Stations on the Great Lakes were equipped with a lifeboat or sometimes a smaller surfboat. Additionally, they were equipped with a beach apparatus on a hand-drawn cart to effect rescues by breeches buoy when a shipwreck was close enough to shore to be reached by a small cannon-thrown line. Drills in launching and righting capsized boats and rigging the breeches buoy were often well attended by the interested public. The Life-Saving Service often recognized heroic rescues by awarding the Gold or Silver Life Saving Medal.

In January 1915, the Life-Saving Service was merged with the Revenue Cutter Service, forming the Coast Guard. The Life-Saving station at Oswego became the new Coast Guard lifeboat station. The Life-Saving Service keeper, in turn, became the officer in charge of Coast Guard Station Oswego. The original Life-Saving Service station facility was moved, and in 1915, a Chatham-style two-story barracks was built.

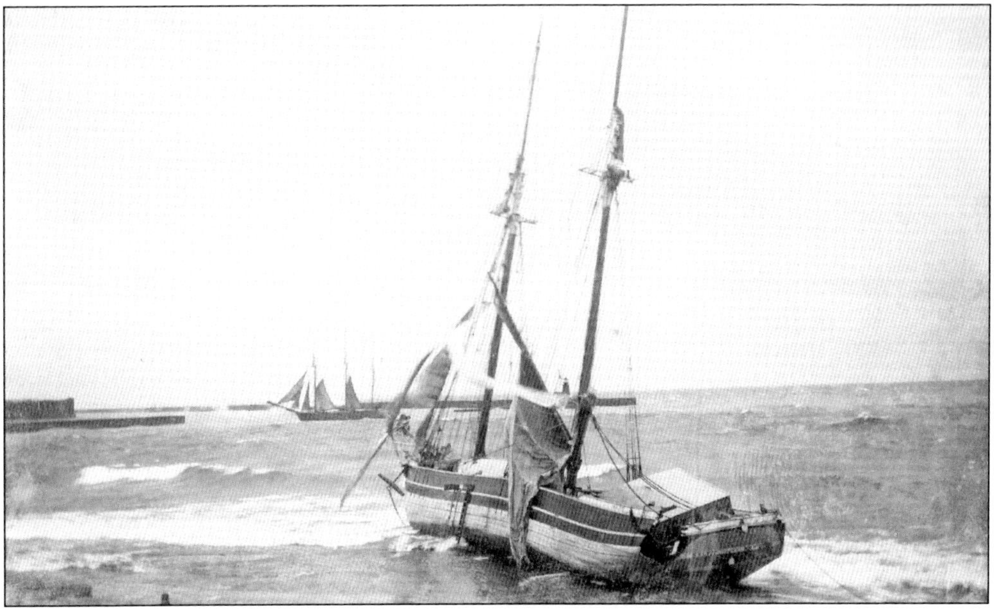

On November 24, 1894, the schooner *Baltic* of Hamilton, Ontario, ran aground right in front of the Oswego Life-Saving Station. The crew from Station Oswego rescued all six from the wreckage, including the captain's wife, using the beach apparatus. Sailing on the Great Lakes late in the year was extremely challenging, even for the best of sailors. Attempting to make port at Oswego in a storm often exceeded the capability of vessels and crew and even of the tugs sent out to assist them. The next day, the crew went onboard the wreck and saved a horse, a pet dog, and the crew's personal effects.

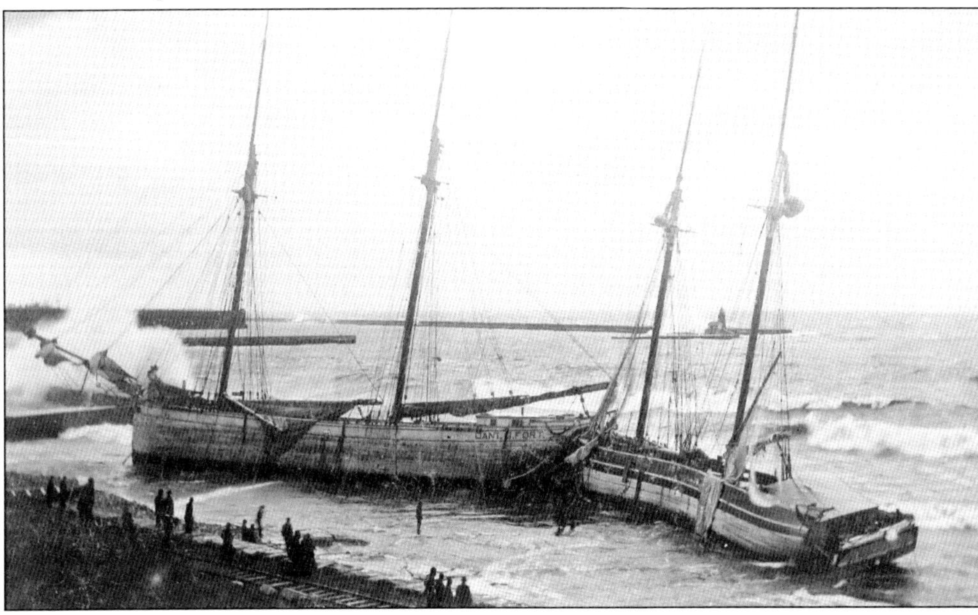

Baltic was joined three days later by the schooner *Daniel G. Fort* of Oswego, which, in spite of valiant assistance from a tug, met with disaster at the same location. Fortunately, the crew of the Oswego Life-Saving Station, under the direction of Keeper Frederick Anderson, rescued all seven of the crew, which required two trips of the station's lifeboat.

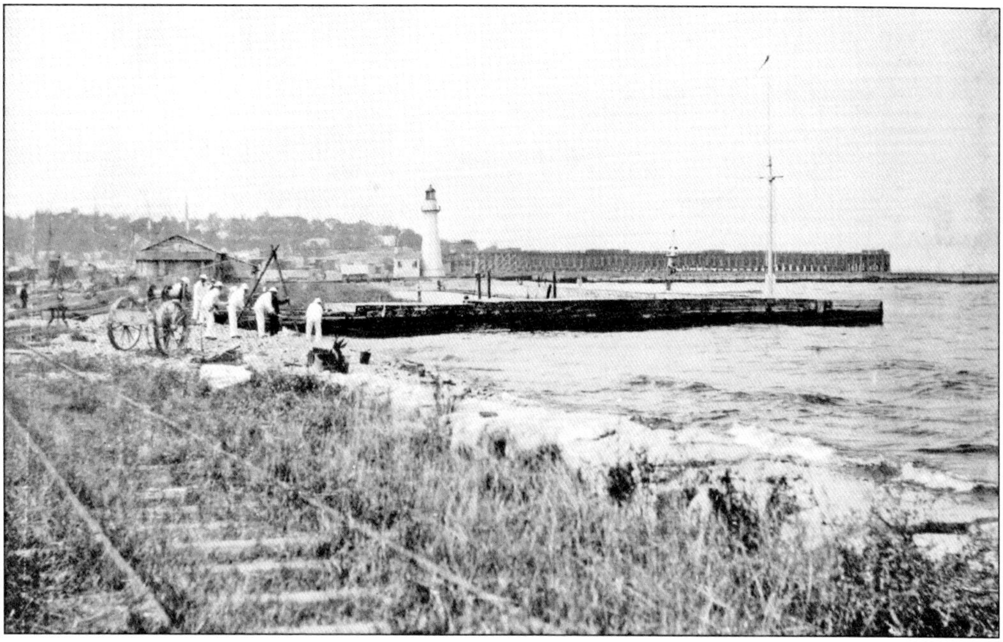

The Life-Saving crew from Oswego is seen here drilling with the beach apparatus, the method used to rescue the crew of the *Baltic*. The equipment was moved on the wheeled cart, and the tall pole, known as the drill pole, was a stand-in for the mast of a shipwreck. A light line was fired out to the wreck using a small cannon, called a Lyle gun, which could reach roughly 500 yards from shore. This was used by those on the shipwreck to haul out a block, or pulley, with a medium-weight line running through it. Attached to the block were instructions on how to rig it.

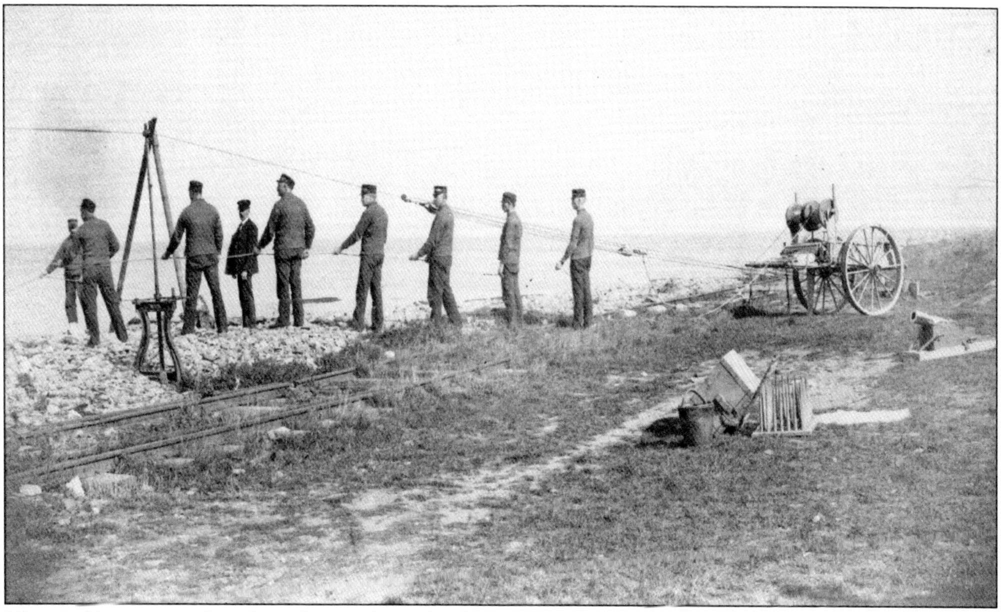

The drill continued with eight surfmen hauling a heavy hawser out to the shipwreck using the medium-weight line, or whip. The hawser also came with instructions on how to secure it to the vessel. As seen above, the hawser, now secured on the vessel, is made fast on shore with a tackle so it can be made taut. A wooden crutch held the hawser in the air clear of the surf.

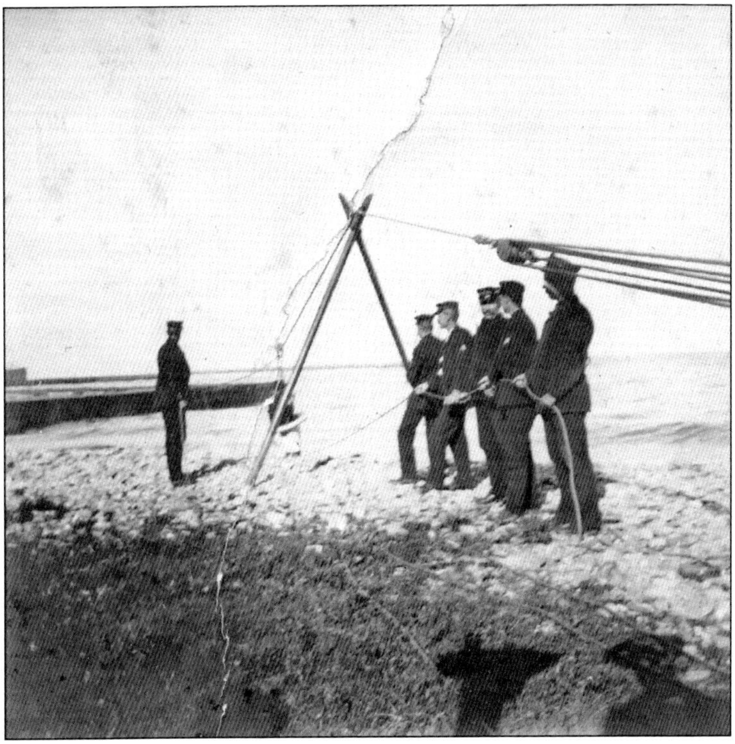

Once all the lines were secure, the rescue began. The first survivor reaches shore in the breeches buoy at left during the same drill. The crew's goal was to have the first survivor ashore within five minutes. During drills, once the light line had been fired, one of the surfmen was sent out to rig the whip and hawser lines and act as the first survivor. Occasionally, a member of the public was invited to volunteer as the first survivor. This drill was conducted twice a week, on Mondays and Thursdays.

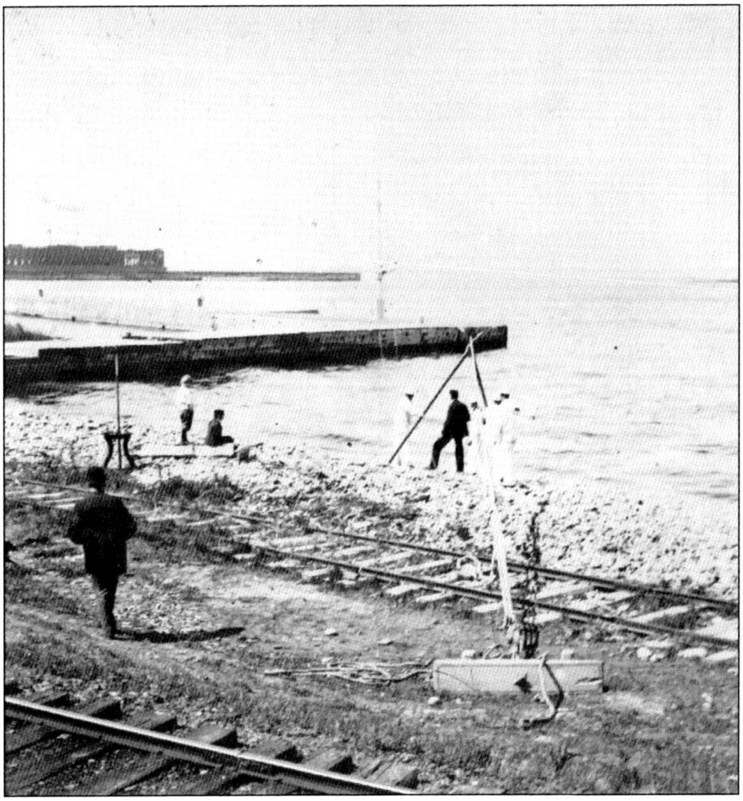

In this view of the rigged beach apparatus, the keeper observes the surfmen as they man the whip to bring survivors ashore. The large timber in the foreground serves to anchor the tackle and apply tension to the hawser line. Two young men and an interested local can be seen observing the drill.

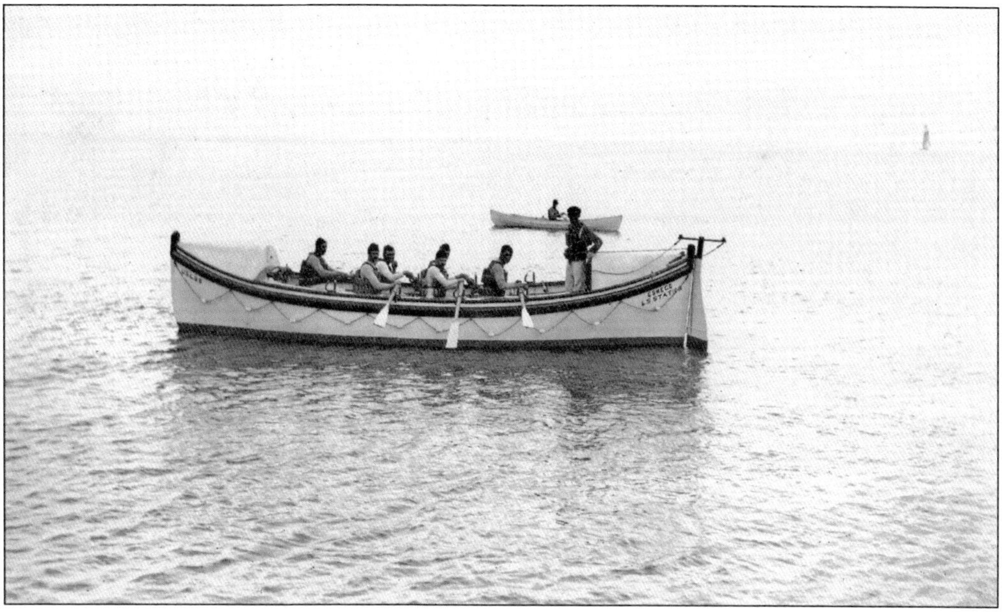

If a shipwreck was farther from shore than the Lyle gun could reach, a rescue required launching the lifeboat. The Oswego Life-Saving Station was equipped with two lifeboats, a 26-foot Merryman type assigned to the station in 1876 and again in 1893, and a 24-foot Dobbins type in 1884 named *Dreadnaught*. The lifeboats were rowed, but some could be equipped with sails.

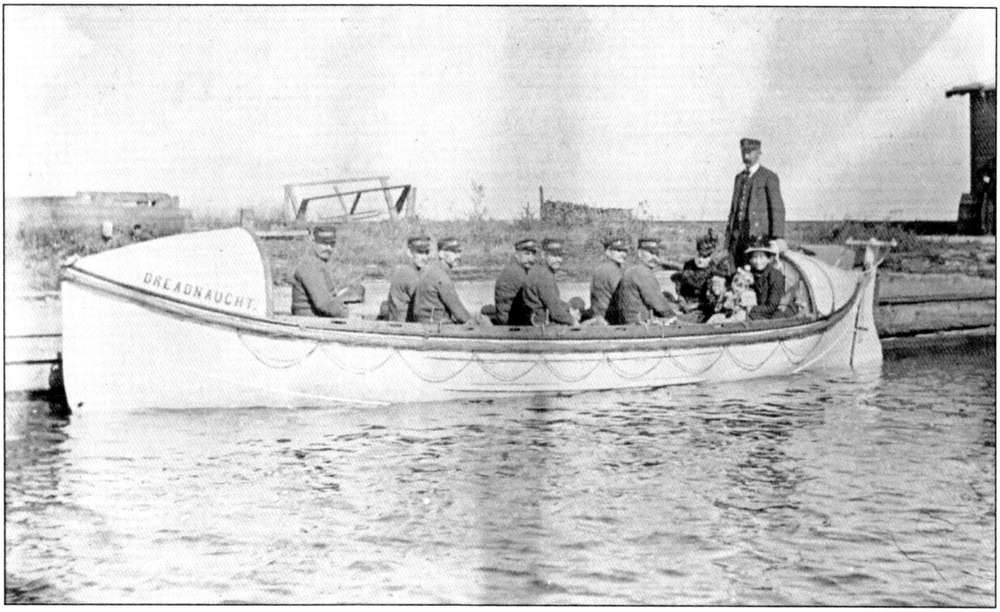

The 24-foot Dobbins-type lifeboat *Dreadnaught* was assigned to Station Oswego in 1884. In this photograph, the passengers in the stern of the boat indicate that the crew is not going out on a rescue or for a capsize drill. Wednesdays were reserved for lifeboat drills, including righting a capsized boat, and were frequently observed from shore by large groups of the public. Some stations, including most on the East Coast, also had a light surfboat that was brought to the scene of a shipwreck along the beach by cart and launched through the surf. On the Great Lakes, lifeboats were usually launched inside a harbor and rowed out to effect the rescue.

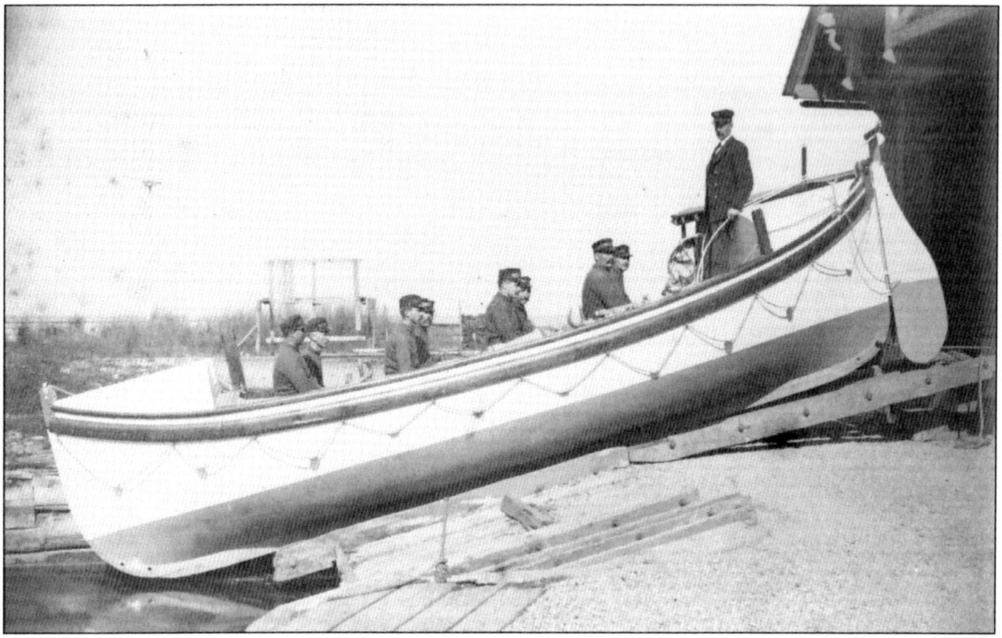

The 26-foot Merryman-type lifeboat was launched down the ramp on the west side of the Oswego Station with the crew of eight surfmen and the keeper at the steering lines. Station Oswego required a ramp because railroad tracks lined the north and west sides of the building.

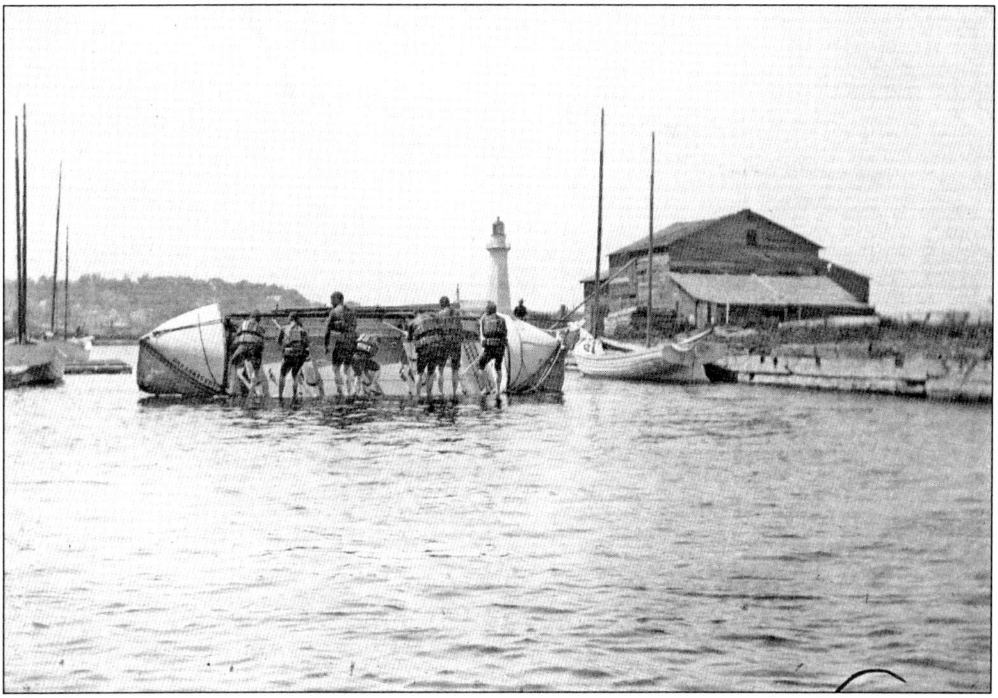

The 24-foot Dobbins-type lifeboat is seen being used for a capsize drill in the slip just west of Station Oswego with the 1837 Oswego Harbor Lighthouse in the background. Six surfmen and possibly the keeper are participating. The keeper may also have a surfman act as coxswain of the lifeboat for practice.

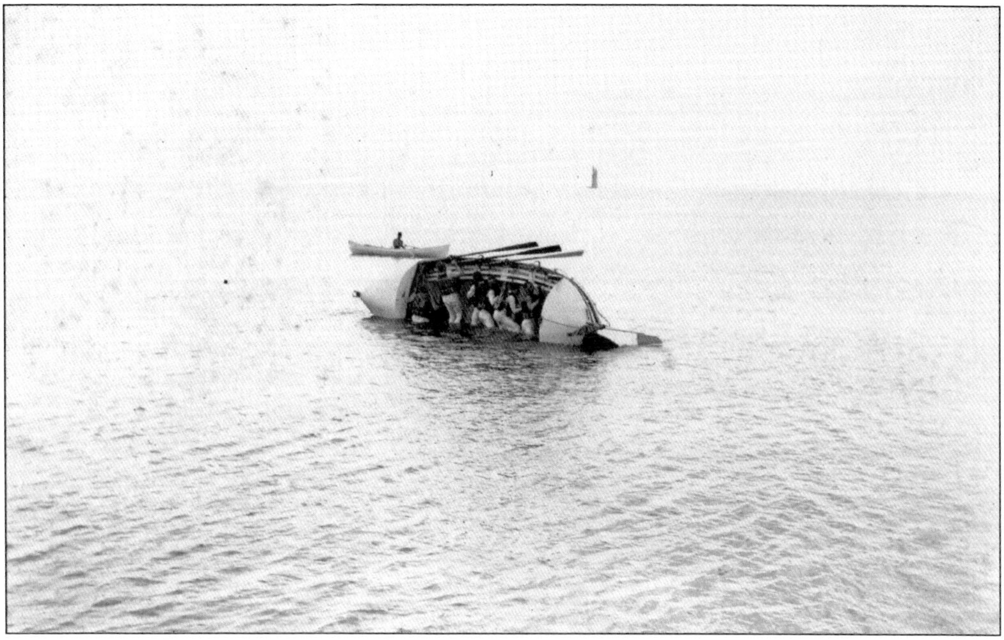

The larger 26-foot Merryman-type lifeboat is being used during this capsize drill, held out in Lake Ontario. There are only five or six crewmen drilling on this calm day, quite different than doing it for real in the high winds and 10-foot waves that caused shipwreck conditions. In the background is possibly the keeper observing the drill from the small skiff.

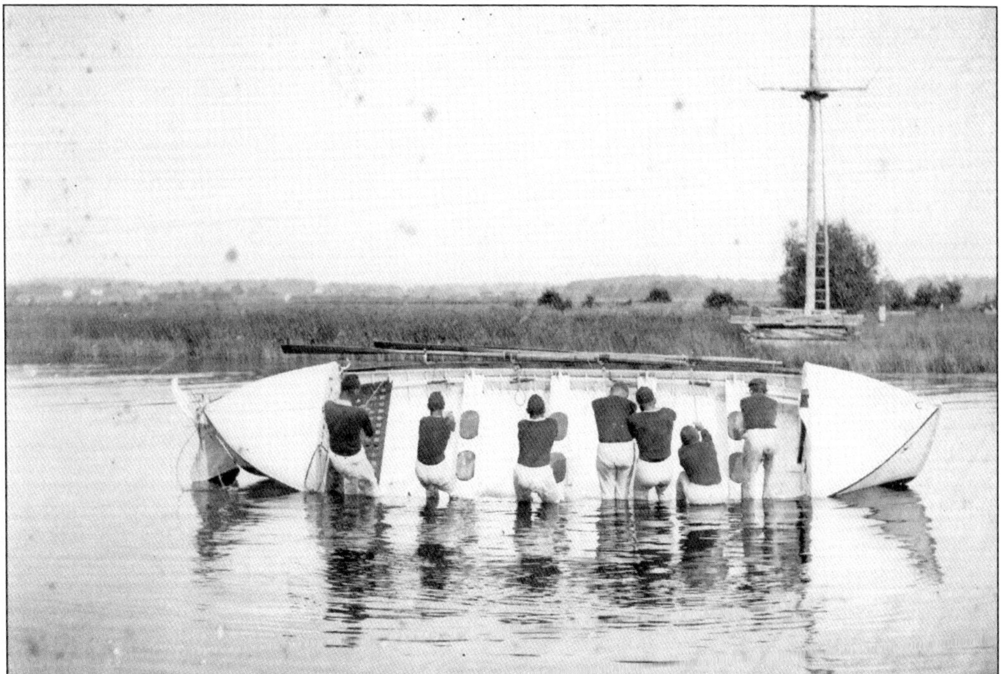

The keeper of US Life-Saving Station Oswego, Fredrick W. Anderson, was previously stationed at the Stoney Point Life-Saving Station, where this photograph was taken. The drilling surfmen are not wearing life jackets, and a drill pole is seen in the background.

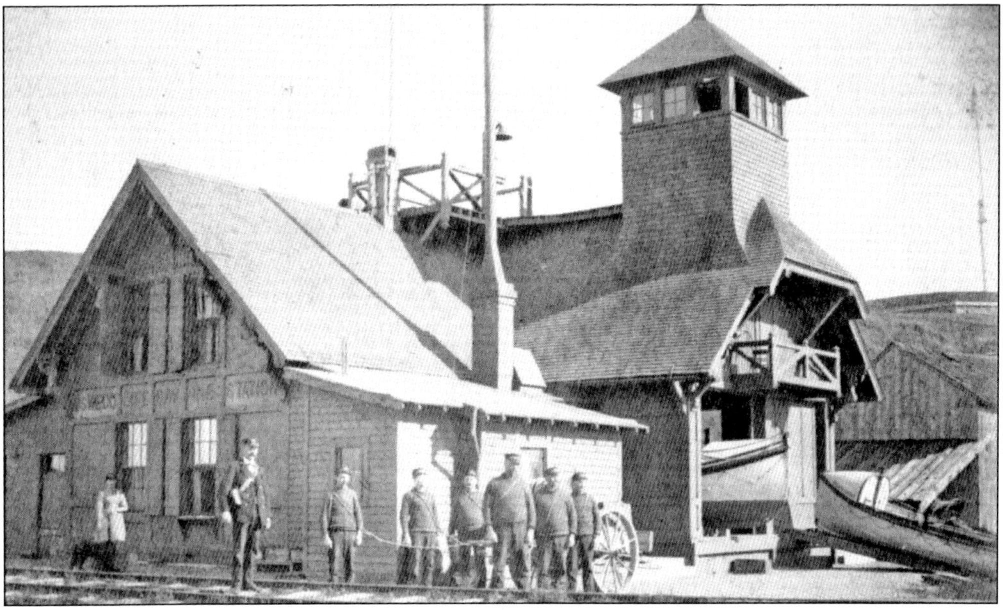

Standing in front of the Oswego Life-Saving Station are the keeper, six surfmen, and a woman (left) with the station mascot. A beach apparatus drill is about to unfold, as the surfmen are harnessed to the beach cart and the keeper is carrying his pouch containing powder charges for the Lyle gun. The beach cart was pulled to the scene of the shipwreck with manpower. The two lifeboats are also visible at the door to the boathouse.

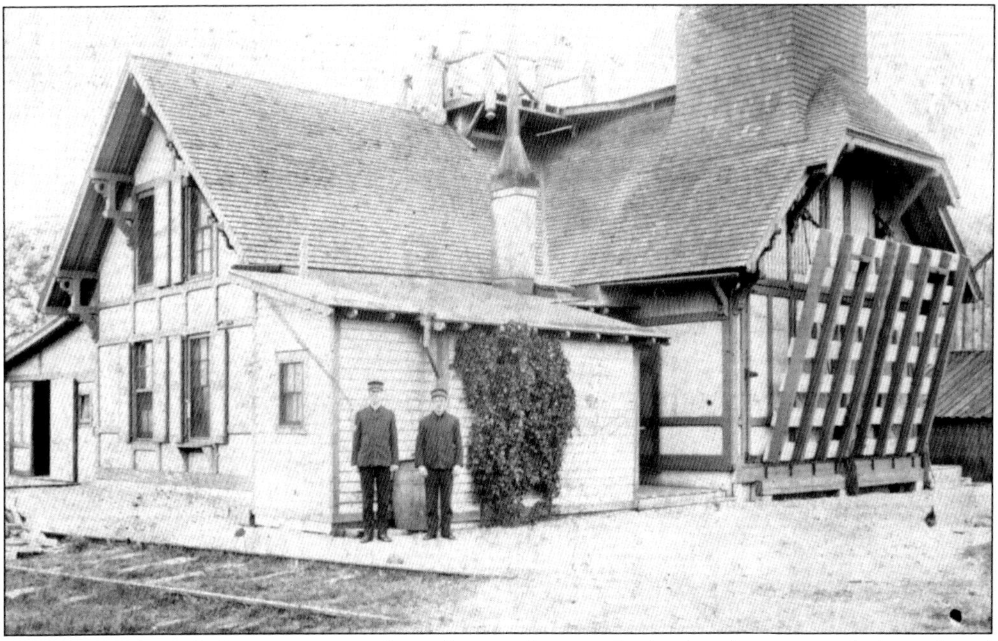

Looking at the Life-Saving station from the northwest, the bridge that covered the railroad tracks for launching the lifeboats is raised just in front of the boathouse doors. Two surfmen are standing next to the tracks that pass in front of the station. A crewmember from Station Oswego stood watch from the lookout tower during daylight hours. At night and in times of bad weather, a beach patrol was also conducted.

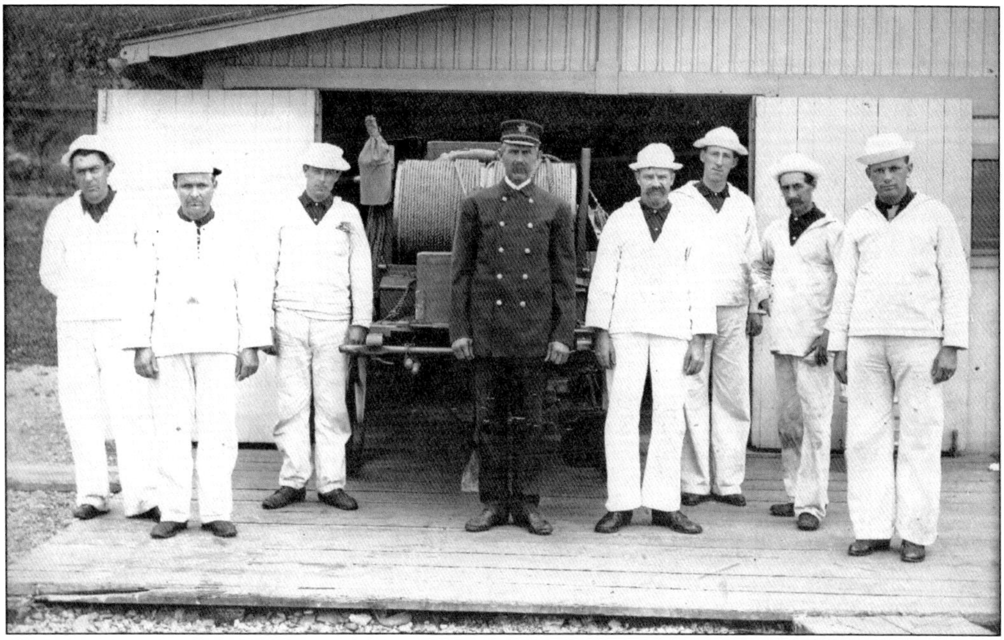

Capt. Frederick W. Anderson served as keeper of the Oswego Life-Saving Station from October 31, 1892, until January 27, 1915. On that date, the US Life-Saving Service and the US Revenue Cutter Service merged to form the US Coast Guard. Captain Anderson was made officer in charge of the new Coast Guard station until August 15, 1916, when he retired. He is seen here standing with seven surfmen in their summer working white uniforms in front of the beach cart.

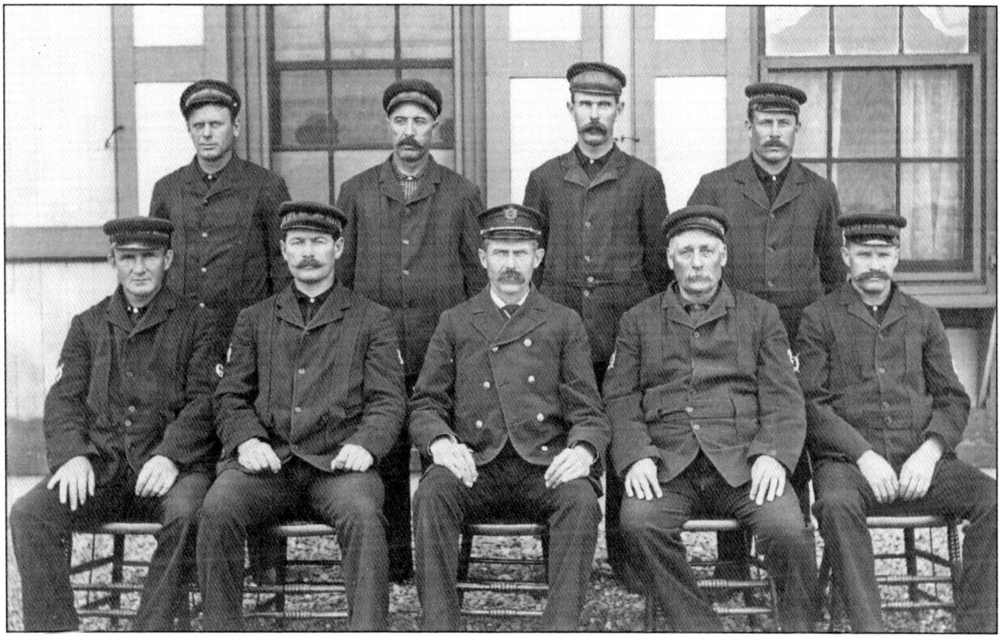

Captain Anderson (seated at center) and the eight surfmen of Station Oswego pose for a formal station photograph. The surfmen have the US Life-Saving Service logo on their right sleeves. On their left sleeve is their surfman rank. Surfman No. 1 is seated second from left, and surfman No. 2 is seated second from right. Surfman No. 6 is seated at far left.

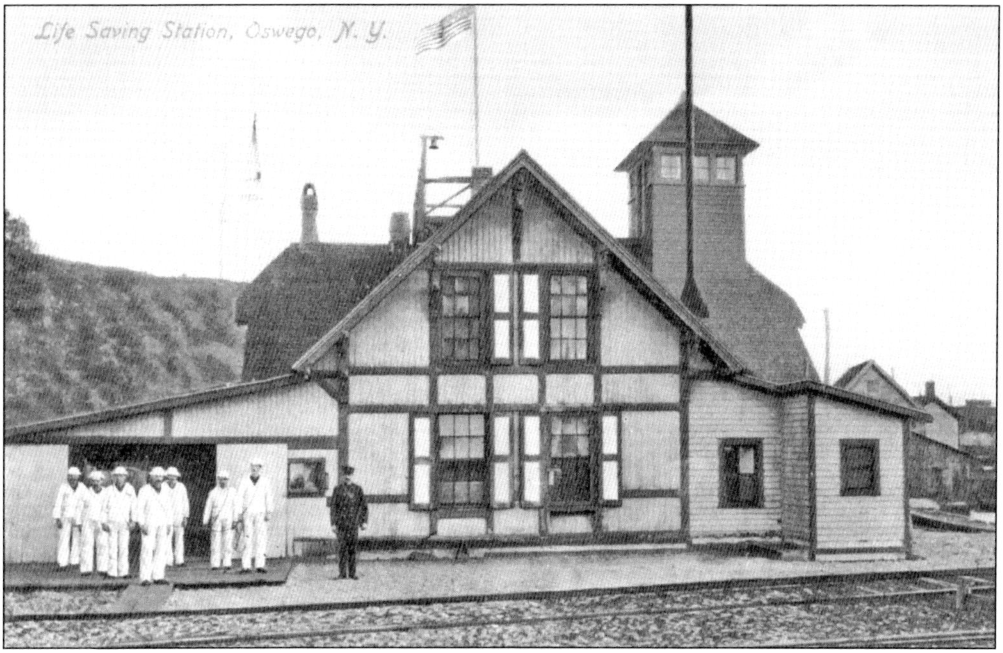

This postcard image shows the keeper and seven surfmen of Station Oswego preparing for a beach apparatus drill. The surfmen are harnessed to the cart, and the keeper is carrying his pouch with Lyle gun charges. The US flag is flying from the station flagstaff, usually used to display signal flags.

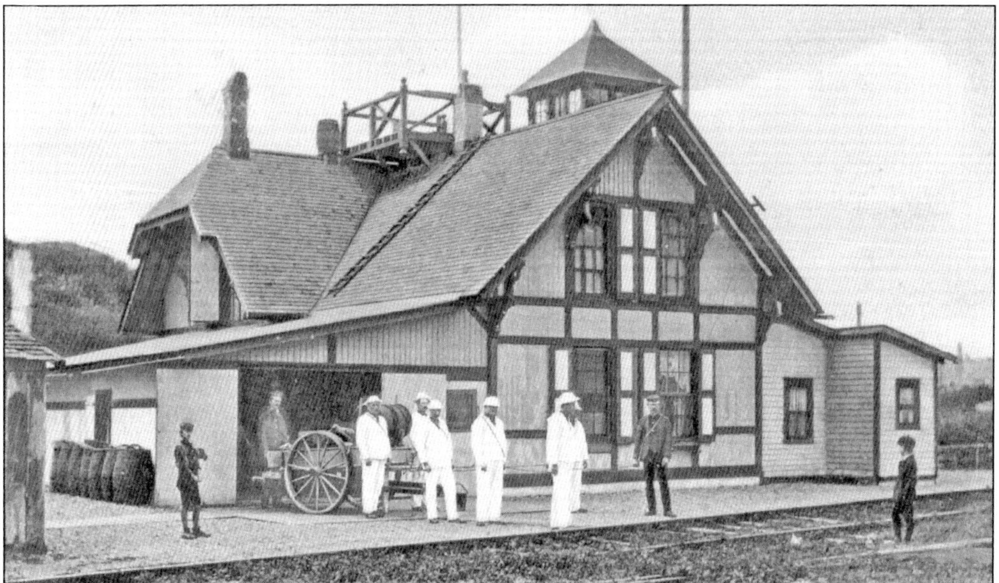

This postcard of the Oswego Life-Saving Station shows the beginning of a beach apparatus drill underway as the beach cart is pulled out and six surfmen are harnessed to it. Two very interested young men are observing the process, perhaps contemplating joining the US Life-Saving Service when they are of age.

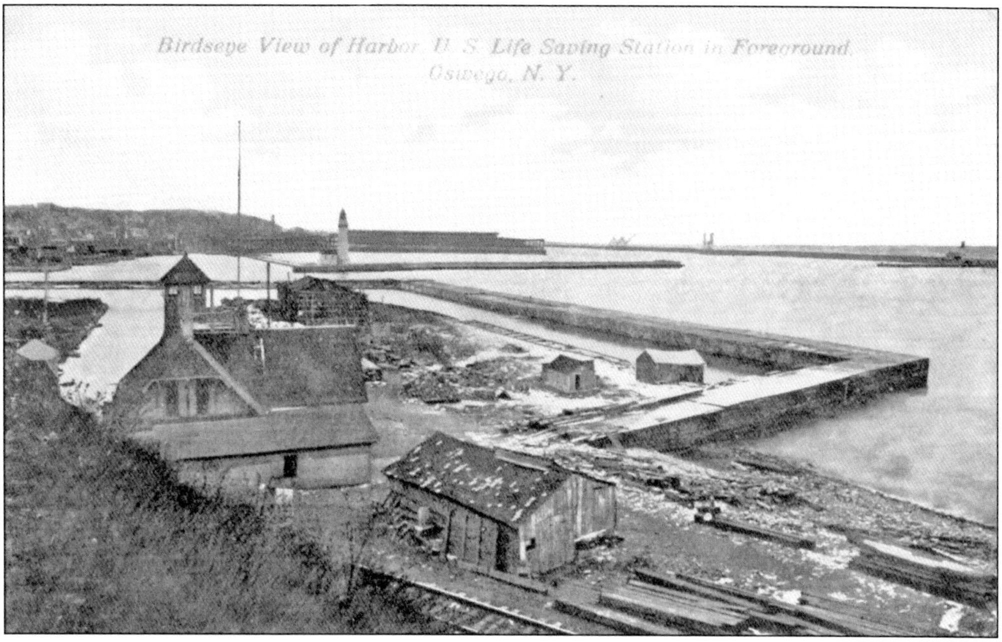

Viewed from the walls of Fort Ontario, this postcard view shows the slip where the lifeboats were launched from just west of the station. Interestingly, the railroad tracks have been moved behind the station, and railroad timbers are stacked next to the tracks.

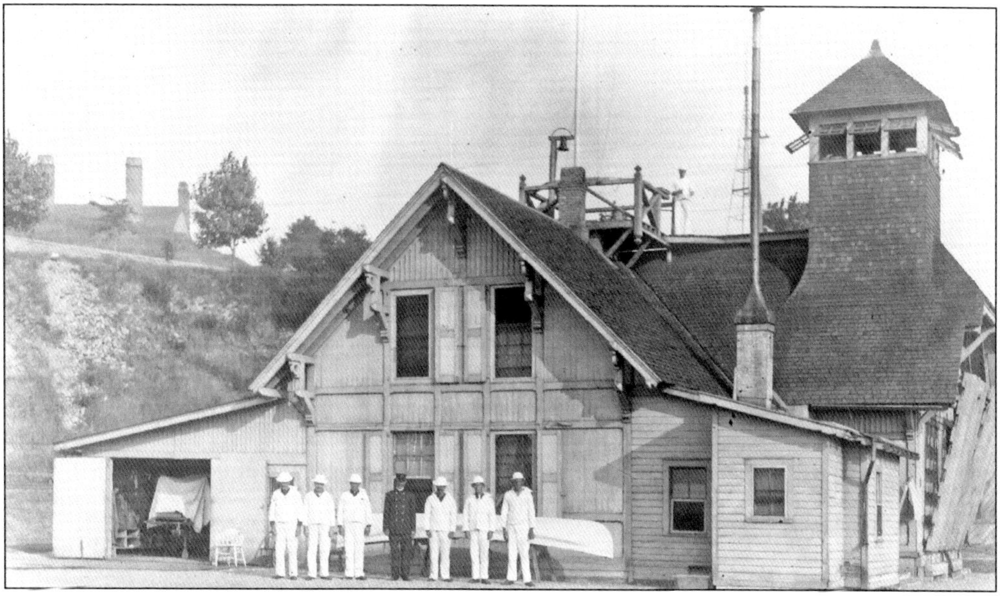

Captain Anderson and six of the surfmen from Station Oswego stand on the north side of the station, and two other surfmen are visible. One stands on the platform on top of the station, and another is just visible in the left window of the lookout tower. The surfmen are wearing their summer white working uniforms, and the beach cart rests inside the door to the lean-to on the east side of the station. The second floor contained a dormitory where the surfmen slept. The keeper's quarters, kitchen, and mess hall were on the ground floor.

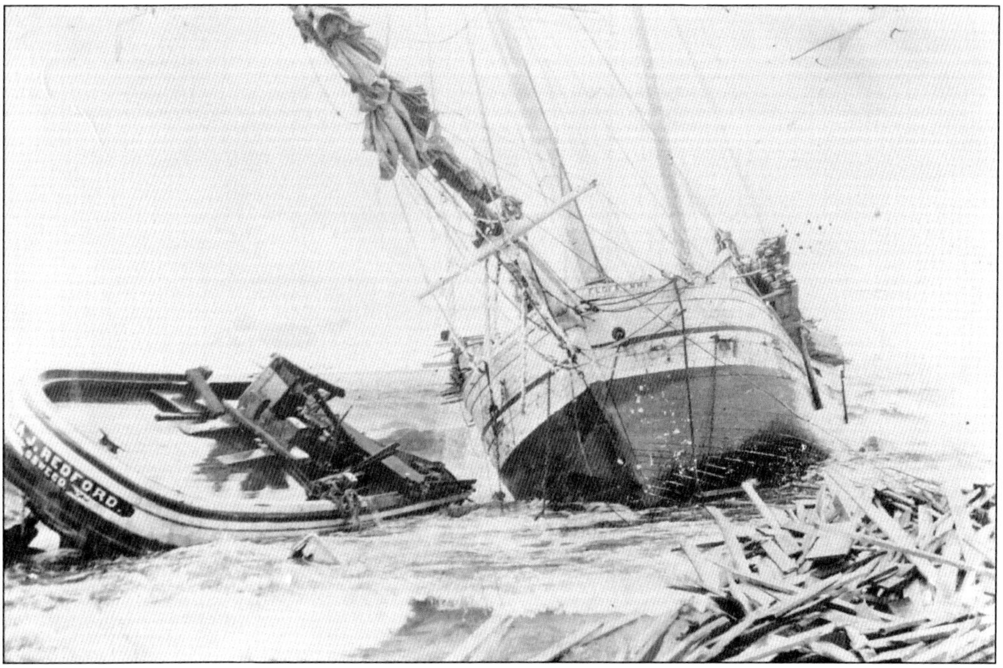

During a gale on November 15, 1893, the schooner *Flora Emma* broke adrift from its moorings in Oswego Harbor and was driven onto the shore in front of the Oswego Life-Saving Station. The tug *Eliza J. Radford*, while attempting to assist, was disabled and also driven ashore. The station crew used the lifeboat to attempt to assist the tug to no avail. Using the beach apparatus, though, they rescued the captain, his wife, and their son from *Flora Emma*. Three of the crew from the tug reached the pier safely, but the captain unfortunately lost his life.

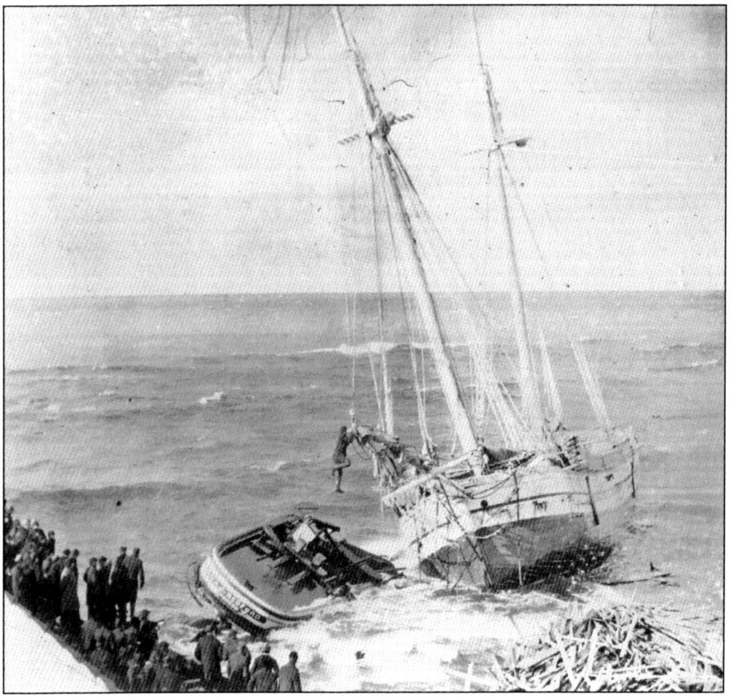

Likely taken from the station's lookout tower, this photograph shows the salvage effort underway to secure the lumber cargo from *Flora Emma*. The Life-Saving station crew likely assisted in this effort, as the *Annual Report of the United States Life Saving Service* valued the cargo of vessels assisted by the service over the course of a fiscal year in addition to the number of rescues, lives saved, and vessels assisted.

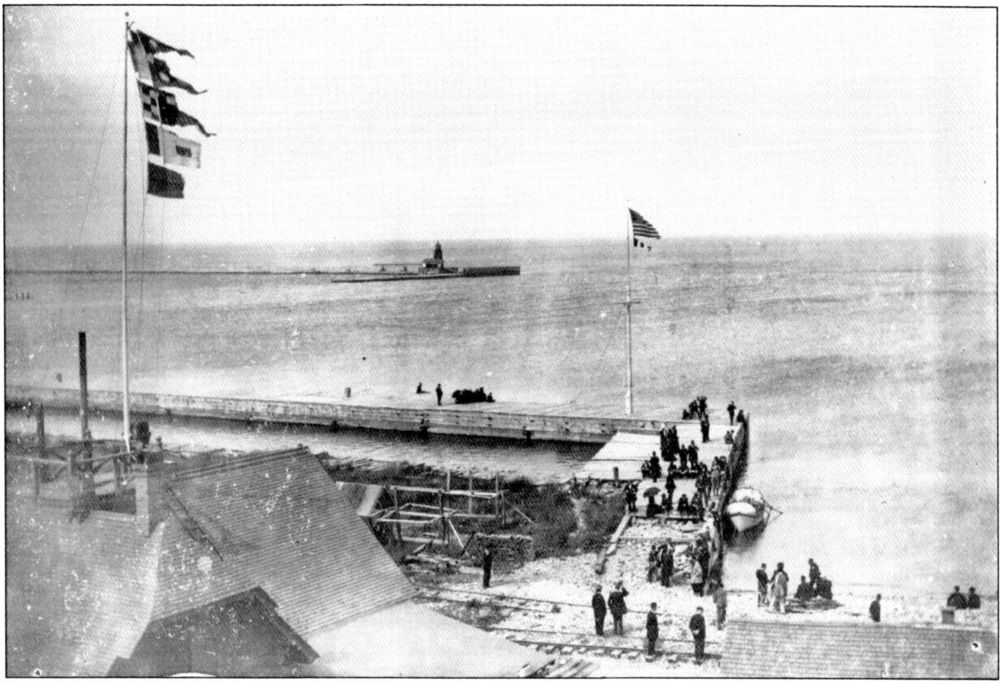

A large crowd has gathered in front of the Oswego Life-Saving Station, and many appear to be looking out into Lake Ontario with anticipation. A lifeboat is moored alongside the breakwater, and the station is flying several signal flags and a pennant below the American flag on the drill pole. Stations were equipped with a full set of signal flags, which were used to communicate with and identify vessels offshore and relay the station's identification number to the vessels. (Courtesy of Mark Slosek, City of Oswego historian.)

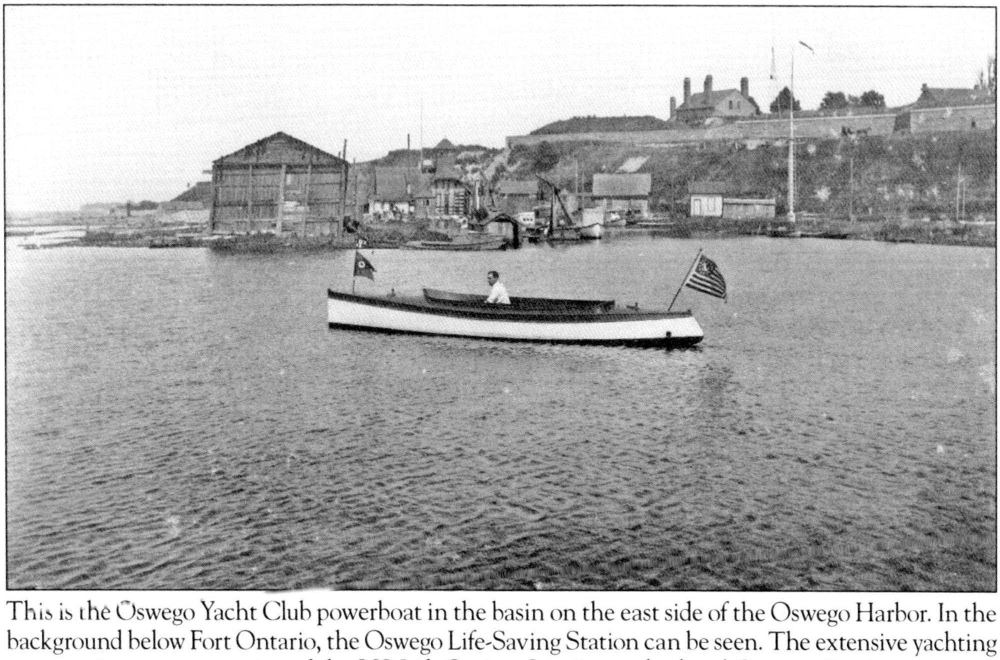

This is the Oswego Yacht Club powerboat in the basin on the east side of the Oswego Harbor. In the background below Fort Ontario, the Oswego Life-Saving Station can be seen. The extensive yachting community was supportive of the US Life-Saving Service at the local Oswego Station.

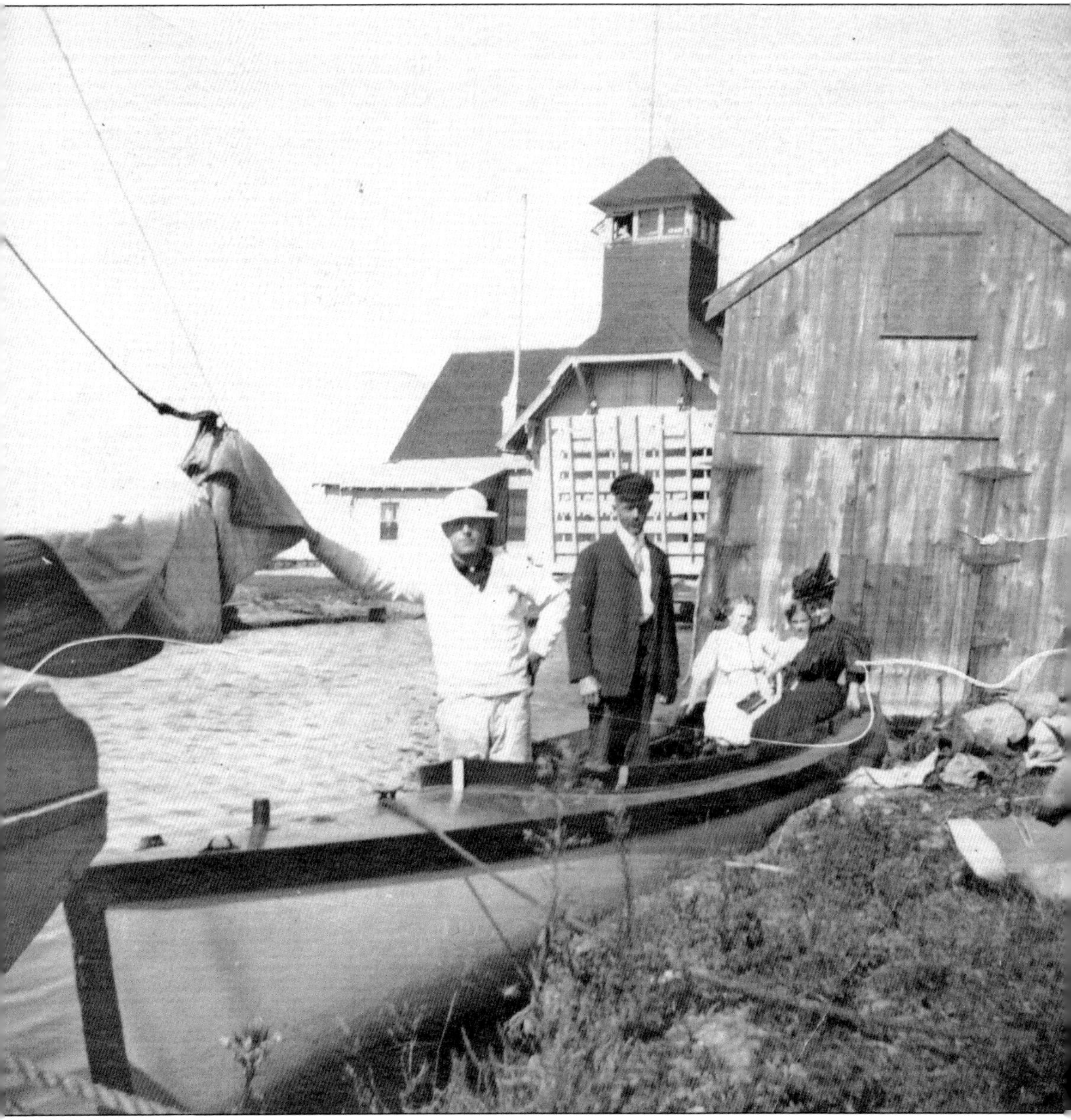

This photograph shows two women and a child in the stern of a motorboat that looks very similar to the one on the previous page. The man standing at right is believed to be Captain Anderson in his civilian clothes. A Life-Saving Service surfman is standing at the bow, and the station, with the drawbridge in the up position, is in the background.

Seven

EARLY COAST GUARD 1915–1945

When the Life-Saving Service station became the Coast Guard station in 1915, the station's crew added law enforcement to its mission in Oswego. After the passage of the Volstead Act in 1919, Prohibition became law, and it was evident that the few large Coast Guard cutters on the Great Lakes were not adequate for the greatly increased law enforcement requirements. As such, a series of 75-foot and 100-foot specialized patrol boats were constructed, many of which were stationed on the Great Lakes, including at Oswego.

By the mid-1930s, motorized rescue boats (specifically the 36-foot motor lifeboat) augmented the pulling lifeboats at Great Lakes Coast Guard stations. Oswego's fleet grew in the early 1940s, when a 38-foot picket boat and a 30-foot rescue boat were added. In July 1939, when the Coast Guard assumed responsibility for all US lighthouses, it also acquired all Lighthouse Service property on the west side of Oswego Harbor, which included a boathouse, several outbuildings, and the station launch. The responsibilities of Coast Guard Station Oswego—now under the command of a military officer—expanded yet again as it assumed oversight of other nearby lighthouses and beacons.

On December 4, 1942, a serious tragedy occurred in Oswego Harbor when six Coastguardsmen, including the station's commanding officer and an assistant lighthouse keeper, lost their lives during an exchange of keepers at the Oswego West Pierhead Lighthouse. During World War II, as the station's responsibilities and personnel expanded, the limitations of the small area on the east side of Oswego Harbor became evident. Plans were made to move the station to the west side of the harbor on the property of the former US Lighthouse Service. The transition occurred during 1944 as single-story buildings were added to the existing facilities on the west side. When no longer needed, the Coast Guard dismantled the old facilities on the east side of Oswego Harbor.

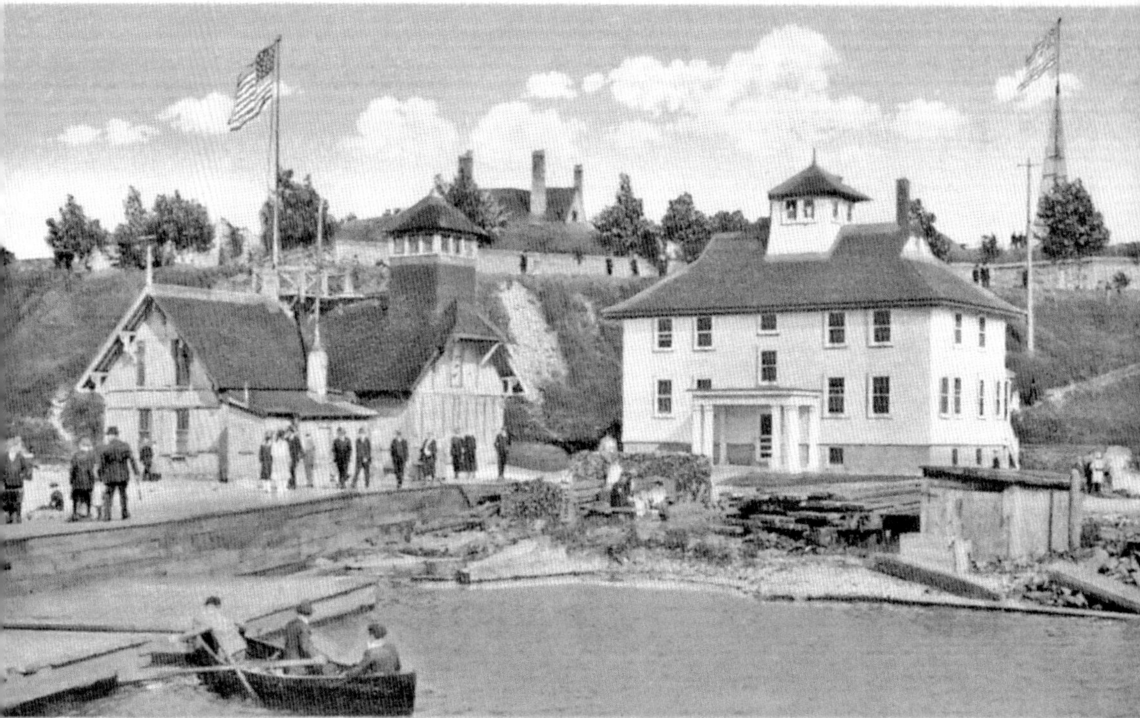

LIFE SAVING STATION AND FORT ONTARIO IN REAR, OSWEGO, N. Y.

In January 1915, when the Coast Guard was formed, in order to accommodate the larger crew to handle the expanded mission, the barn east of the old Life-Saving Station was removed so that a new barracks could be built, and the old station was moved east. This postcard shows the Oswego Coast Guard Station's new configuration.

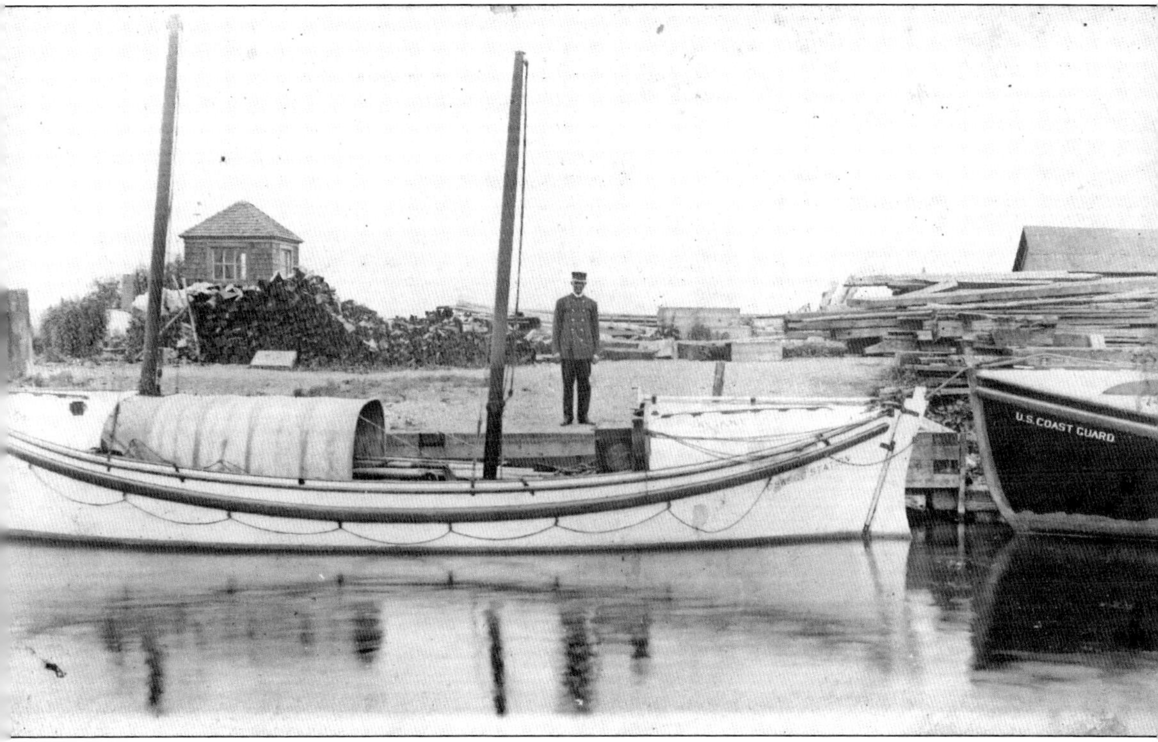

Capt. Frederick W. Anderson became the officer in charge of the new Oswego Coast Guard Station and is seen here inspecting the new Coast Guard lifeboats in the boat slip next to the station. Both boats are motorboats, which were beginning to come into service as the transition from Life-Saving Service to Coast Guard was underway. Captain Anderson remained in charge at Oswego until he retired on August 15, 1916.

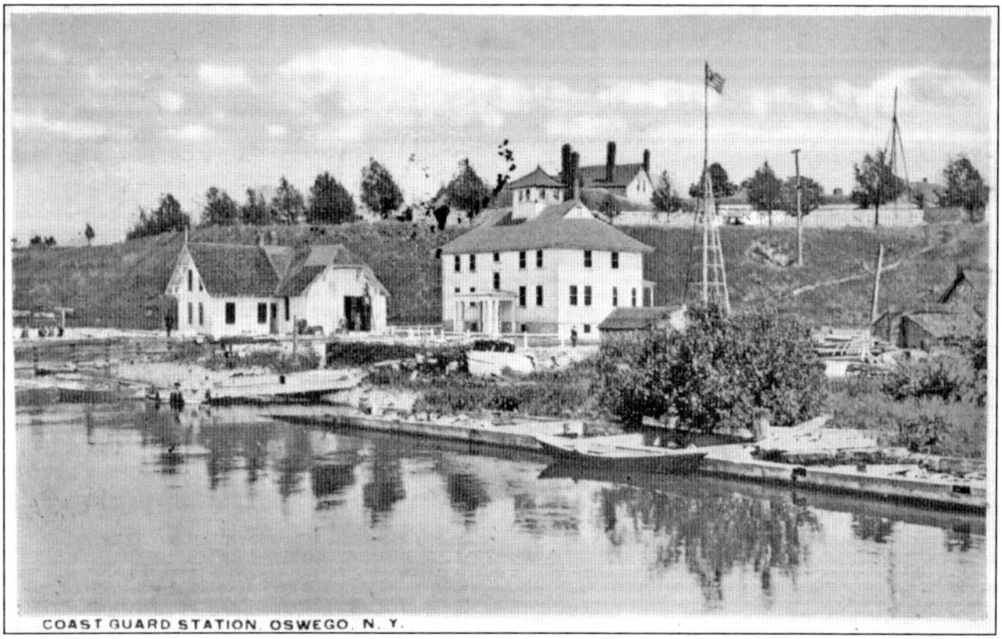

This postcard shows the Oswego Coast Guard Station at a later date, after the lookout tower on the top of the original clipped gable–style Life-Saving station had been removed. The new Chatham-type station included a lookout tower, and two were not necessary. The Chatham type was widely used in the Great Lakes and along both the Atlantic and Pacific coasts. They are long-lived structures, and many are still in use today.

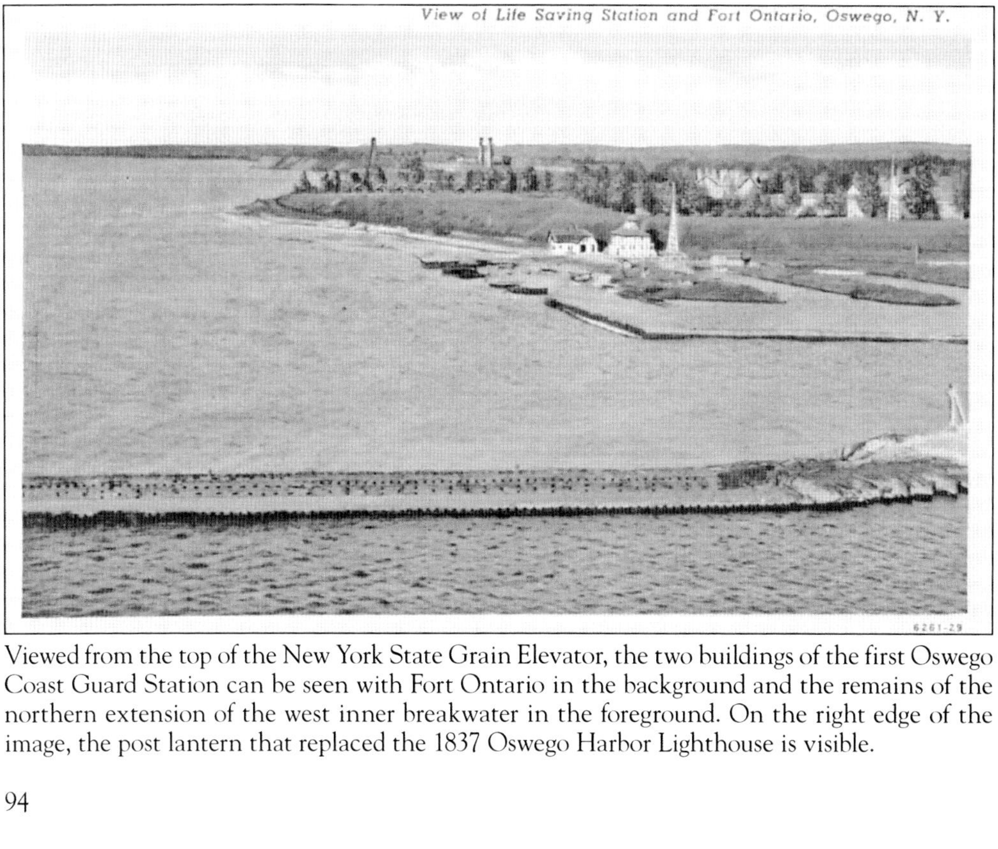

Viewed from the top of the New York State Grain Elevator, the two buildings of the first Oswego Coast Guard Station can be seen with Fort Ontario in the background and the remains of the northern extension of the west inner breakwater in the foreground. On the right edge of the image, the post lantern that replaced the 1837 Oswego Harbor Lighthouse is visible.

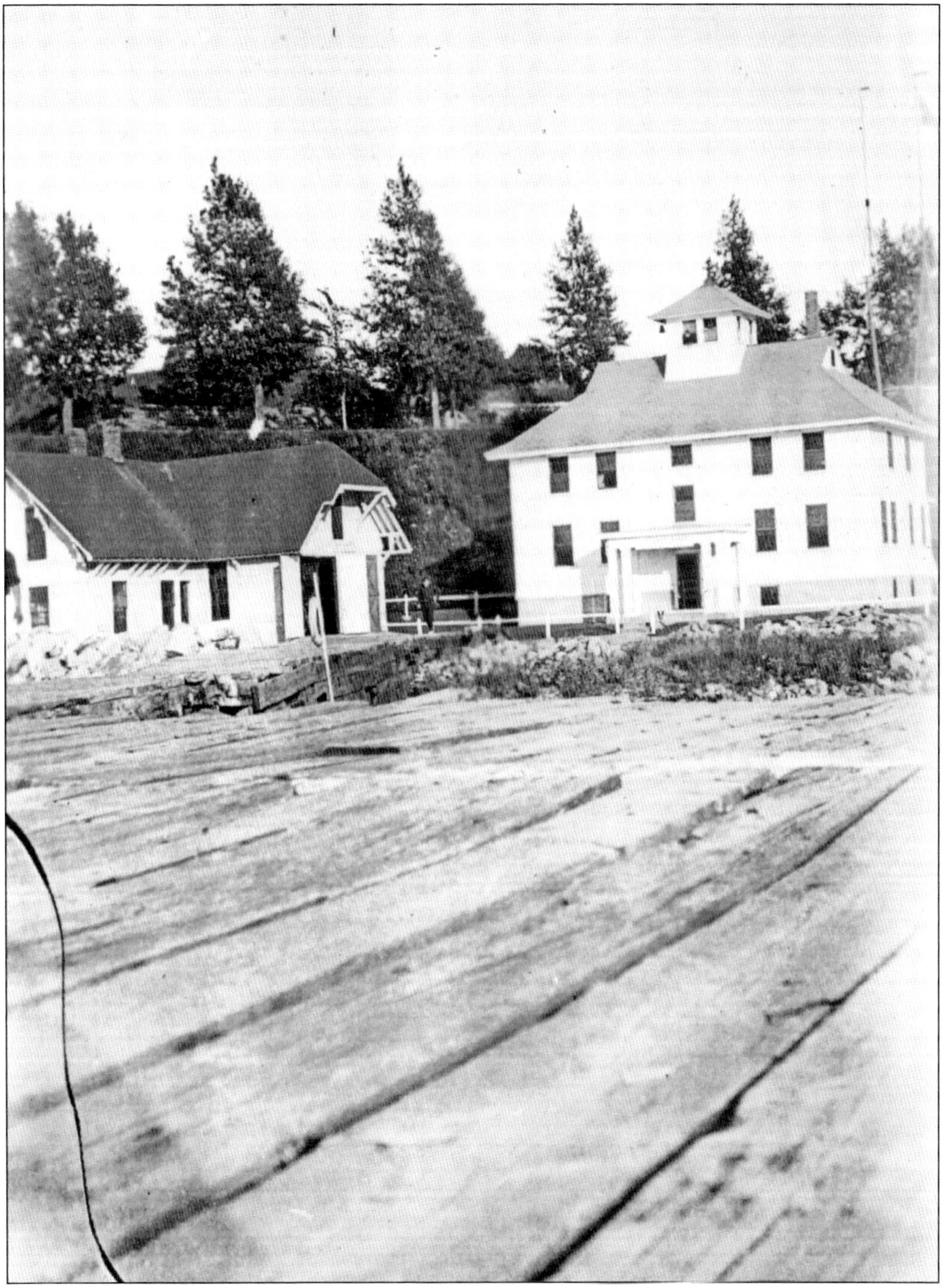

This photograph shows the Oswego Coast Guard Station buildings in the late 1930s or early 1940s. The earthen parapet walls of Fort Ontario are in the background. In the foreground, the deteriorated condition of the timber surface of the east breakwater, which protects the station, is very evident. The condition of this breakwater, along with the lack of room to expand below the fort, likely influenced the decision to move the station across the harbor during World War II. (Courtesy of the Oswego Coast Guard Station.)

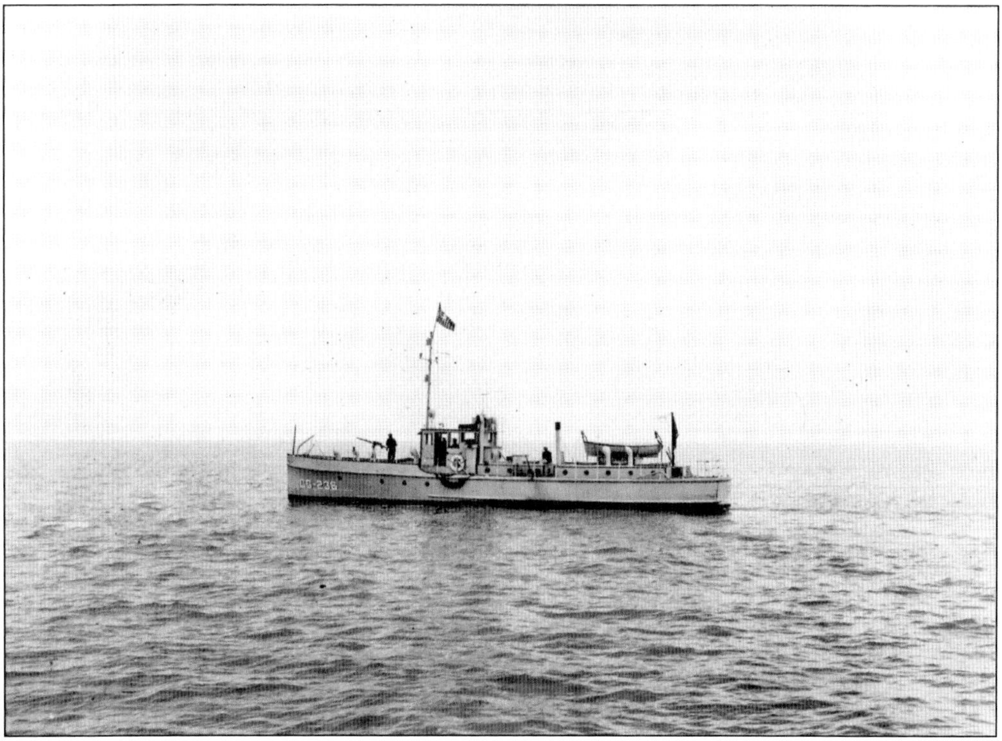

When the Volstead Act was passed in 1919, the US Coast Guard was tasked with enforcing Prohibition along the coastal waterways and in the Great Lakes. Large numbers of patrol vessels were required, and the 75-foot patrol boat and 100-foot patrol boat were the result in Oswego. Over two hundred 75-foot patrol boats were built, and CG-236 (above) was stationed in Oswego from 1924 to 1933. It was replaced by the 100-foot patrol boat *Forward* (below), which remained in Oswego until 1938.

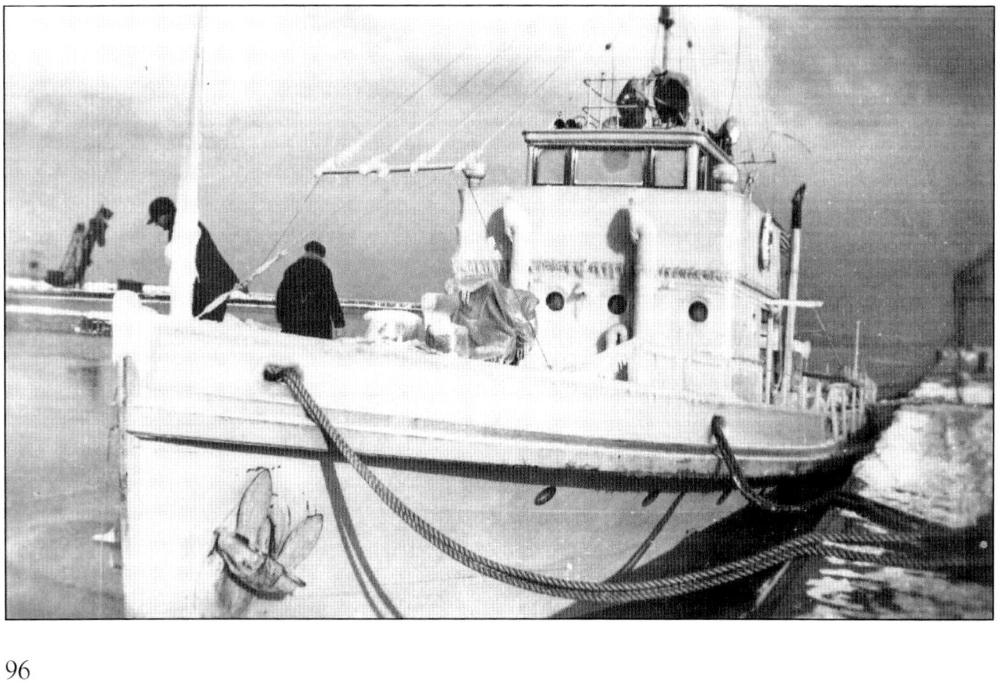

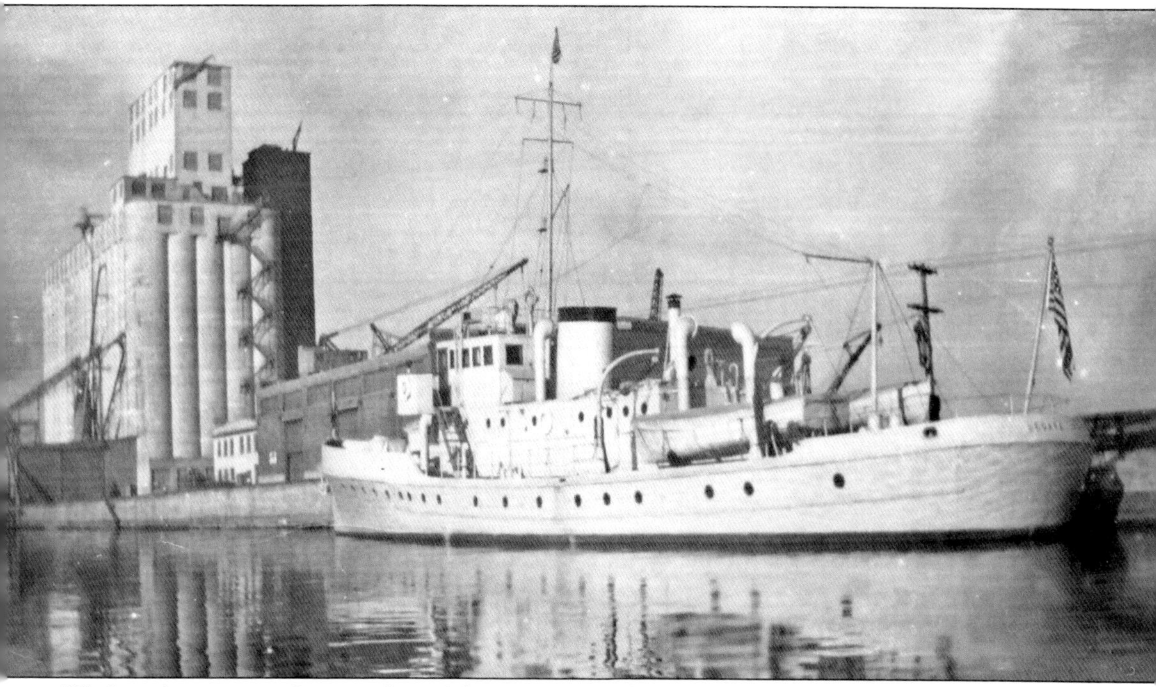

While making port at Oswego, the 125-foot Coast Guard patrol boat *Legare* is shown moored along the New York State Grain Elevator pier on Oswego's west side sometime prior to World War II. *Legare* was a member of one of the most successful classes of cutters in Coast Guard service; it was commissioned in 1927 and served for more than 40 years.

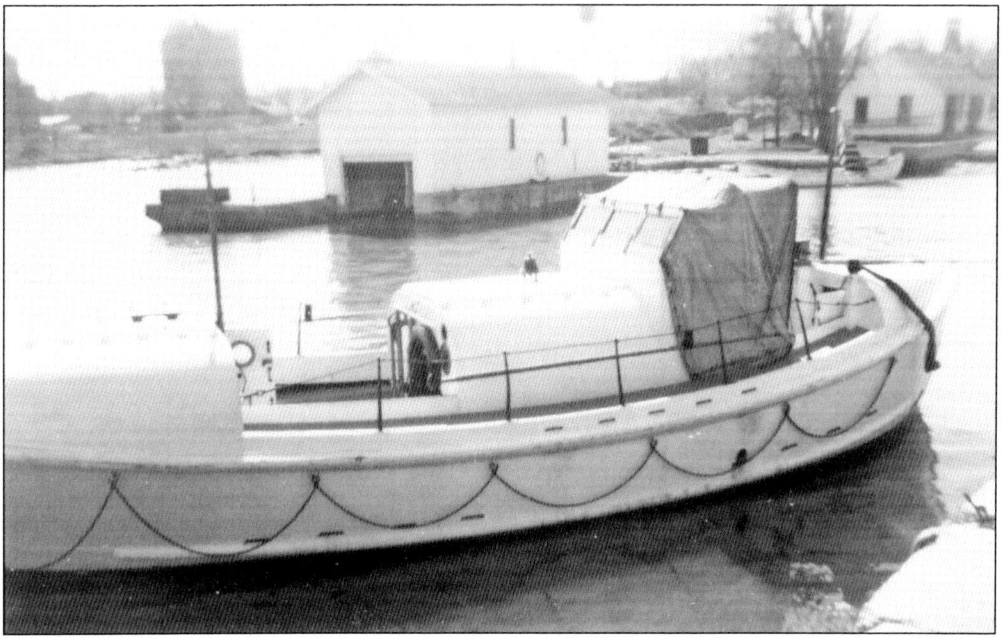

By the time the US Coast Guard was formed in 1915, motorized lifeboats and surfboats were already being developed. By 1928, the 36-foot motor lifeboat design was becoming standard for Coast Guard rescue operations. Oswego received one of the first 36-foot motor lifeboats in 1931. The self-righting and self-bailing boat came in three different types between 1928 and 1956, had a crew of three, and could carry 30 survivors. The last 36-foot motor lifeboat at Oswego was not replaced until 1963. (Both, courtesy of the Oswego Coast Guard Station.)

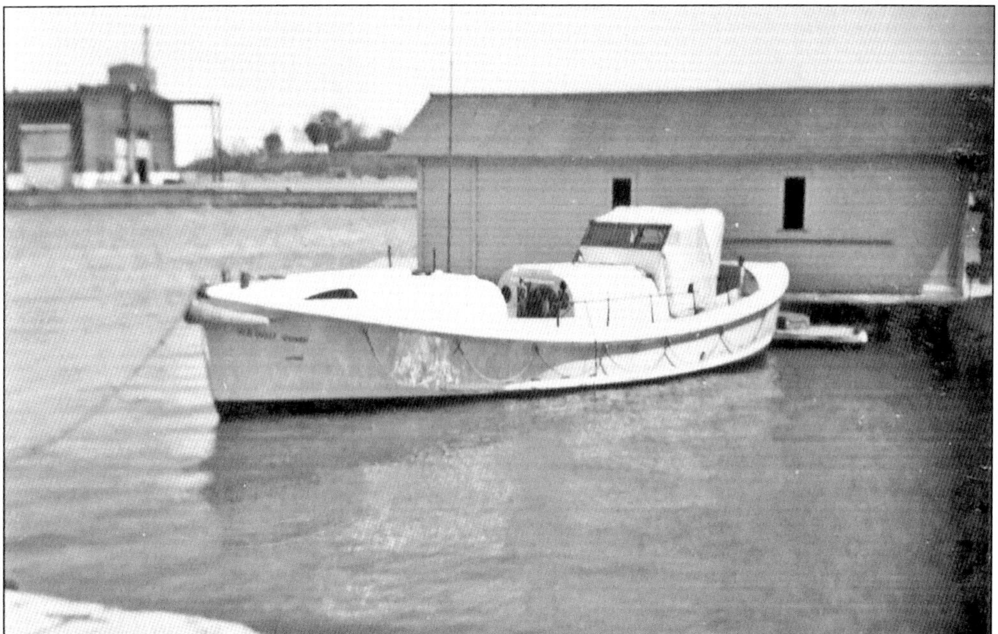

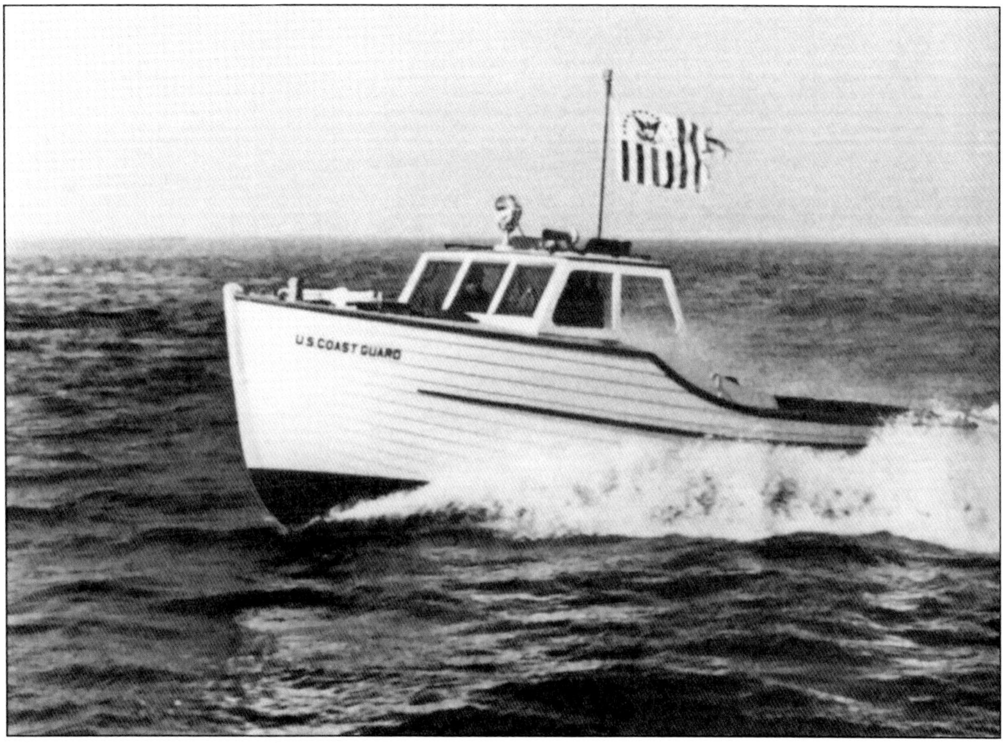

The Oswego Coast Guard Station was also equipped with a 30-foot motor rescue boat, a craft capable of quick response in moderate seas that could cruise at 20 knots for 135 nautical miles carrying 18 people. Seventy-one of these rescue boats were built between 1938 and 1953.

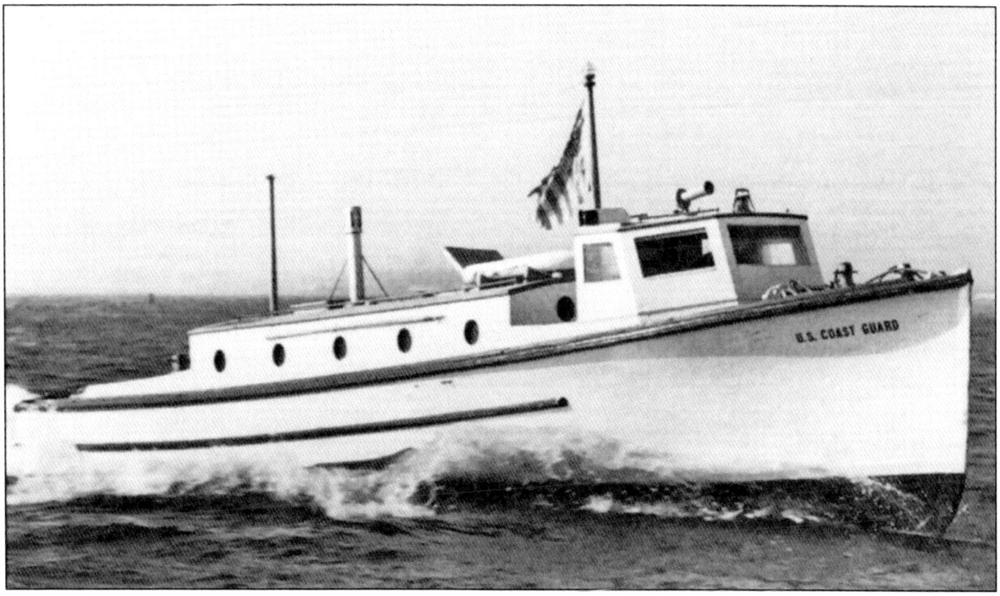

The Coast Guard 38-foot cabin picket boat was the third type of rescue boat assigned to the Oswego Coast Guard Station prior to World War II. A larger vessel, it was designed for patrolling harbors and protected coastal waterways and was capable of 19 knots with a crew of four. Over 500 of these watercraft were built between the early 1930s and the mid-1940s.

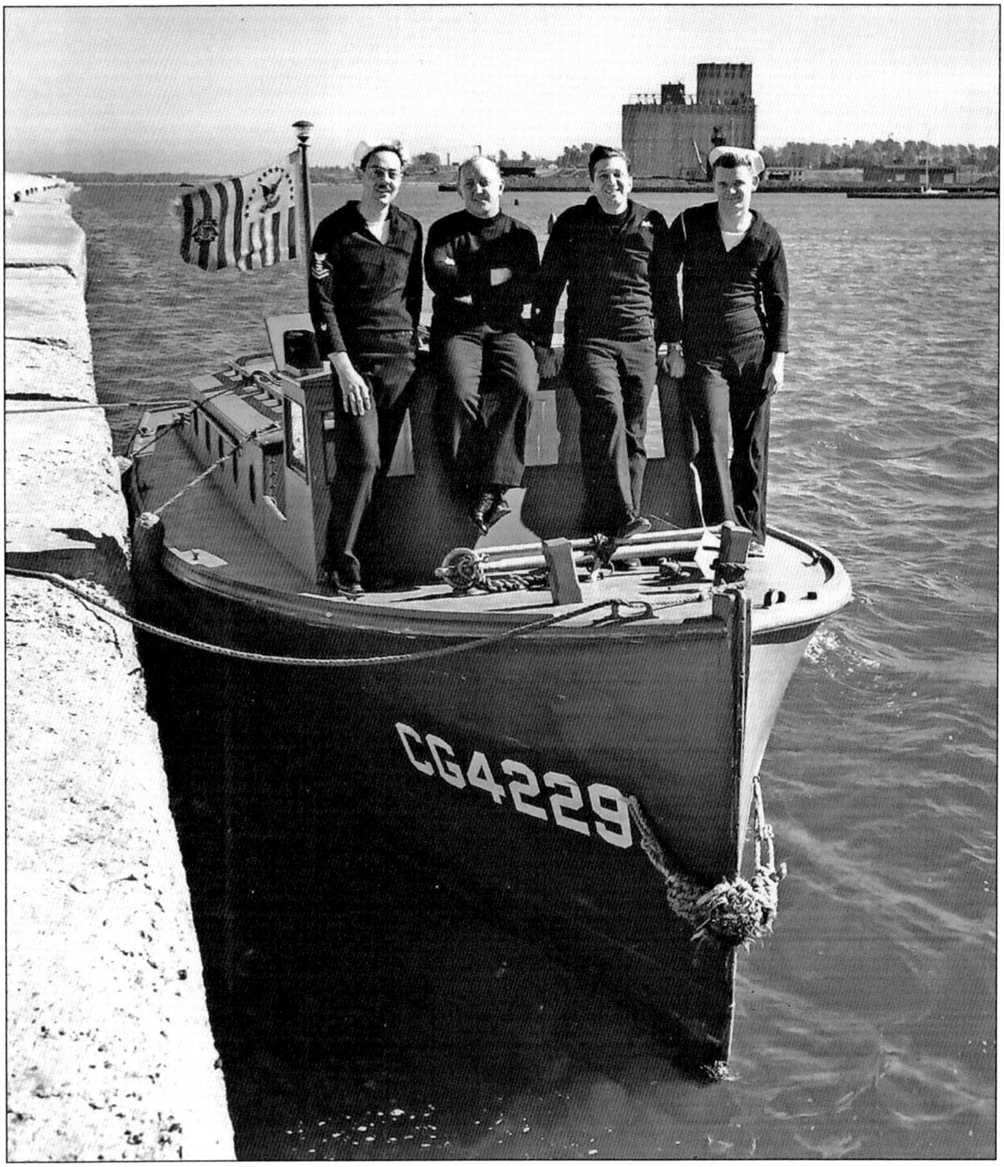

Picket boat CG-4299 and its crew are seen here moored alongside the outer breakwater with the New York State Grain Elevator in the background. This boat and its crew, First Assistant Keeper Karl Jackson, and the Oswego Coast Guard Station commanding officer, Lt. (jg) Altson Wilson, lost their lives during an exchange of keepers in Oswego Harbor on the morning of December 4, 1942. Keeper Karl Jackson had been stranded at the Oswego West Pierhead Lighthouse for several days and was anxious to return. Lieutenant Wilson believed the exchange of keepers could be accomplished safely. The exchange was successful, but as the picket boat left the lighthouse the engine stalled, and it could not be restarted. Unable to anchor successfully, it drifted onto the east arrowhead breakwater, where it sank. Station Oswego launched the 36-foot motor lifeboat to effect a harrowing rescue in winter conditions lasting over an hour. The two survivors from CG-4299 and two additional station personnel on the breakwater as part of an earlier rescue attempt were finally rescued from the east side of the east breakwater. (Courtesy of the Oswego County Historical Society.)

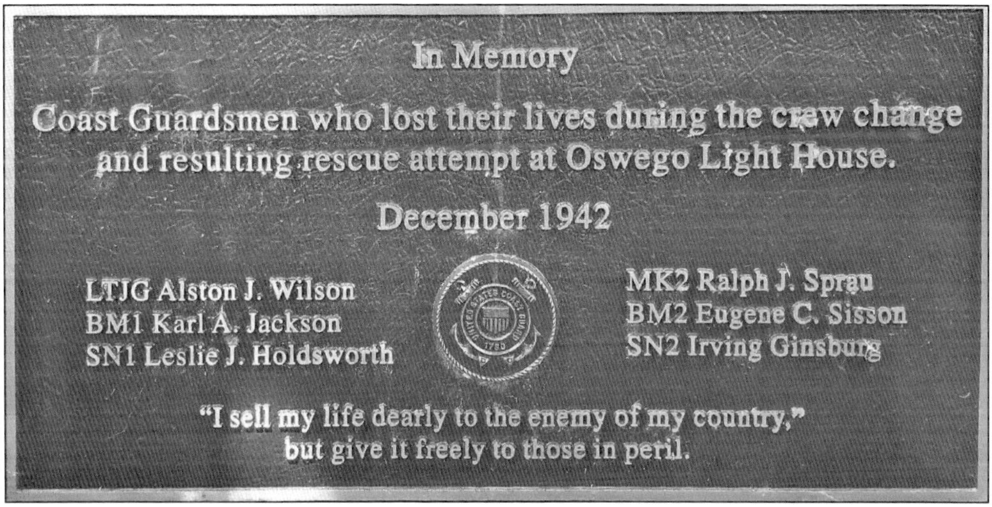

This bronze plaque was placed in the Oswego Veterans Park on the west side of the Oswego River by the City of Oswego on August 4, 1997. Descendants and family members of the Coastguardsmen who lost their lives on December 4, 1942, attended the ceremony.

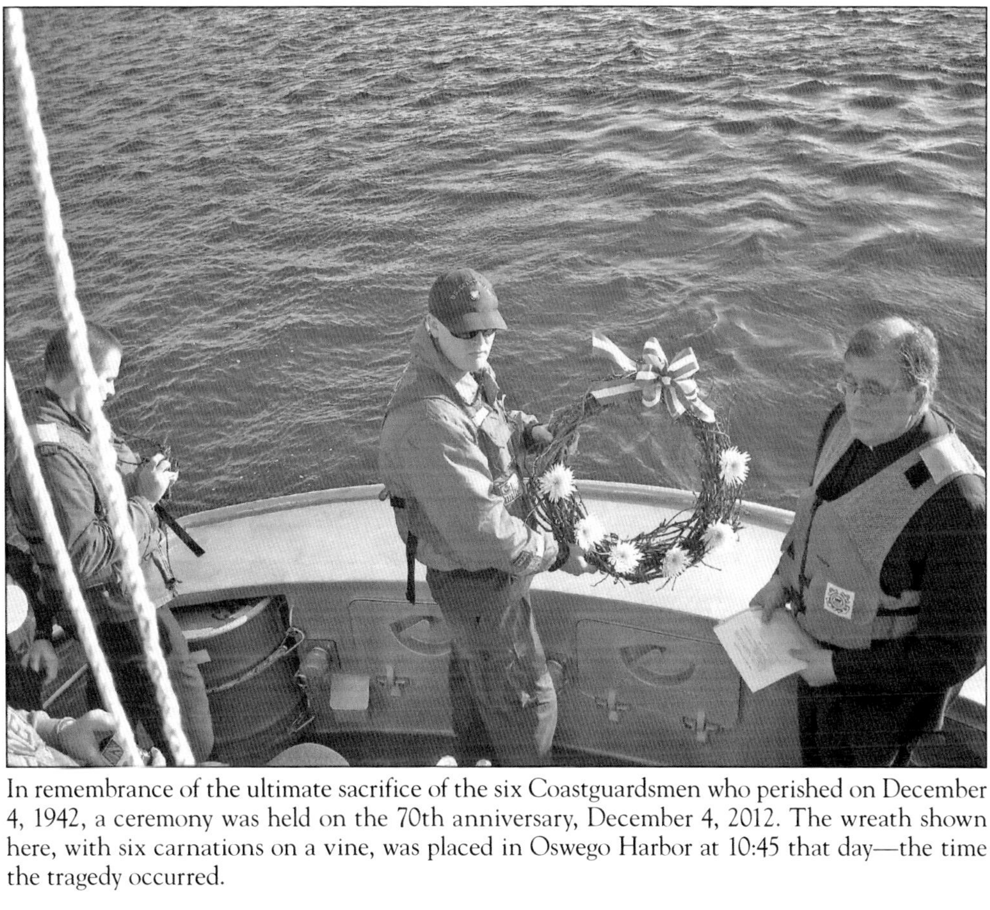

In remembrance of the ultimate sacrifice of the six Coastguardsmen who perished on December 4, 1942, a ceremony was held on the 70th anniversary, December 4, 2012. The wreath shown here, with six carnations on a vine, was placed in Oswego Harbor at 10:45 that day—the time the tragedy occurred.

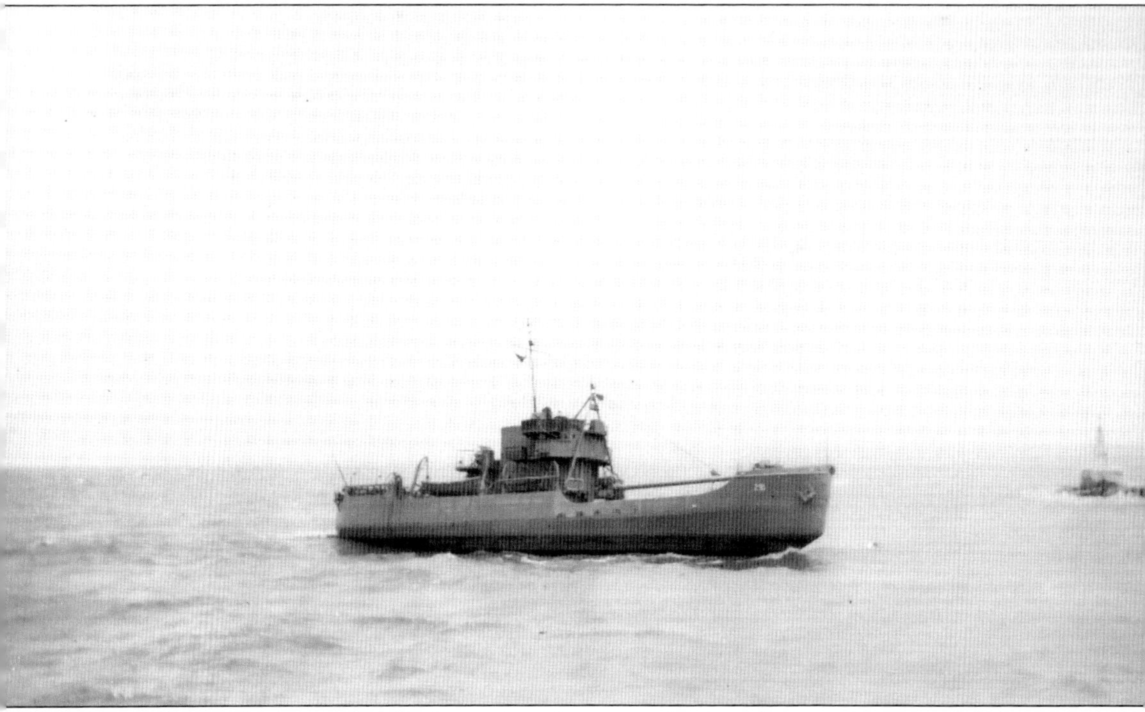

During World War II, the US Coast Guard buoy tender *Laurel* enters Oswego Harbor. It was built in Duluth and served in the Atlantic theater. Clearly seen are the guns on the topside of the bridge and the antisubmarine depth charge racks on the stern. *Laurel* is painted the standard World War II Navy gray, with the number 291 on its bow.

Eight

LATER COAST GUARD 1945–2017

When World War II began, Coast Guard Station Oswego's responsibilities significantly increased. Security of the Port of Oswego and the many war-related cargos coming and going were added to the traditional law enforcement and search and rescue missions. The station's location on the east side of the Oswego River became too confining. Fortunately, with the absorption of the US Lighthouse Service in 1939, a larger tract of land was acquired on the west side of the harbor. Former Lighthouse Service buildings were available, additional buildings were constructed, and the move across the river was made. This move also facilitated launching boats and protected the station from northwest storms.

After World War II, plans were made to build a modern station and improve the boat basin behind the original inner breakwater. A new administration building was commissioned in 1950. The boat basin, once the site of an Oswego shipyard, was expanded to accommodate larger Coast Guard vessels. This allowed a large three-bay boathouse and shop building to be added to the east side of the administration building. At that time, the Oswego Coast Guard Station also became the headquarters of Group Oswego, responsible for the Coast Guard station at Galloo Island and lighthouses at Oswego, Stony Point, and Galloo Island. A large boat storage shed was added to the station to house boats in the winter, when the harbor was frequently frozen and not accessible.

When they were no longer needed, the older buildings were removed. Part of that space is now occupied by a US Geologic Survey research facility and the research vessel RV *Kaho*, which is moored in the Coast Guard station's basin. New postwar Coast Guard boats were assigned to the Oswego station: a 30-foot, 40-foot, and later a 41-foot utility boat and a boat to service the lighthouse. A new 44-foot motor lifeboat, MLB-44390, replaced the older 36-foot motor lifeboat in 1963. It was in turn replaced by a 47-foot motor lifeboat. The complement of the station was one chief petty officer as officer in charge and 16 enlisted personnel, augmented by members of the Coast Guard Reserve and the all-volunteer Coast Guard Auxiliary.

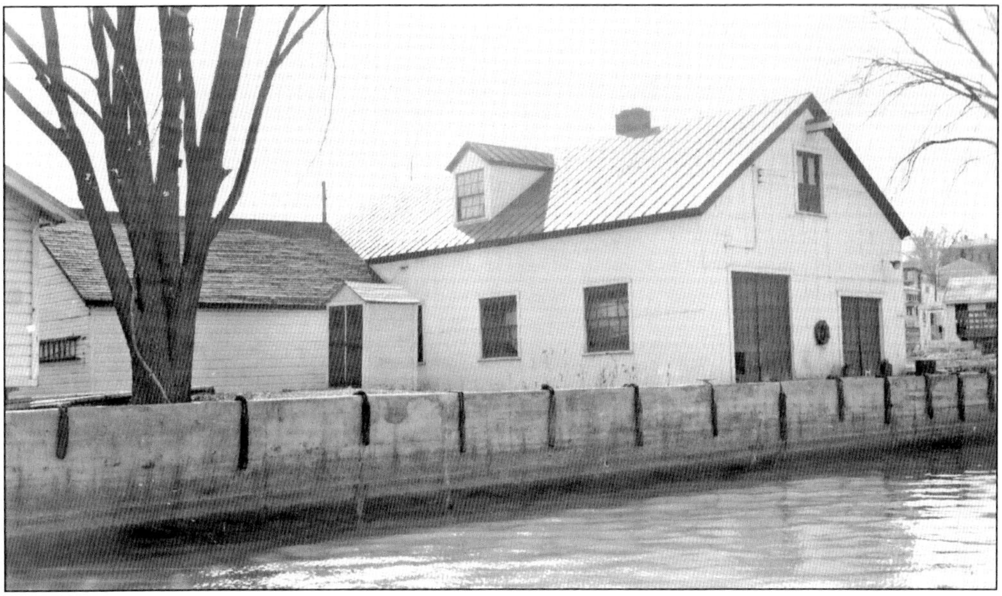

When World War II began, the responsibilities and personnel attached to Coast Guard Station Oswego greatly increased. The small station on the east side of Oswego Harbor was no longer sufficient, and plans were formulated to move to the west side of the harbor. Fortunately, when the Coast Guard acquired responsibility for lighthouses in 1939, it also acquired a large tract of land on the west side of the harbor, where the Lighthouse Service had several buildings inherited from the Army Corps of Engineers after the most recent Oswego Harbor expansion was completed. The Coast Guard, in turn, added several single-story buildings to the tract that became its new station around 1944.

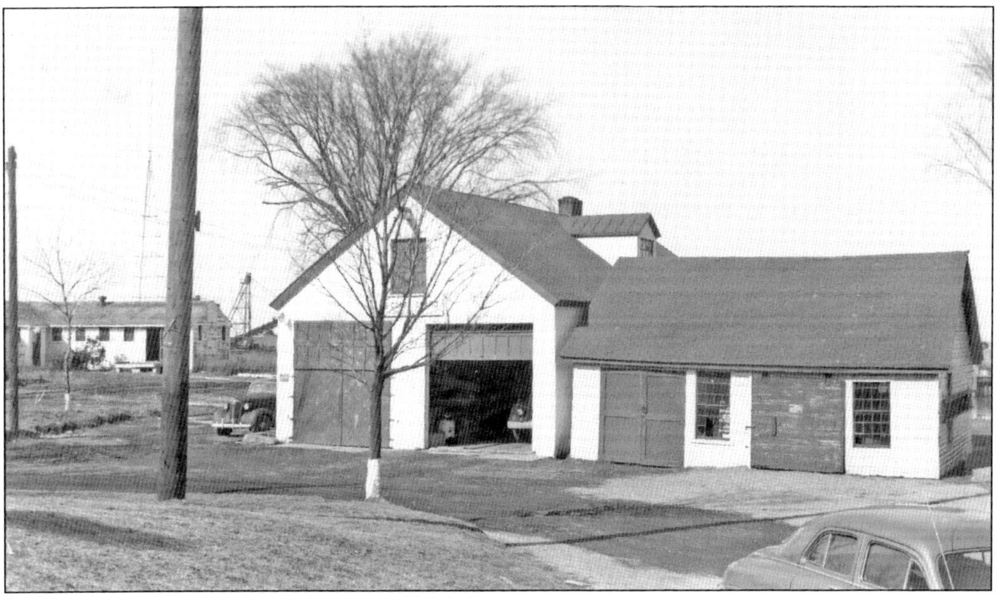

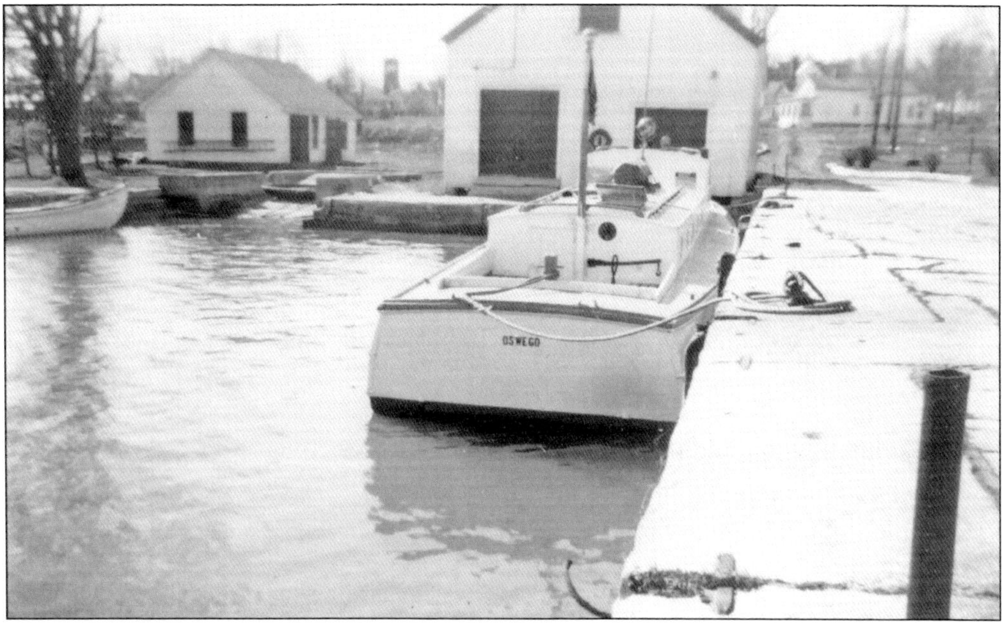

The boat basin on the west side of Oswego Harbor at the new Coast Guard station is shown here. Above, the station's 38-foot picket boat is moored in front of the buildings inherited from the Lighthouse Service, and the pulling surfboat is in front of the old Lighthouse Service boat slip. Below, with the New York State Grain Elevator in the background, the 38-foot picket boat is moored to the remains of the old inner harbor breakwater, with the 36-foot motor lifeboat in the foreground.

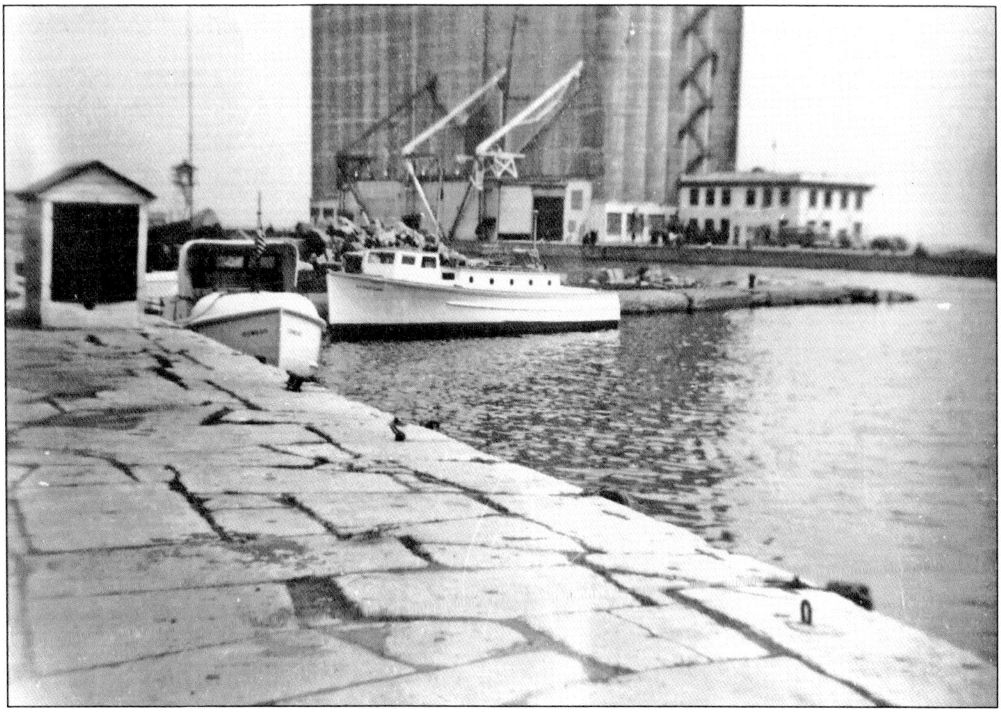

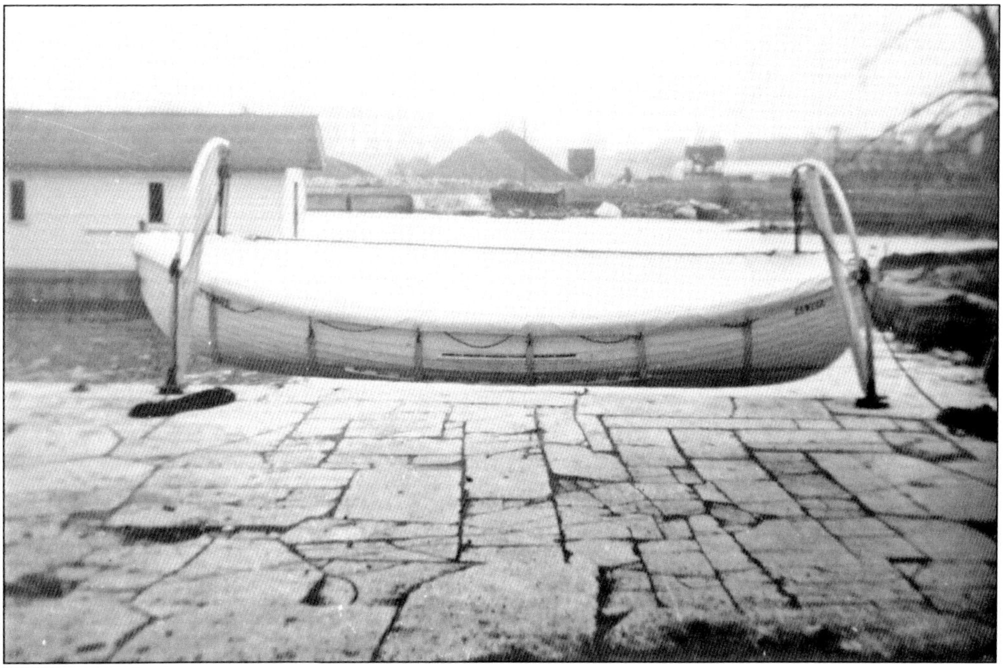

The US Coast Guard rigged a set of boat davits on the shore end of the old inner harbor breakwater in order to hoist the surfboat to the top of the breakwater. This kept the boat out of the water but ready to launch at a moment's notice.

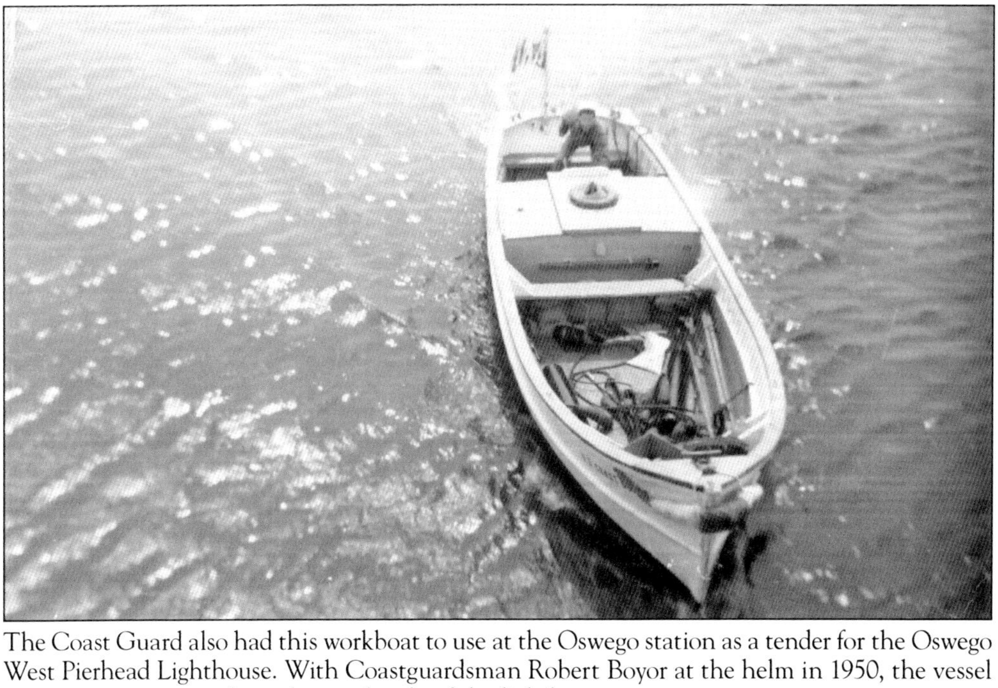

The Coast Guard also had this workboat to use at the Oswego station as a tender for the Oswego West Pierhead Lighthouse. With Coastguardsman Robert Boyor at the helm in 1950, the vessel is preparing to moor along the south side of the lighthouse.

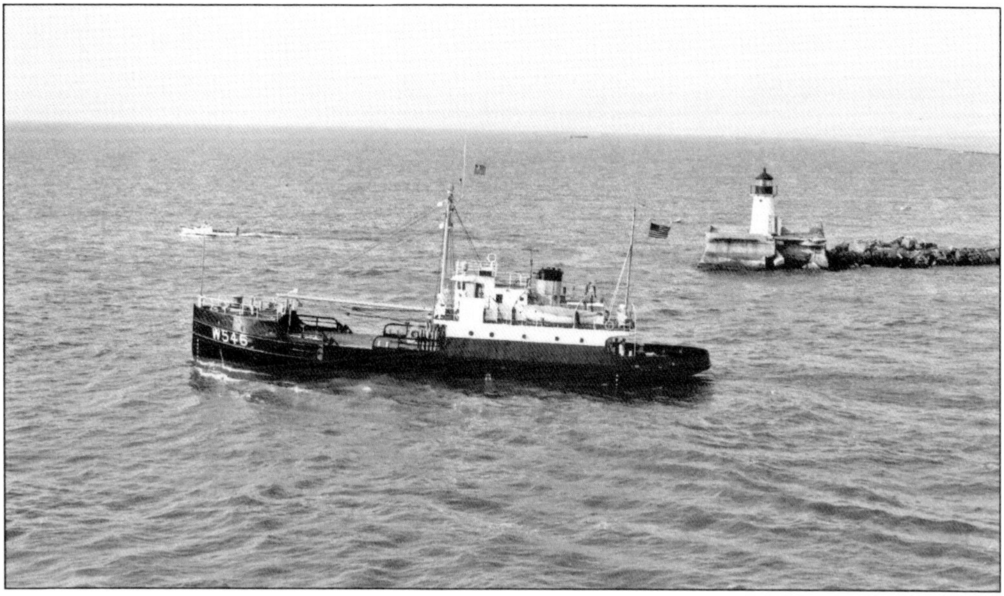

The Coast Guard buoy tender WLM-546 *White Lupine* is shown departing the harbor at Cleveland with the Cleveland East Pierhead Lighthouse in the background. *White Lupine* began life in Erie, Pennsylvania, in 1944 as a 133-foot Navy cargo lighter, YF-446, with no name. In 1947, YF-446 and seven sisters were transferred to the US Coast Guard to be converted into buoy tenders. Subsequently it was sent to the Great Lakes and while at Ogdensburg, New York, was responsible for servicing all lighthouses and aids to navigation on Lake Ontario. (Courtesy of the Library of Congress, HAER Collection.)

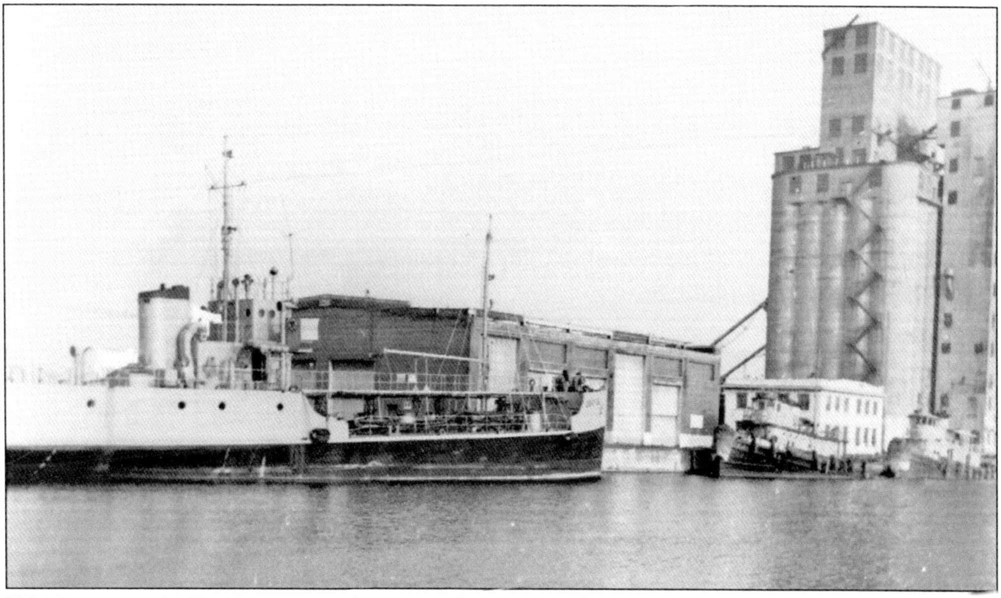

US Navy vessel YO-68 is pictured visiting Oswego Harbor. YO-68 is a yard oiler and is moored alongside the State Grain Elevator pier. The vessel was built in 1943 and carried over 6,000 barrels of fuel oil to refuel Navy ships in port. These vessels had a crew of one officer and 20 enlisted personnel. After World War II, the US Navy maintained vessels on the Great Lakes, including a minesweeper in Oswego, to train Naval Reserve officers and men. The YO-68 served until the end of 1973.

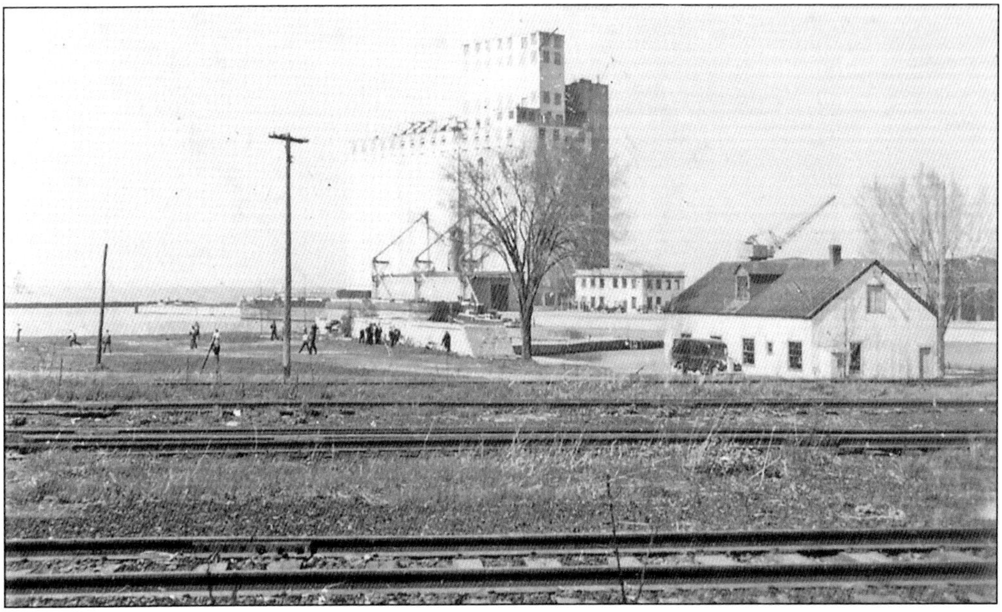

At the Oswego Coast Guard Station, sports were always a welcome diversion from watch duty and work. A baseball game is underway on the west-side Coast Guard property. The New York State Grain Elevator is in the background, with its support building to the right.

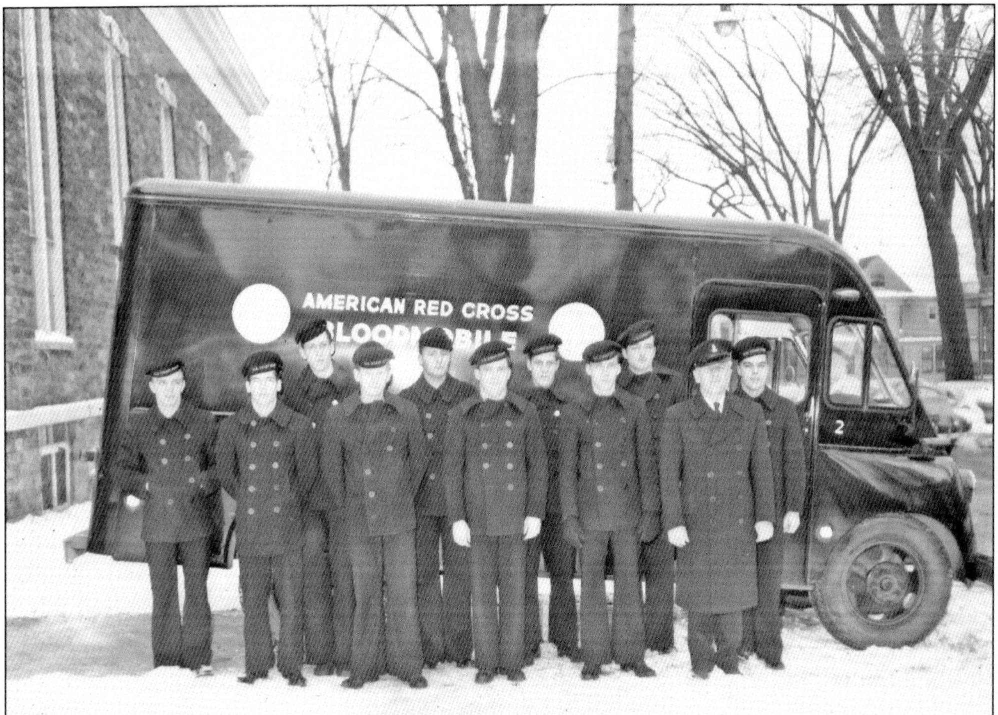

In addition to sporting events, community service was a welcome chance to get away from the station and support the local community. Here, some of the crew including possibly Chief Petty Officer Kenneth Outten (front right) are preparing to donate blood at the Red Cross Bloodmobile.

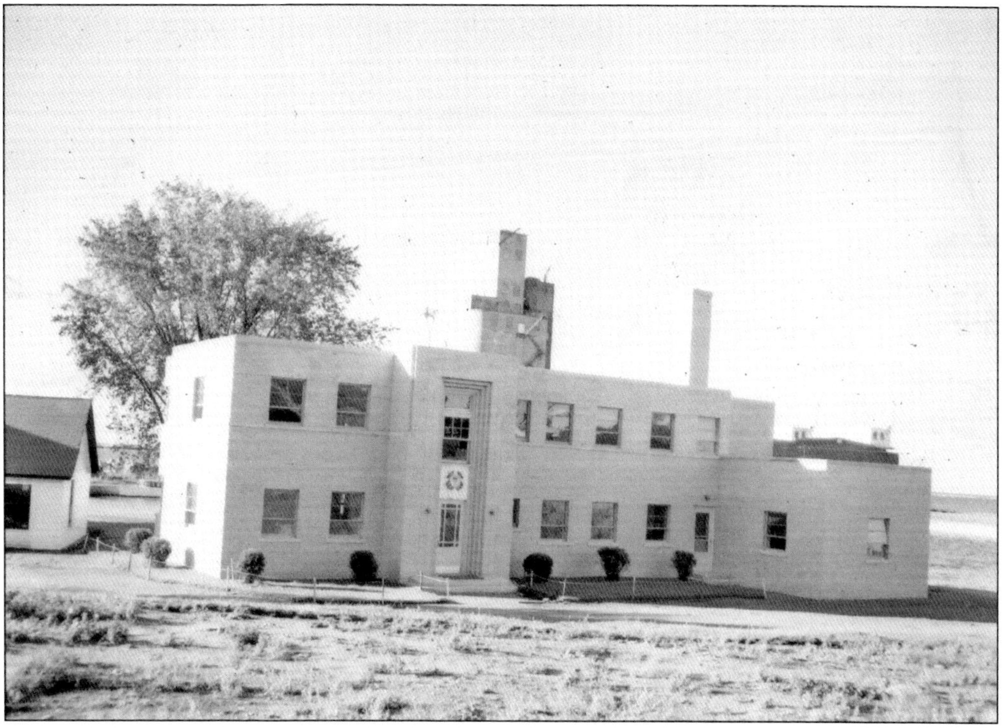

In 1950, the new Oswego Coast Guard Station administration building was completed on the west side of Oswego Harbor. The building contained communication facilities and administration offices on the ground floor and crew quarters on the second floor. This was the first phase of construction in a nearly $625,000 Coast Guard station facility intended to command all other Coast Guard facilities in the eastern Lake Ontario region.

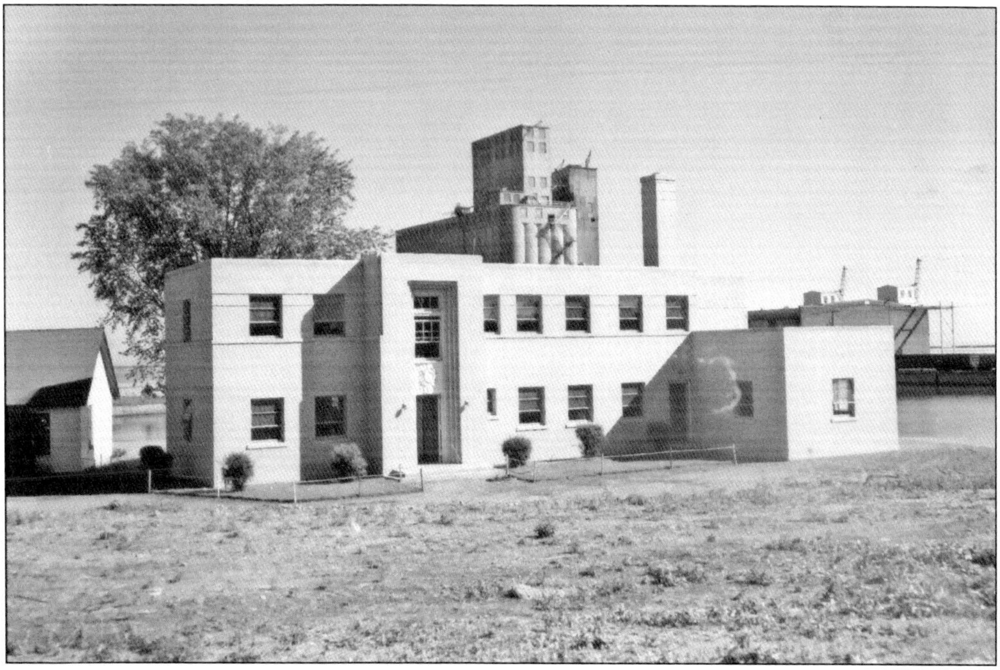

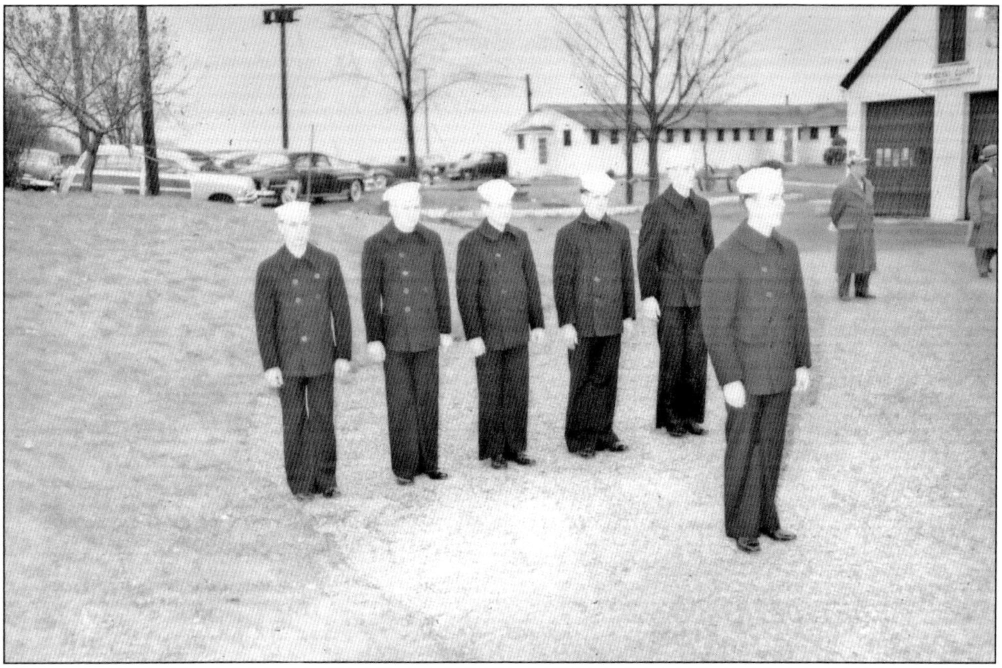

In November 1950, a special commissioning ceremony was held with multiple branches of the armed services present to welcome the new facility. Members of Coast Guard Station Oswego stand in rank for the ceremony.

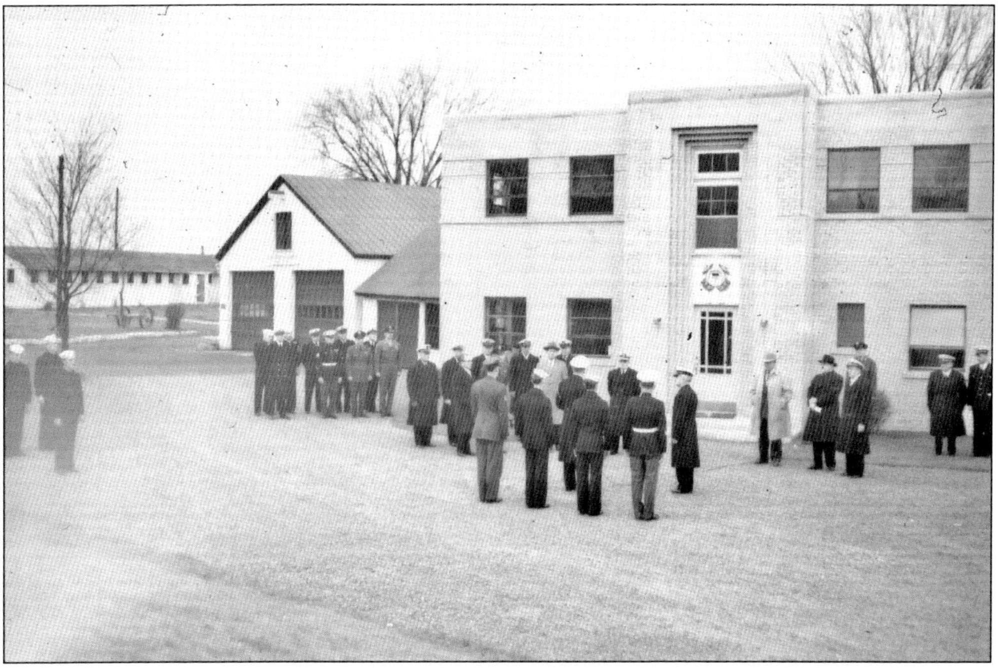

In addition to the crew of the Oswego Coast Guard Station, local dignitaries and representatives from the Navy, Marine Corps, Army, and Air Force were in attendance at the new station's commissioning. The former Army Corps of Engineers and Lighthouse Service facilities still stand just left of the new station.

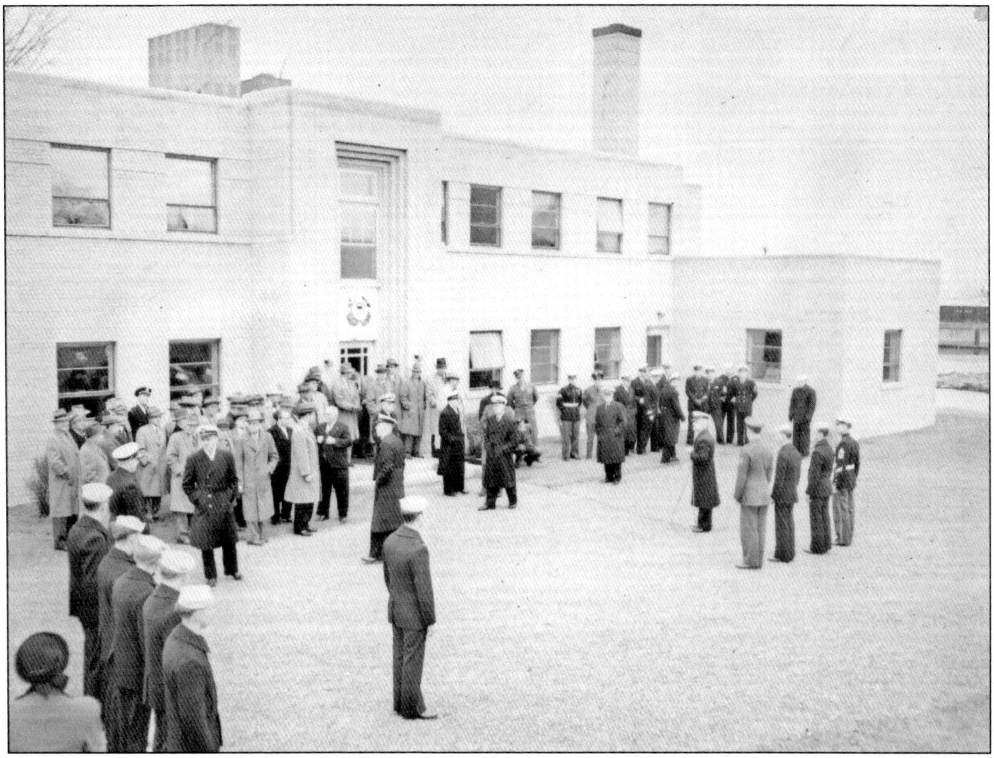

With all the branches of the armed services present, preparations are seen here just prior to the commissioning of the new Oswego Coast Guard Station. Seen from the south side of the facility, the New York State Grain Elevator towers over Oswego Harbor in the background.

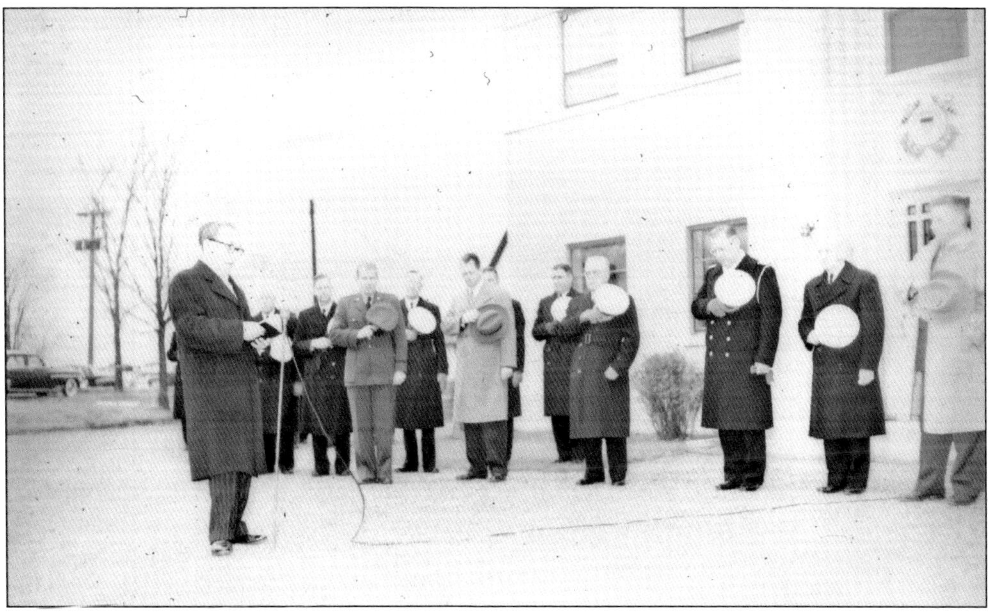

The commissioning began with an invocation, which may have included a blessing for those who place themselves in peril on the sea. One wonders if anyone at the ceremony remembered what happened on December 4, 1942.

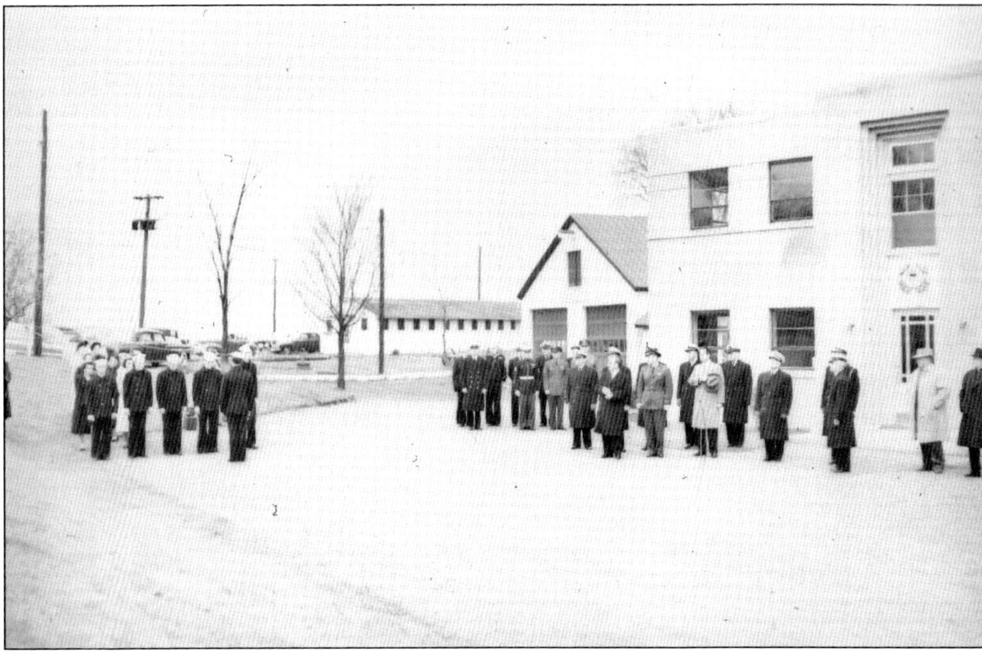

As the commissioning ceremony continues, all in attendance are looking to their right at the crew of Oswego Coast Guard Station standing in rank. Behind the crew of Station Oswego, a small group of women joins the celebration.

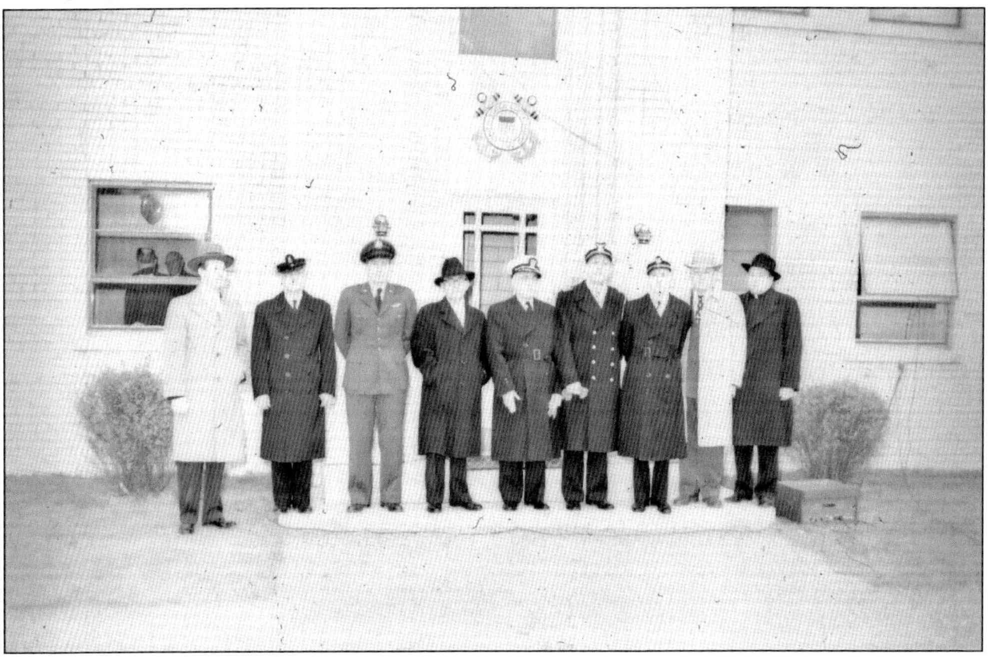

The dignitaries pause to pose for the camera after the ceremony's conclusion. At center, with gloves in hand, is a Coast Guard staff captain likely representing the commandant of the Ninth Coast Guard District Headquarters in Cleveland. Standing next to a civilian and second from the left is CPO Kenneth T. Outten, the officer in charge of the Oswego Coast Guard Station in November 1950.

Colors, or the raising of the flag, is a daily occurrence at Coast Guard Station Oswego. Here, the flag is raised as part of the commissioning ceremony of the new station with assistance from several other service branches.

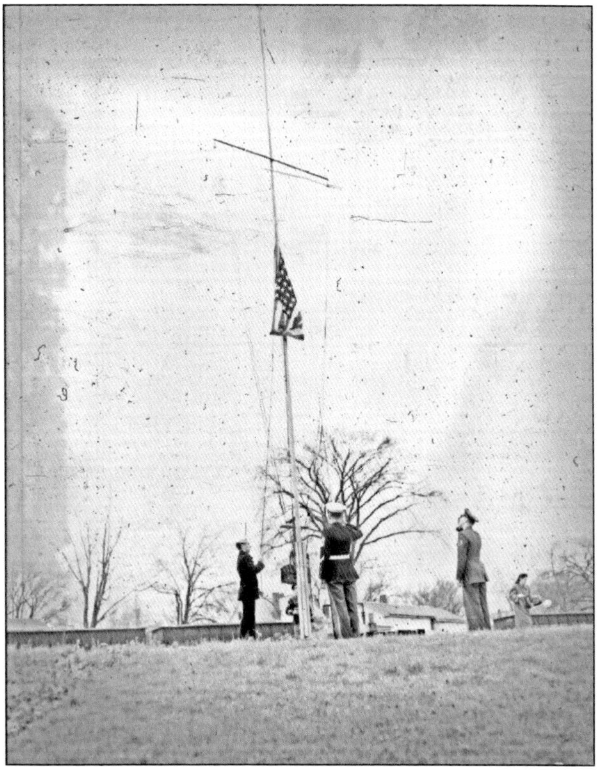

The evening of the commissioning ceremony featured a formal dinner. Seated left of the speaker is a Coast Guard staff captain from the Ninth Coast Guard District, and seated right of the speaker are a Navy commodore and the new station's officer in charge, Chief Outten.

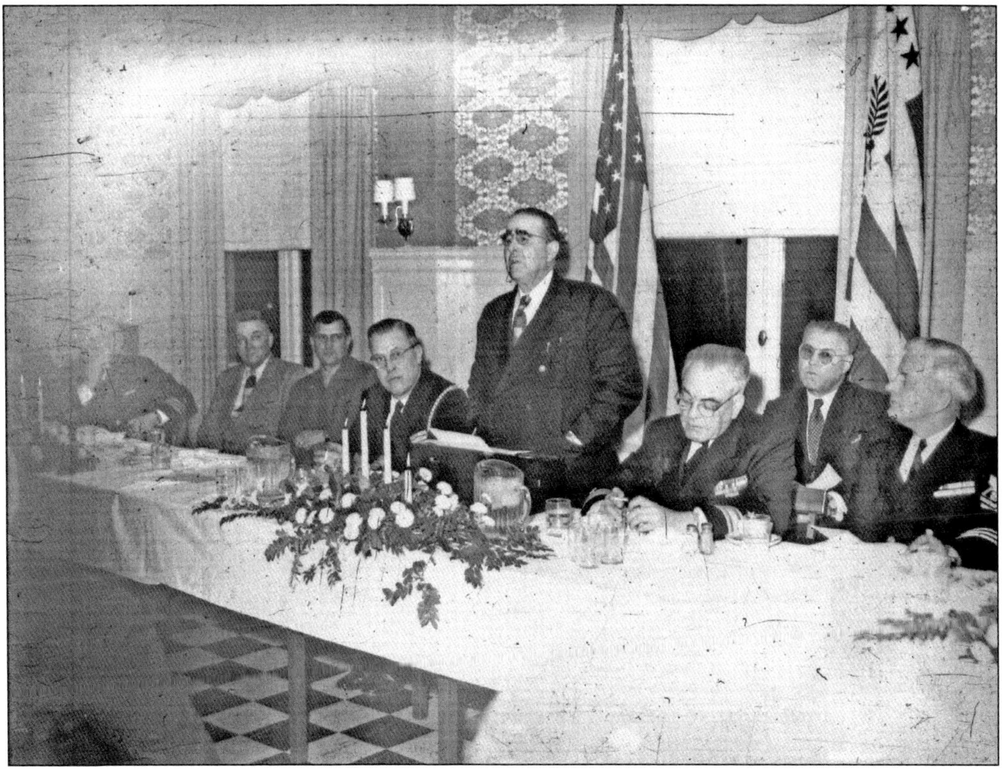

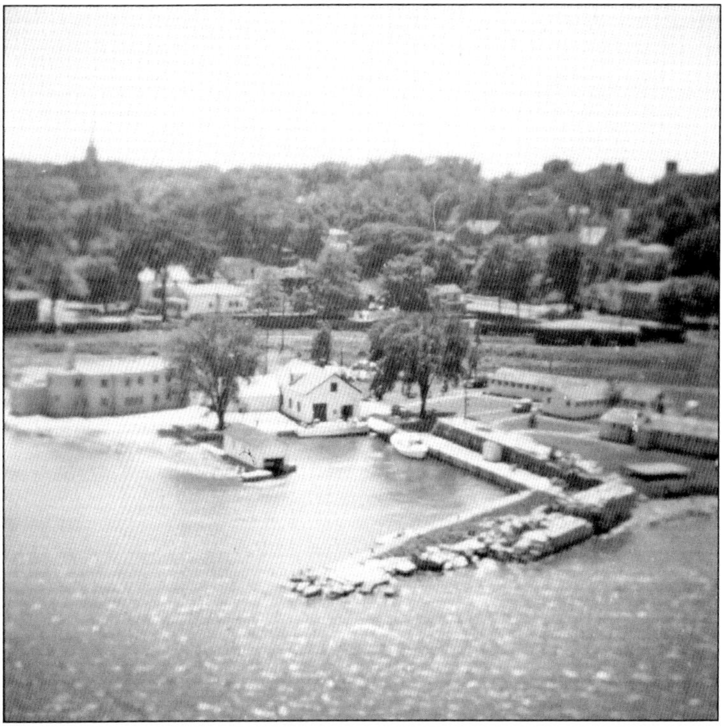

As Coast Guard Station Oswego continued to expand, improvements to the boat basin were necessary. Viewed from the air at left is the boat basin prior to reconstruction around 1950, with the station's three vessels moored along the old portion of the inner breakwater. Enhancements to the station's boat basin required a coffer dam (below); work is seen well underway.

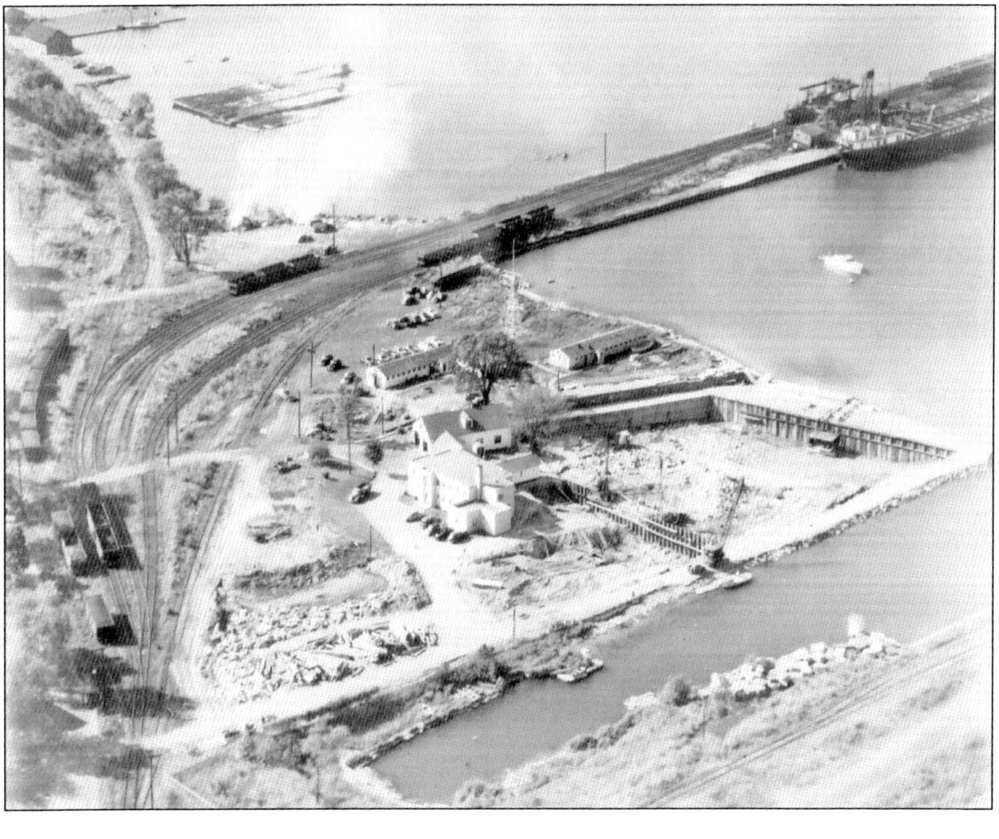

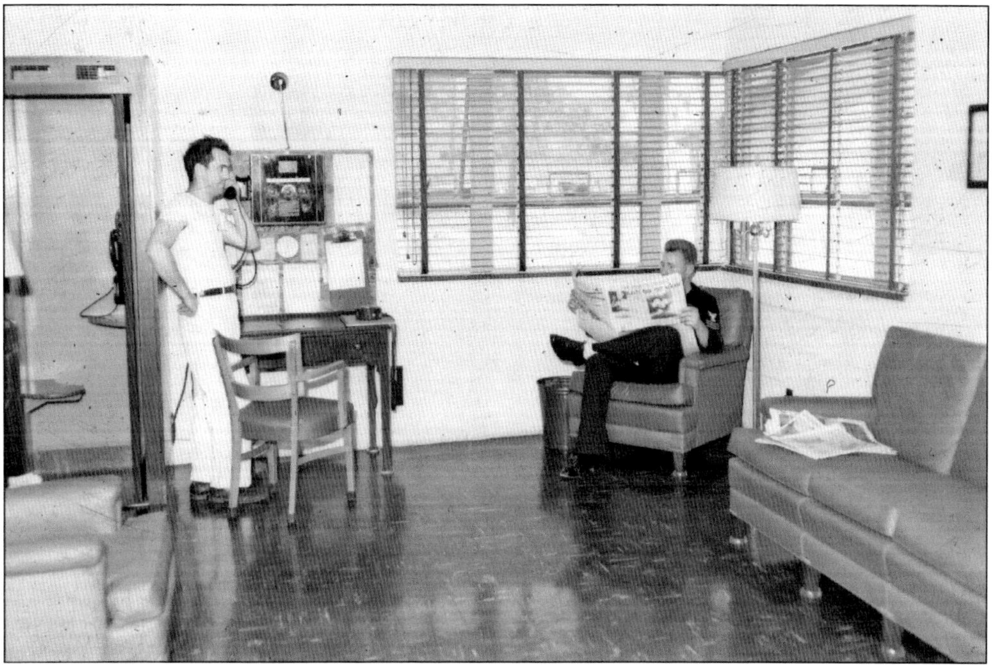

The communications facilities at the new Oswego Coast Guard Station were located in the northwest corner of the building, where they still reside today although much more elaborate. Shown to the left of the communications equipment in both photographs is a telephone booth for use by station personnel.

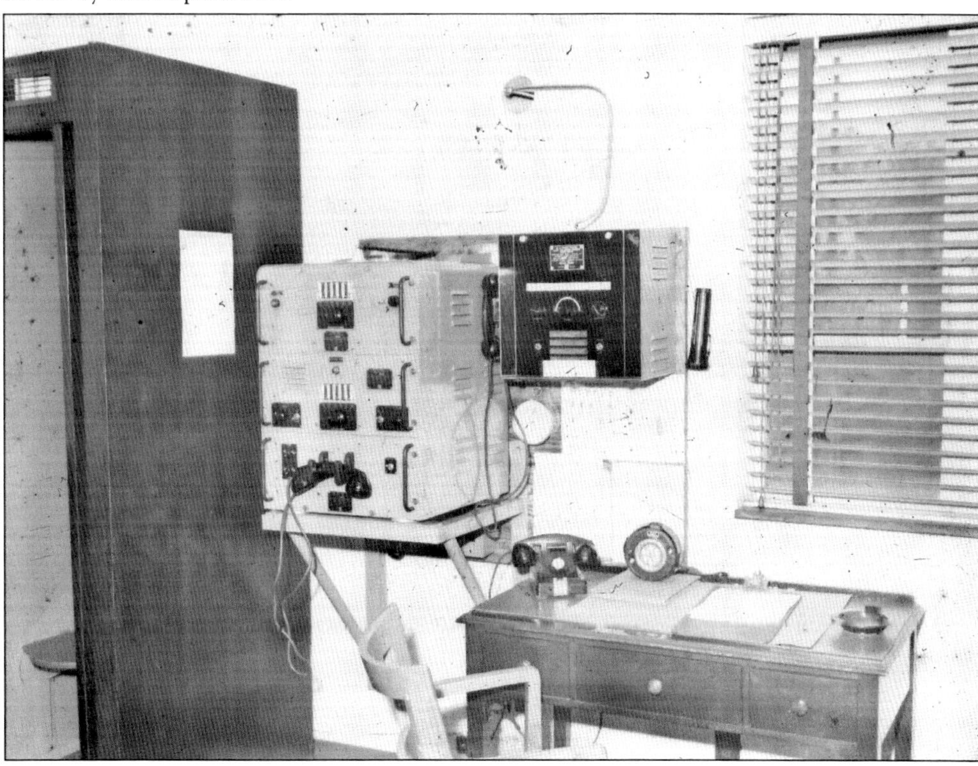

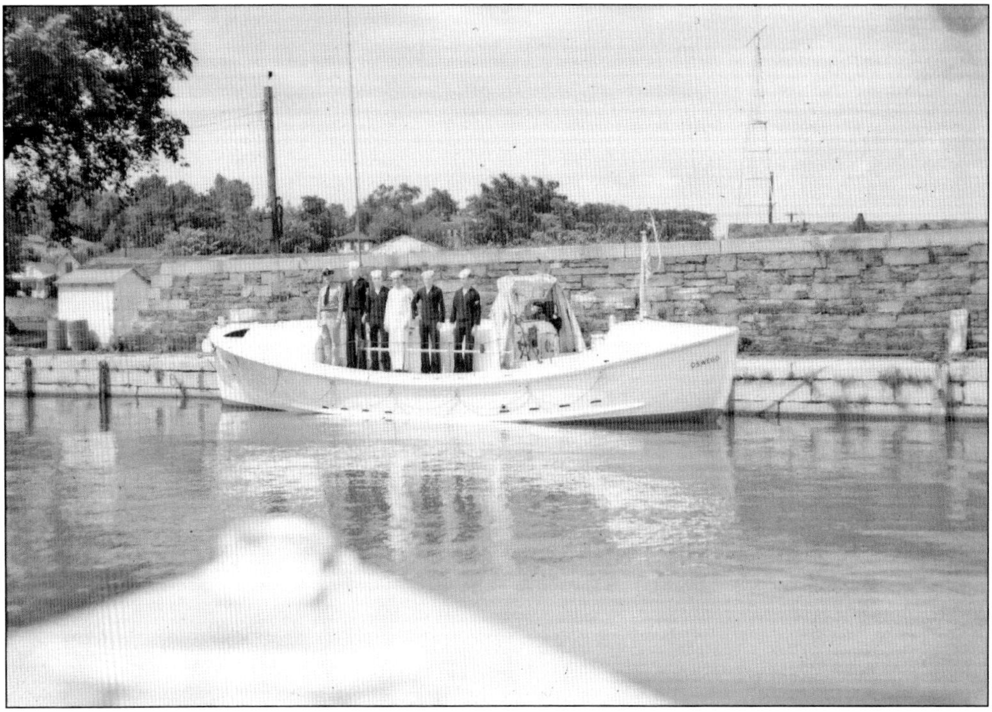

At the Oswego Coast Guard Station, training for rescues and inevitable inspections was a rather routine daily task. The crew of the station's 36-foot motor lifeboat above is seen falling in with the station officer in charge onboard the boat for inspection. The motor lifeboat below is underway on a calm Lake Ontario day conducting a routine patrol.

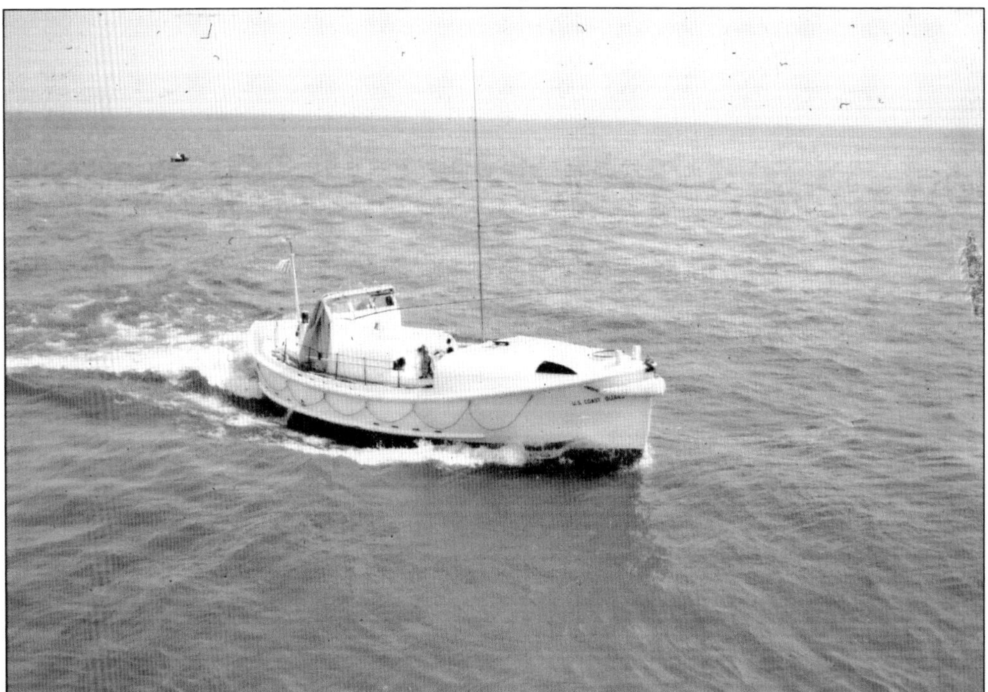

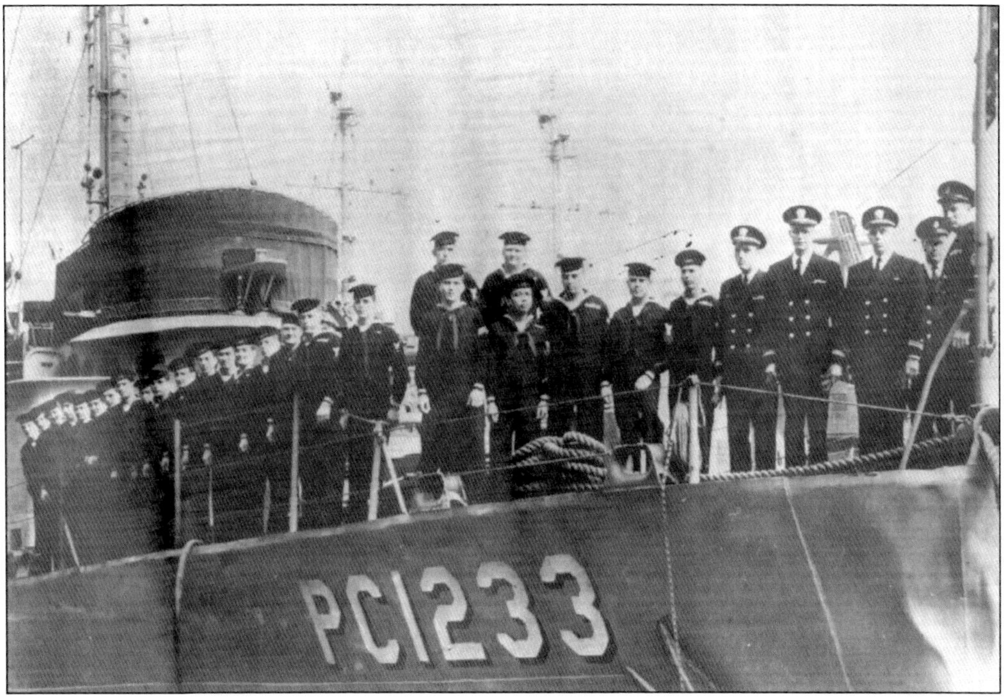

USS PC-1233, stationed at Oswego in the early 1950s, was laid down in September 1942 and launched on January 11, 1943, at the Sullivan Dry Dock and Repair Co. in Brooklyn. PC-1233 served in the European Theater during World War II and returned to be stationed on the lower Great Lakes between 1946 and 1954. Here, the crew is pictured onboard in Oswego Harbor. PC-1233 was decommissioned on July 26, 1954, and transferred to Taiwan, where she was renamed *Kung Kiang*.

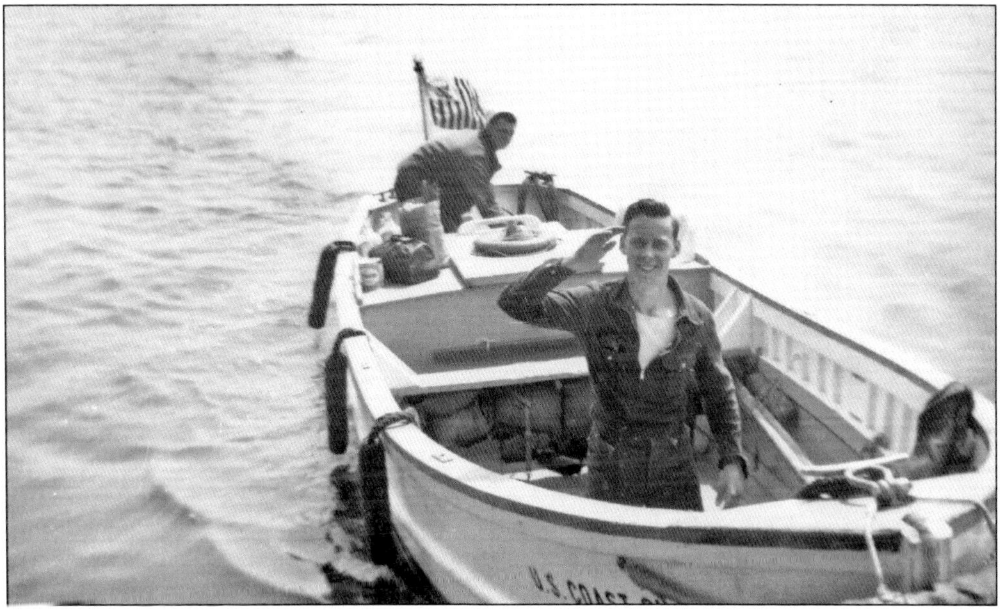

When the US Coast Guard acquired the Oswego West Pierhead Lighthouse in 1939, it fell under the jurisdiction of Station Oswego's officer in charge. Seen here, Conrad T. Brickman salutes while preparing to moor the station's workboat at the Oswego West Pierhead Lighthouse.

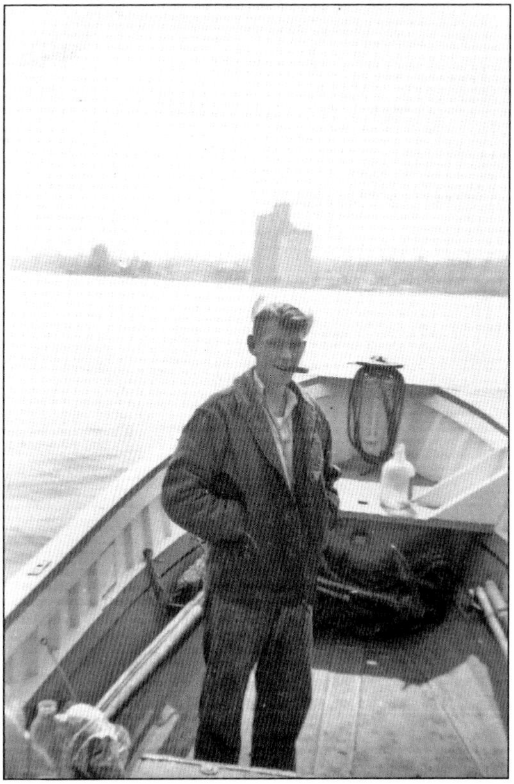

Supplying the lighthouse was a continuous task for the crew of Coast Guard Station Oswego, but it ensured the lighthouse operated reliably. Apparently, boat trips to and from the lighthouse were a time to enjoy a good cigar, as Edmond Mason is seen doing here in 1950.

The 36-foot motor lifeboat was reliable and had a long life at the Oswego Coast Guard Station. This stalwart rescue craft was kept always ready for rescue operations on Lake Ontario until finally retired in 1963.

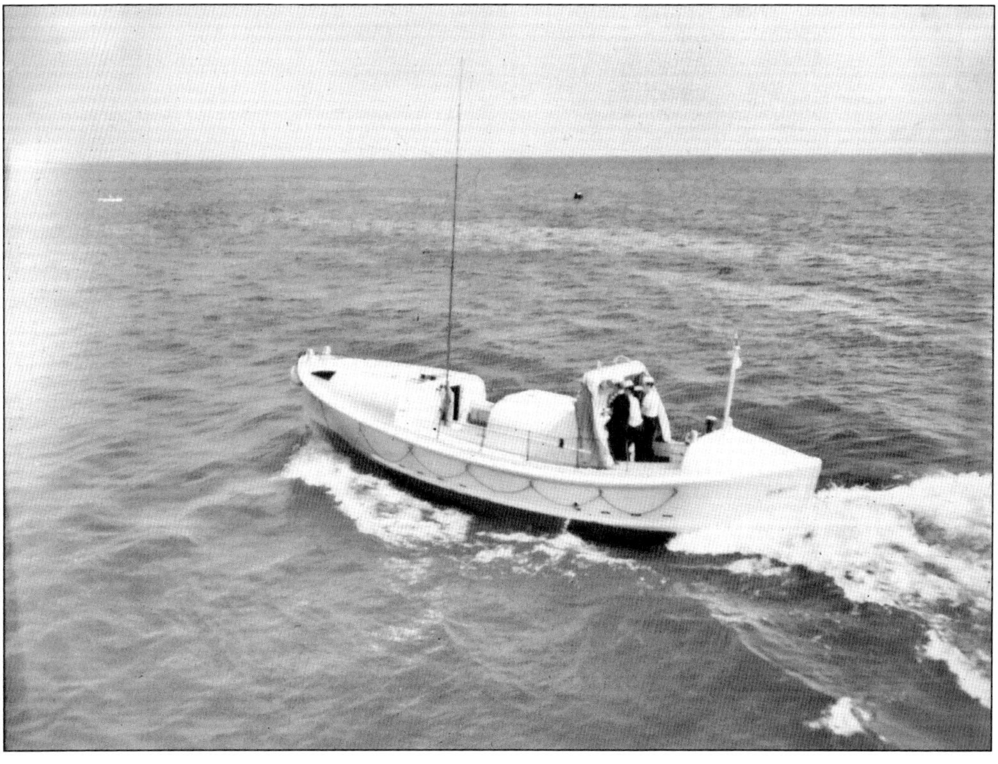

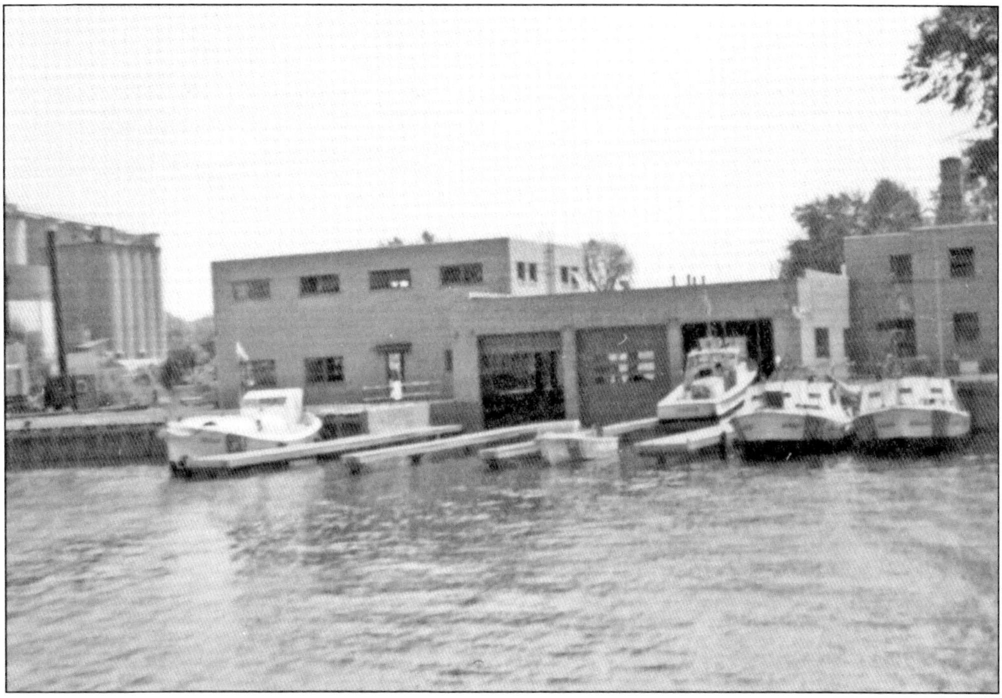

These two photographs, taken around the late 1950s or early 1960s, show the new west-side Coast Guard station with the new three-bay boathouse and shop building to the left. The new station administration building, commissioned in 1950, is on the right. Various boats attached to the station can be seen moored alongside the piers and on a boat launch at the boathouse. (Both, courtesy of the Oswego Coast Guard Station.)

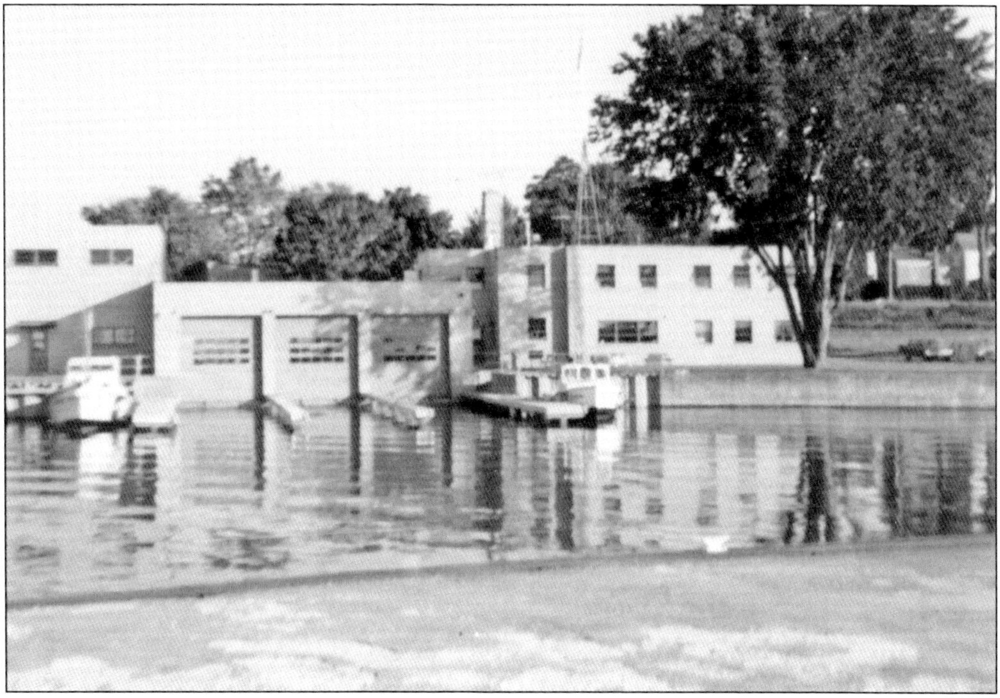

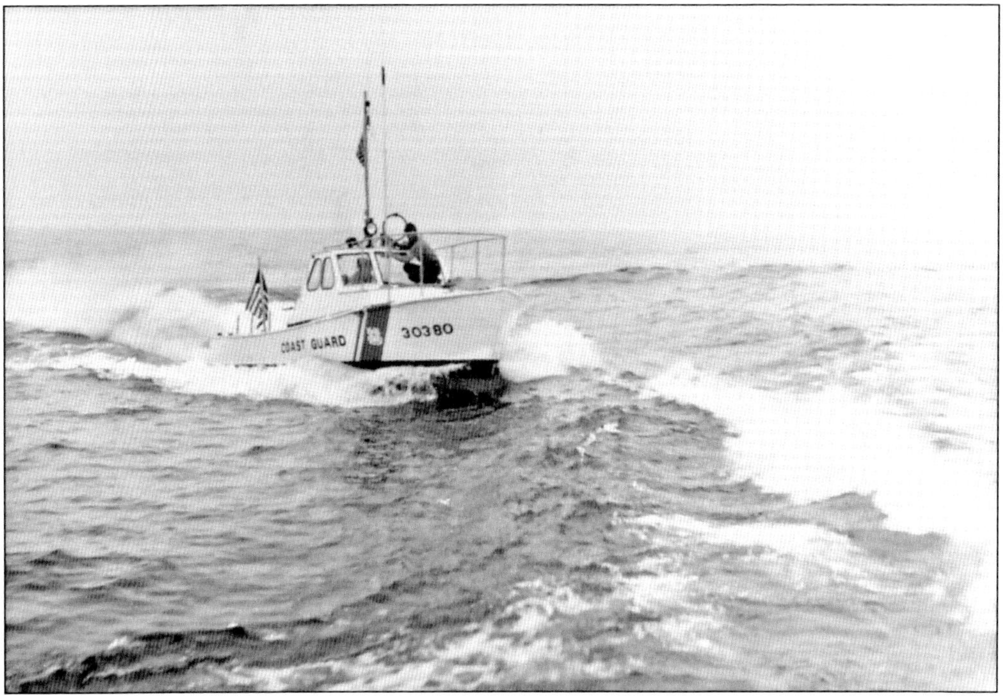

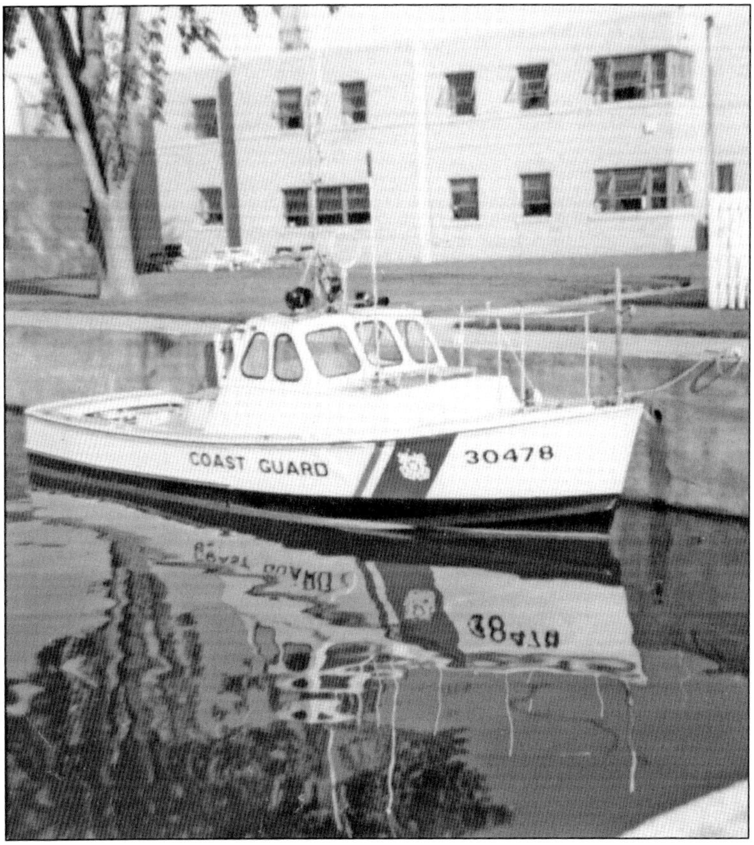

By the late 1950s and early 1960s, many of the Coast Guard's small boats, built during the World War II era, were aging and in need of replacement. The Coast Guard developed two sizes of utility boat, a large 40-foot and a medium 30-foot. The Oswego Coast Guard Station had one of the former and two of the latter. CG-30478 is moored at the station in front of the administration building at left, and CG-30380 is underway on Lake Ontario above. (Both, courtesy of the Oswego Coast Guard Station.)

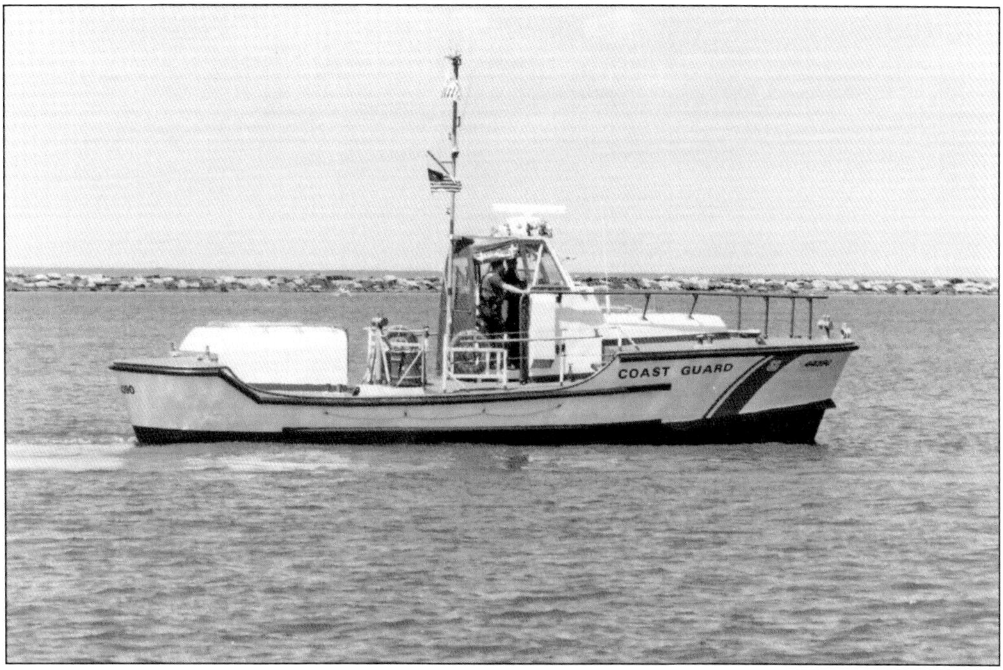

The 44-foot motor lifeboat CG-44390 replaced the 36-foot motor lifeboat at the Oswego Coast Guard Station in 1963. This steel-hulled self-bailing and self-righting boat was designed for rescues in the worst conditions. It had a crew of four and could carry 25 survivors at 14 knots for 164 miles. The Coast Guard yard at Curtis Bay, Maryland, built 110 of these between 1963 and 1972. Above, Oswego's CG-44390 is underway in the west harbor, and below, it is moored alongside Coast Guard Station Oswego. (Both, courtesy of the Oswego Coast Guard Station.)

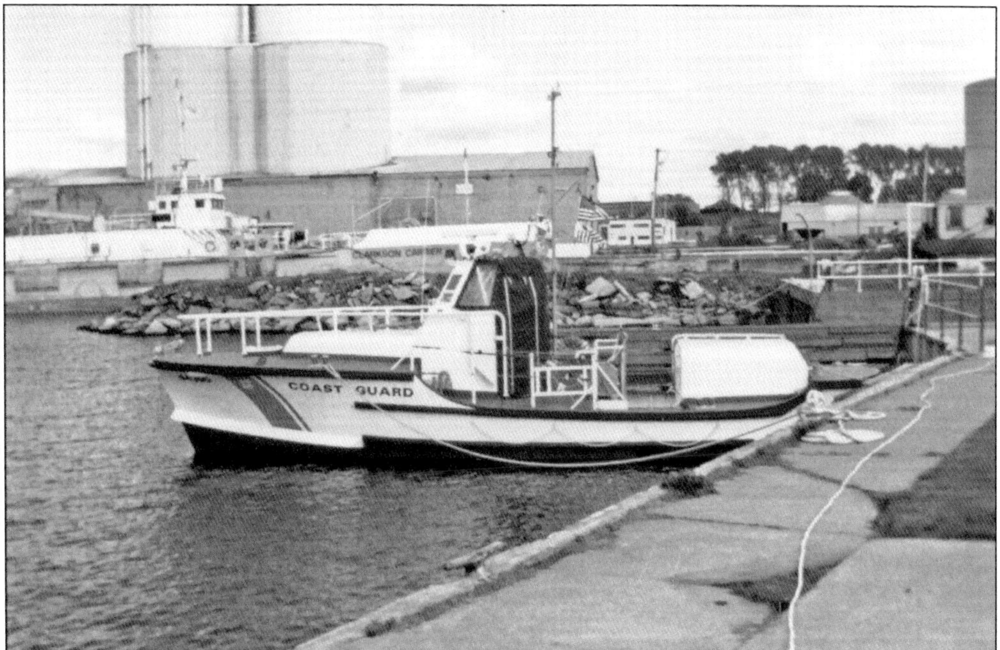

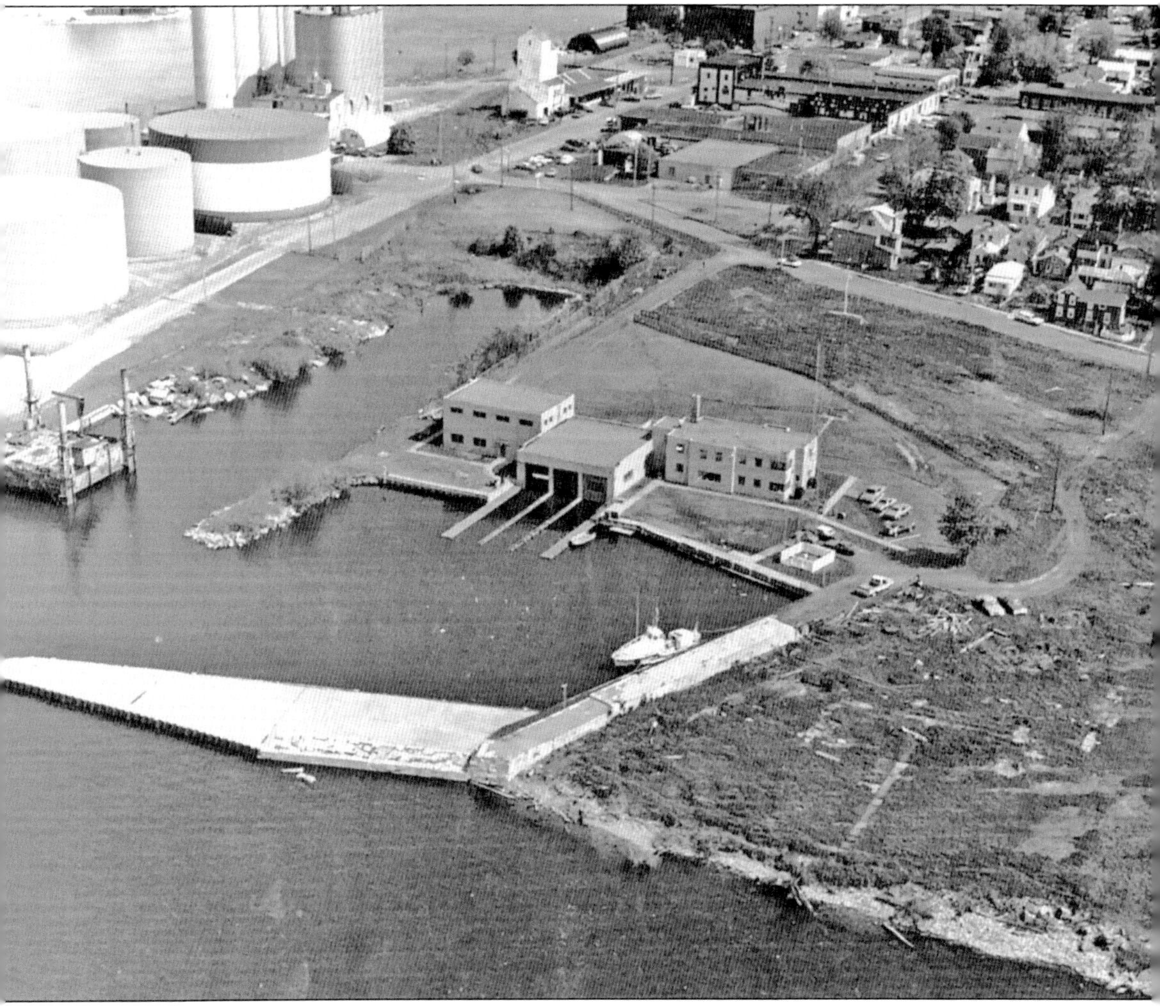

This c. 1960s aerial view of the Oswego Coast Guard Station shows the expanded buildings, including the three-bay boathouse and shop building. The 44-foot motor lifeboat is moored to the last remaining part of the old inner harbor breakwater, and all of the wooden World War II buildings have been removed. They have not all disappeared, however, as one building currently resides about 25 miles south of Oswego on the Oswego Canal, where it is used as part of a Coast Guard Auxiliary station.

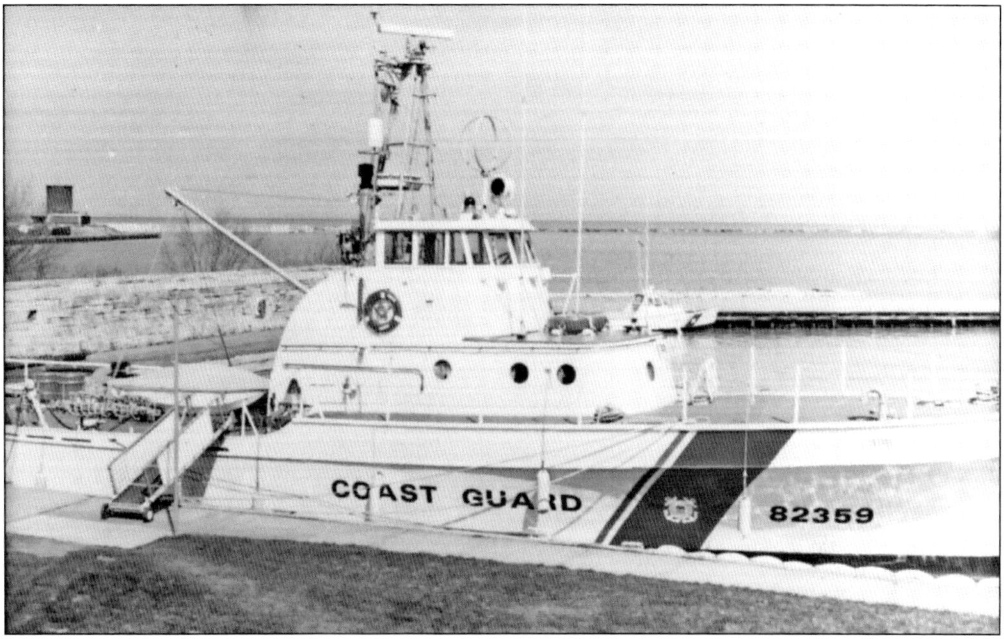

The US Coast Guard 82-foot patrol boat *Point Steel*, WPB-82359, is moored at the Oswego Coast Guard Station. This patrol boat, one of 78 built between 1960 and 1970, was built at Tacoma, Washington, and commissioned in 1967. The 82-foot patrol boats, which had a complement of two officers and eight men, were all named for geographic points. *Point Steel* had a top speed of over 20 knots and an operating radius of over 500 miles. It was stationed in Oswego from 1970 to 1980 and was transferred to Key West in 1981. (Courtesy of the Oswego Coast Guard Station.)

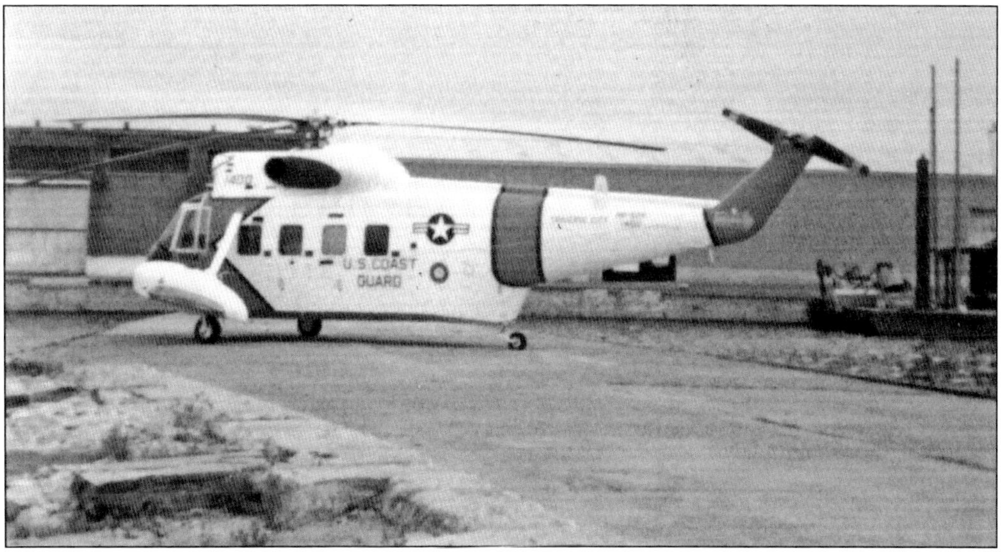

The Coast Guard HH-52A Seaguard search and rescue helicopter is pictured on a visit to Coast Guard Station Oswego. Introduced in 1961, it could land on water and was capable of cruising at 85 knots for 400 nautical miles. Sikorsky Aircraft built 99 of them for the Coast Guard and another 75 for other customers. Because of its amphibious capability, it was sometimes referred to as a flying lifeboat. The HH-52A was assigned to two Coast Guard air stations on the Great Lakes: Chicago and Traverse City, Michigan. (Courtesy of the Oswego Coast Guard Station.)

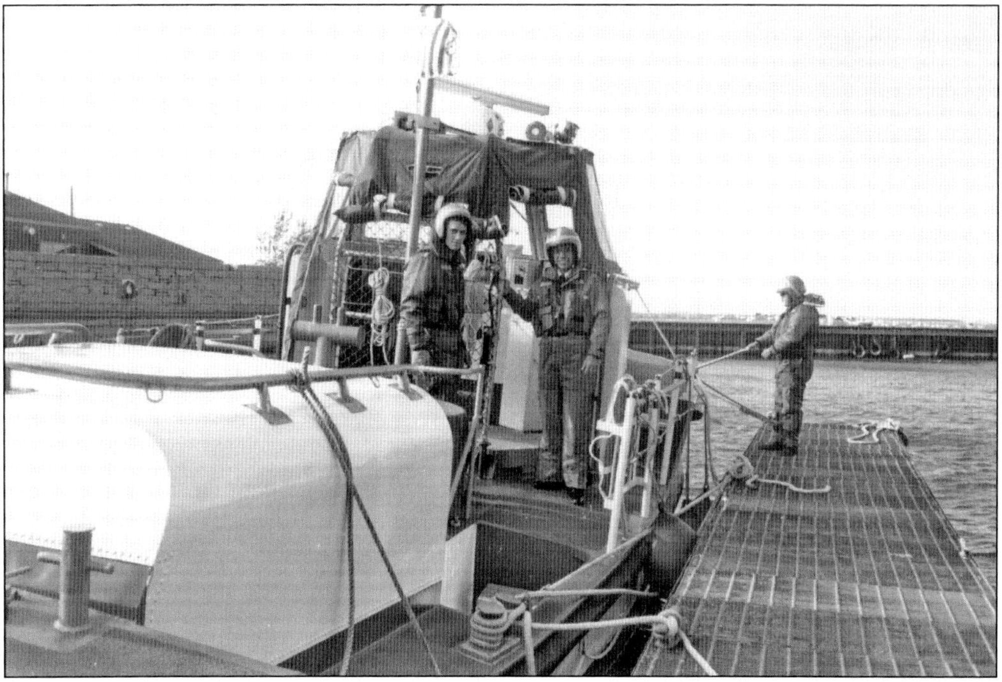

Above, the crew of CG-44390 moors the motor lifeboat alongside the floating pier at the Oswego Coast Guard Station. The crew is wearing helmets, along with life jackets and probably exposure suits, which are necessary equipment for rescue operations in bad weather. Below, the crew of CG-44390 practices responding to a capsized recreational boat. This is taking place in the boat basin in front of the Coast Guard station with the New York State Grain Elevator and support building in the background. (Both, courtesy of the Oswego Coast Guard Station.)

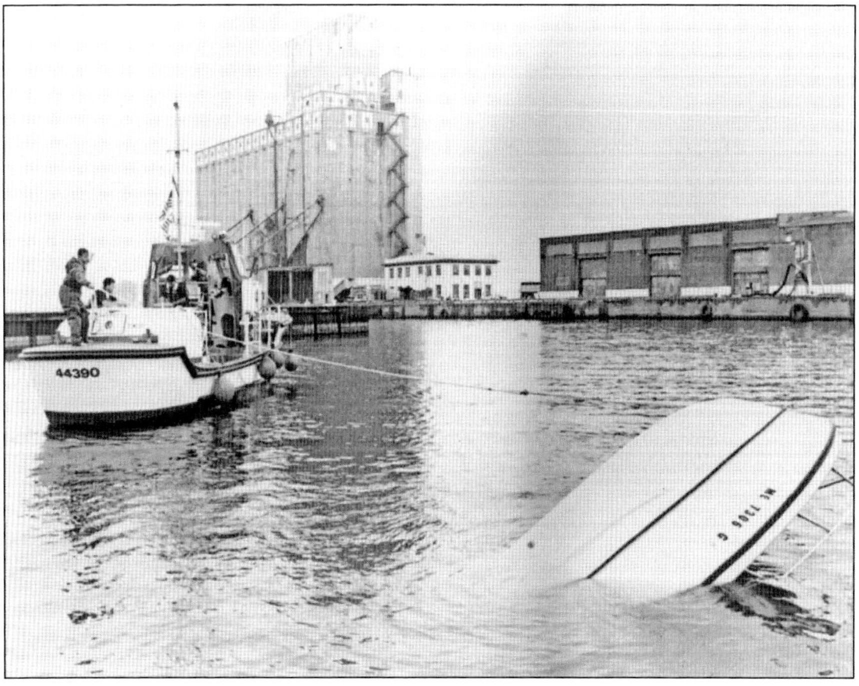

This is the US Coast Guard's premier search and rescue vessel, the 47-foot motor lifeboat. It is the successor to the 44-foot motor lifeboat and entered service at Oswego in the early 2000s. Textron Marine and Land Systems of Slidell, Louisiana, built 227 of these starting in 1997. The all-aluminum self-righting vessel is built to operate in 60 knots of wind (hurricane strength), 30-foot waves, and 20-foot surf. It is capable of 25 knots with a cruising range of 200 nautical miles and carries a crew of four with room for 30 survivors.

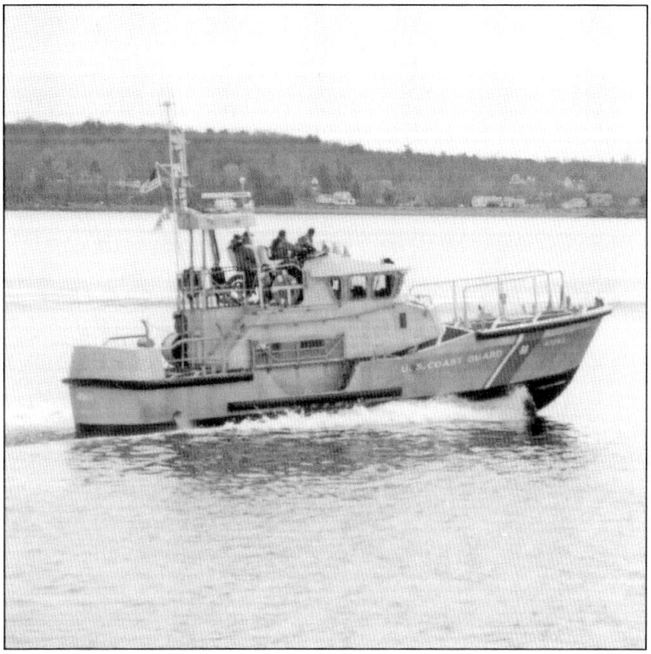

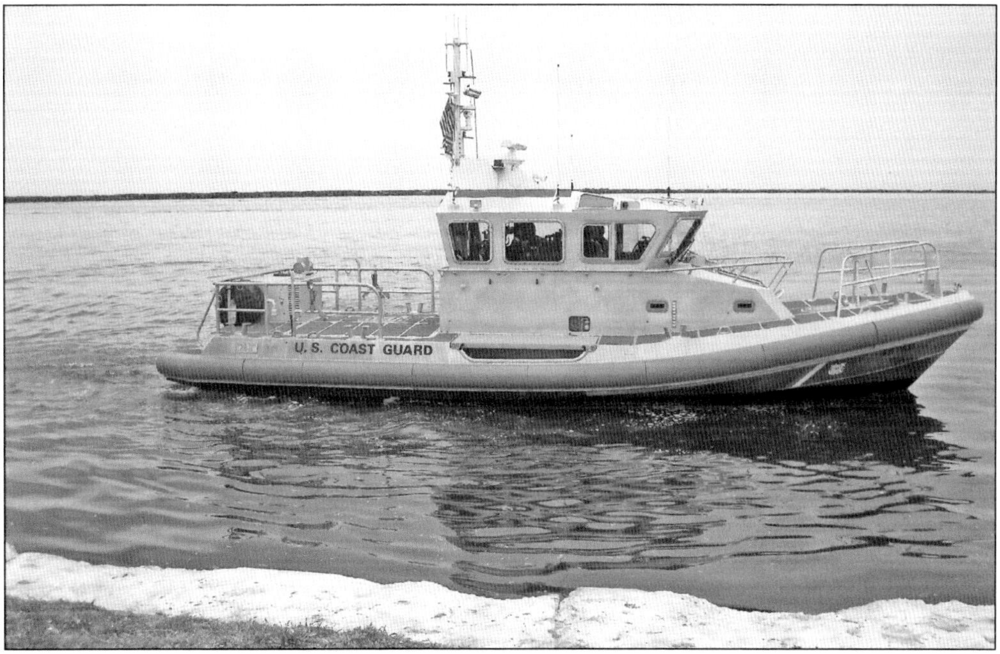

Pictured is the Oswego Coast Guard Station's 45-foot response boat–medium. Deliveries of this vessel began in 2008 as a replacement for the Coast Guard's 41-foot utility boats, which were averaging 30 years of service. Plans are to acquire 170 vessels. At Great Lakes Coast Guard stations, they usually replace the 47-foot motor lifeboat. The 45-foot response boat–medium is primarily a search and rescue vessel, but it is also capable of other varied missions, making it more versatile in the Great Lakes. The 47-foot motor lifeboats can then be transferred to the coasts, where their unique heavy-weather capabilities are more useful. The vessel is water jet propelled, cruises at 30 knots for 250 nautical miles, and has a crew of four.

About the H. Lee White Maritime Museum at Oswego

The mission of the H. Lee White Maritime Museum at Oswego is "to promote, protect, enhance and collect the historical resources associated with the Oswego River and its drainage basin, the Oswego Canal, and Lake Ontario." As such, the H. Lee White Maritime Museum has been serving the central New York area since 1982. Open all year, it offers a wide variety of educational programs for all ages, many free and open to the community. The campus is comprised of several sites, including a museum building, a fleet of historic vessels, and a boating education center. The museum houses exhibits and artifacts telling over 400 years of regional maritime history, while its fleet of vessels includes the national historic landmark World War II tugboat LT-5; New York State's 1927 Derrick Boat 8, listed in the National Register of Historic Places; and the last American commercial fishing vessel on Lake Ontario, *Eleanor D.* Further, it serves as the steward of the Oswego West Pierhead Lighthouse, listed in the National Register of Historic Places, and facilitates the restoration, interpretation, and public access of that site.

H. LEE WHITE MARITIME MUSEUM AT OSWEGO

Bibliography

Laws of New York, Chapter 164, Section I, Passed March 27, 1821.

Laws of the United States, 16th Congress, Session 2, Chapter 52, Sections 1 and 3. Passed March 3, 1821.

Oswego Letters Patent to the United States. *Book of Patents* No. 25, p. 450. July 13, 1821.